COURT SECURITY

COURT SECURITY

A Guide for Post 9-11 Environments

By

TONY L. JONES

CHARLES C THOMAS • PUBLISHER, LTD.
Springfield • Illinois • U.S.A.

Published and Distributed Throughout the World by

CHARLES C THOMAS • PUBLISHER, LTD.
2600 South First Street
Springfield, Illinois 62704

©2003 by CHARLES C THOMAS • PUBLISHER, LTD.

ISBN 0-398-07419-4 (hard)
ISBN 0-398-07420-8 (paper)

Library of Congress Catalog Card Number: 2003048428

With THOMAS BOOKS *careful attention is given to all details of manufacturing
and design. It is the Publisher's desire to present books that are satisfactory as to their
physical qualities and artistic possibilities and appropriate for their particular use.*
THOMAS BOOKS *will be true to those laws of quality that assure a good name
and good will.*

Printed in the United States of America
SR*R-3*

Library of Congress Cataloging-in-Publication Data

Jones, Tony L.
    Court security : a guide for post 9-11 environments / by Tony L. Jones.
        p. cm.
    Includes bibliographical references and index.
    ISBN 0-398-07419-4 (hard) -- ISBN 0-398-07420-8 (paper)
        1. Courthouses--Security measures--United States. 2. Terrorism--United States--
Prevention. I. Title

KF8733.7.J66 2003
347.73'1068'4--dc21

                                                                    2003048428

This book is dedicated to the people who have experienced courtroom violence. These people have experienced the incalculable costs of death, emotional distress, physical injury, facility destruction, disruption of legal processes, negative public perception, civil/criminal lawsuits, and the resulting embarrassment these acts generate. These people need to know that they are not alone; nearly everyone in a community is often touched in some way when courtroom violence erupts.

INTRODUCTION

Courtrooms are intended to be a place for peaceful, calm, reasoned resolution of disputes, and most courts are safe. However, in recent years, there has been a sharp rise in acts of violence in the courts. These acts of violence range from minor disturbances and physical assaults to senseless acts of murder, injury, and mass destruction, and are used as a means of expressing personal anger or public dissent. Security risks at a courthouse are perhaps more visceral than in other environments, running the gambit from vandals at night, to revenge-seeking relatives, to galleries packed with rival gang members during a murder trial. One must also consider the number of arrestees awaiting bond, trial, or sentencing. At any time, there are angry people entering and leaving a courthouse complex. For example, the Supreme Court of Ohio and the Ohio Judicial Conference Committee on Court Security conducted a survey of court officials in 1994 and found the following statistics:

Types of Incidents (in order of frequency)

1. Escape or escape attempt
2. Physical assault with no weapon used
3. Disorderly conduct
4. Physical assault with a weapon
5. Suicide or suicide attempt
6. Vandalism
7. Hostage situation
8. Bomb threat
9. Theft
10. Bomb explosion

Courts in Which Incidents Occurred

1. General trial court, criminal—54%
2. Juvenile and domestic relations—17%

3. Municipal court—11%
4. General trial court, civil—8%
5. Justice/arraignment/first appearance courts—6%
6. Small claims court—8%
7. Traffic court—1%

Location of Incidents

1. Courtroom—41%
2. Lobby—18%
3. Offices—12%
4. Holding cell—9%
5. Public hallway—8%
6. Judges' chambers—4%
7. Elevator—2%
8. Jury room—1%

Type of Case Being Heard at the Time of the Incident

1. Criminal—56%
2. Divorce—11%
3. Juvenile offense—8%
4. Traffic—4%
5. Other domestic—9%
6. All other—18%

Victims of the Incident

1. Bailiff or court security officer—81%
2. Judge—24%
3. Defendant—8%
4. Plaintiff—6%
5. Witness—5%
6. Prosecutor—5%
7. Defense attorney—3%
8. Spectators and others—18%

Injuries Sustained

1. No injuries—54%
2. Minor injuries/no medical attention—19%

3. Minor medical attention—10%
4. Serious injury/hospitalized—10%
5. Death—4%

Stage of Case at the Time of the Incident

1. Sentencing—23%
2. Arraignment—18%
3. Trial—13%
4. Motions—9%
5. Return of verdict—6%
6. Other and unknown—31%

Reason for the Incident

1. Revenge—39%
2. Escape—39%
3. Intimidation—14%
4. Influence court—7%
5. Political—1%

Disposition of the Assailant

1. Arrested—68%
2. Suicide—2%
3. Escaped—2%
4. Injured—2%
5. Killed—1%

Even if people decide to ignore these statistics, they cannot ignore the fact that the world will never be the same after September 11, 2001. In the immediate aftermath of the events of September 11, 2001, the security action of choice was to place armed officers virtually everywhere. Uniformed police were suddenly besieged to protect so-called critical facilities and infrastructures of every description. The country asked these officers to protect valuable vulnerable assets with little or no training. Problems soon transpired in areas having highly technical on-site-responsibilities. It soon became clear that the nation could not afford full-time police officers at every critical facility and without special training the only thing the officers were truly providing was a method to evacuate a facility and the timely contacting of response teams such as hazmat personnel. Therefore, every pre-September 11th security procedure must be evaluated. In this evaluation, every security vulnerability and loophole must be addressed through the implementation of advanced state-of-the-art technologies, policies, and procedures.

Courtrooms must be secure because violence diminishes the respect for the institution as a place for peaceful resolution; if not, the chaos of violence may replace the rule of law. During the Judicial Conference of the United States, held on March 11, 1982, the United States Chief Justice and Attorney General emphasized the importance of court security by stating; "If we cannot ensure the safety of all participants in the judicial process, we cannot maintain the integrity of the system, we cannot—in sum—'establish justice,' as mandated in the preamble to the constitution of the United States." Sadly, many courts at all levels of the judicial system have been slow or even reluctant to implement adequate security procedures.

The potential exists for violence to occur in any court system regardless of size or geographical location. Indeed, no court system is immune from security problems or violence. Court personnel and security officers are frequently called upon to "handle" aggressive or physically violent people. When court personnel fail to calm down an agitated person or are forced to engage in "physical management," the risks of injury and liability for the officer, bystanders, and even the aggressor are significantly increased. In light of these facts, courts must move from the traditional reactive security mode to the proactive mode. Indeed, with the increasing incidence of sophisticated and complex security threats, it is imperative that security operations focus their energies on preventing, policing and remedying threats and attacks from both external sources and internal threats. Therefore, many bailiffs, constables, deputy sheriffs, police officers, marshals, and others charged with court security and the transportation of prisoners must reevaluate current methods of safeguarding the judicial process.

Philosophical changes and standards establishing "what" a court should do is a start. However, in the author's experience, the "how to" portion of the security equation is left up to each court. As many bailiffs, constables, deputy sheriffs, police officers, marshals, and other personnel charged with court security duties have found, the "how to" process is very hard to complete without consulting specialized in-depth information.

The purpose of this book is to provide information concerning state-of-the-art court security operations and technologies, help determine areas where security improvements ought to be made, and shed some light on upgrading procedures for court security and the transportation of prisoners. The ultimate goal of this book is to clarify the fact that security, in today's world, must be reexamined and revamped to protect human and physical assets. A dynamic and adaptive security system is required to address the evolving nature of security threats. Time is running out!

CONTENTS

LIST OF FIGURES

COURT SECURITY

Chapter 1

PERPETRATORS PLANNING AN ATTACK

It has been said that for an individual to effectively counter an enemy, one must know his enemy. This statement certainly rings true in the case of courtroom security personnel charged with protecting the court, citizens, and perpetrators. There are generally three types of perpetrators who plan violent courtroom attacks; they are known as reactive offenders, mission offenders, and thrill-seeking offenders.

Types of Perpetrators

Reactive offenders have a perceived sense of entitlement regarding their rights, privileges, and way of life that does not extend to the victim. This offender may react due to a perceived threat that seemingly threatens the perpetrator's way of life, personal relationships, or privilege. A reactive offender typically focuses on protecting and defending against any perceived threat constituted by the presence of outsiders. This offender may resort to using fear and intimidation to send a message that will repel the outsiders. Victims of this offender often fall into the category of an individual or group who are perceived by the offender as constituting a threat. Acts of violence may occur in the offender's own neighborhood, place of recreation, or court. If the threat is perceived to subside, the reactive behavior may also subside. Reactive offenders generally feel little if any guilt because they perceive that violent behavior is a justifiable response to personal feelings of violation.

Mission offenders are often psychotic, suffer from mental illness that may cause hallucinations, have an impaired ability to reason, and often withdraw from other people. The mission offender's motivation revolves around believing that he or she has been instructed by a higher order (God, the Fuhrer, the Imperial Wizard, etc.) to rid the world of an evil. They may also believe that they must get even for any misfortunes they may have suffered. These offenders may also perceive a conspiracy of some kind being perpetuated by the

3

person or groups targeted for violence. This offender may feel a sense of urgency about their violent mission, believing they must act before it is too late. Victims often fall into the category of an individual or group who are perceived as responsible for the offenders' frustrations. All members of a despised group may be targeted for elimination. Acts of violence are likely to occur wherever the targeted group is likely to be found. Their mission often ends in the offender's suicide.

Thrill-Seeking offenders are often trying to fit into a group. Their motivation revolves around gaining a psychological or social thrill, to be accepted by peers, or to gain bragging rights. Victims may constitute any person or vulnerable group perceived as inferior by the offender. Acts of violence are likely to occur wherever the targeted group is likely to be found. Since attacks are random, it is often difficult to identify the offender. Attacks often involve desecration and vandalism, although they can involve more violent actions. Hatred of the victim is relatively superficial; offenders may be deterred from repeating actions if there is a strong societal response condemning the behavior.

Any of these offenders may become what law enforcement professionals call "Active Shooters." These active shooters often intend to kill as many people as possible and may have no plan or intentions of escape. The active shooter may intend to do as much damage as possible and then commit suicide by his or her own hand. Additionally, the active shooter may confront the police and force action or attempt to escape the crime scene. Finally, active shooters can be expected to be heavily armed with more than one weapon and carry a large amount of ammunition.

Perpetrators Planning an Attack

There may be some readers who believe perpetrators commit acts of violence with little thought or preparation. However, this does not appear to be the case with many of the more violent incidents recently witnessed. Indeed, once a perpetrator has targeted a court for attack, an extensive planning phase may be set into motion. Granted, sophistication of an attack and the planning phase for the attack will vary in detail. However, the mechanics of an attack will likely focus on the following areas to some degree: target selection, tactics, operation style, and the completion of a plan of attack.

Target Selection

Once motivated, the perpetrator will select a target court after answering the following questions. Is the target courthouse critical, accessible, easily restored, vulnerable, and what effect will the attack and subsequent death and destruction have on the local and national population? A target courthouse is deemed critical when destruction or damage will have a significant impact upon unique specialized functions. Of course, the criticality of a target courthouse may change with political, economic, and sociological fluctuations.

A target court is accessible when the perpetrator can easily infiltrate the target site. Perpetrators will often gather detailed intelligence concerning the court's location, physical structure, and efficiency of security measures. A target court is easily restored if restoration efforts are considered efficient and quick or if judicial activities can be easily transferred to other locations. This is important as the offenders may consider the effort not worth the risk. However, if restoration will be expensive, difficult, time consuming, or impractical, the target court may become a favored target for attack.

Courthouse vulnerability focuses on whether the court is open to attack by the means and capabilities available to the offenders. Offender means include explosives or bombs, both conventional and unconventional; arson; assassination; raid-type attacks; hostage taking; sabotage; insider assistance; and mob/gang actions, etc. Offender capabilities include available manpower, logistics, support networks, money, training, and the availability of weapons and explosives. A focal point of offender capability lies in the fact that court attacks always enable streamlined assets, when compared to defending assets (it may only require one offender to successfully attack a courthouse protected by numerous security systems and personnel). Offenders will often compare their means and capabilities to the target court's location, type, security systems, security forces, and available assistance.

Finally, the offender will often consider how the public will react to the attack? Will there be economic, political, psychological, and sociological impact? Can a nationwide court system be affected by these attacks or, at the very least, will only a certain area be affected? For example, many local economies cannot afford heightened security measures or the building of new courthouses. Will citizens fear the prospect of entering the courthouse? Will criminal justice and other professionals be afraid of entering the courthouse? Will the government and judicial systems become repressive in order to protect citizens, and will citizens accept or even demand this type of reaction? Can sociological unrest be developed or exploited?

Naturally, each question does not require an affirmative answer for a perpetrator to target a certain courthouse; however, as favorable factors accumulate, chances are that a court will be chosen for attack. Particularly desirable targets are high profile in nature, for example, large courthouses, courthouses located in or around large cities, and courthouses representing a popular landmark for a community.

Perpetrator Tactics

In order to understand the effectiveness of perpetrator attacks, their tactics must be examined. A perpetrator may specialize using only one tactic or utilize several techniques that range from simple acts of sabotage to utilizing weapons and explosives. The tactics chosen usually correspond to the offender's abilities, philosophies, expertise, funds, or by what tactic is most effective at the time. The following list represents goals a perpetrator may seek:

1. Destroy or damage judicial institutions.
2. Gain control of a judicial institution.
3. Eliminate criminal justice officials.
4. Harass judicial institutions and systems.
5. Harass the community.
6. Harass organizations with criminal justice ties.
7. Harass government organizations–this includes police organizations.
8. Attract media attention.
9. Terrorize a society.

Once a goal or goals are identified, the perpetrator will settle on tactics to achieve the desired outcome, for example: the use of subversion, sabotage (passive and/or active), threats or hoaxes, bombs, arson, assassination, media manipulation, armed raids, and hostage taking.

Subversion and Sabotage

Subversion is often the perpetrator's main goal and is best described as actions designed to undermine the economic, psychological, or political strength of a judicial entity. Sabotage (a very effective form of subversion) permits the selective destruction of facilities using a minimum of manpower and resources. Often, sabotage is utilized by subversive offenders or organizations to gain recognition, momentum, support, and to recruit members.

There are two types of sabotage: passive and active. Passive sabotage uses subtle, nonviolent techniques that may be difficult to recognize as a subversive activity. Passive sabotage includes mass absenteeism, demonstrations, protests, or organized substandard employee performance. Active sabotage may be high profile and easier to recognize as an offender activity. Active sabotage includes mechanical, incendiary, explosive, and administrative methods. Mechanical sabotage is the deliberate damaging or destruction of courthouse equipment by deliberate abuse, neglect, or the introduction of harmful additives into the critical parts of expensive or crucial equipment. Incendiary sabotage is the damage or destruction of courthouses by fire. Explosive sabotage is the damage or destruction of courthouses by explosives. Administrative sabotage is the deliberate garbling of instructions or guidance, misdirection, destruction or loss of documents, computer hacking, and the blocking or interference with communications.

Threats or Hoaxes

Threats or hoaxes are intended to force a targeted court to respond without actually carrying out a physical act. Threats or hoaxes disrupt judicial productivity, normal day-to-day activity, and create fear and/or panic. This tactic can cost a judicial system vast amounts of money, damage judicial productivity, disrupt operating efficiency, and tie up valuable law enforcement and emergency response assets. Threats and hoaxes cost the offender nothing. However, if an offender uses this tactic too often, the need to actually carry out violent activity may be committed in order for future threats or hoaxes to be taken seriously.

The dilemma encountered by a targeted court experiencing numerous threats or hoaxes is this: can a threat ever be categorized as just another threat or hoax? (Remember the gamble is life–the pay off may be death.) How much is human life worth? Ultimately, the effectiveness of threats or hoaxes hinges on the value of life! **Note:** The hoax technique may also be a basic technique used by a perpetrator to "test" the effectiveness of response plans and personnel. This act may be a primary technique used by perpetrators to assist in their intelligence gathering efforts when considering potential or real targets. A hoax is often not just a hoax, but a serious analysis of potential targets, and should never be regarded as simply "just some kooky citizen intent on annoying us."

Bombs or Explosives

Bombs/explosives are a favored tactic due to their propensity to maximize casualties, death, destruction, and sensationalism. An added attractiveness is the minimal use of assets and manpower. Bombs may be easily constructed on a low budget and technological base or be extremely sophisticated. A total explosive package may be commercially obtained, stolen, or constructed by improvisation. Bombs include conventional/unconventional types such as: vehicle bombs; suicide bombs; letter bombs; military weapons, i.e., rockets, mines, mortars, hand grenades, and booby traps. Increased technological sophistication and the availability of information may be seen in the use of complex timing devices and fuses.

Arson

Arson is a technique used by perpetrators to destroy judicial facilities through the use of flame-producing devices, but casualties or deaths are often viewed as bonuses. Arson is usually carried out through the use of incendiary devices that are designed to ignite after the offender has left the scene. Fire enhancing devices may also be left at the scene; for example, courthouse fire extinguishers may be filled with flammable liquid in the hope they will be sprayed on the fire. Of course, unsophisticated devices may be used as well.

Assassination

A perpetrator may also employ a tactic known as assassination to kill criminal justice administrators, judges, lawyers, law enforcement officers, jurors, and other support personnel. Assassination targets are selected based upon retaliation, symbolism, and for the publicity the act will generate. Assassination may be extremely attractive if a perpetrator views the target as "easy to attack."

Media Manipulation

The media provides perpetrators with immediate publicity and dramatization of their cause. The media may represent an extremely powerful and effective tool used by offenders to enhance or perpetuate additional violent actions. Fear and intimidation may be spread nationwide and even worldwide through media coverage of a violent act. Media vehicles include exclusive interviews, videotape, audiotape, telephone-tape, and a convenient eye witness.

Armed Raids

Armed raids are usually military style surprise attacks that target judicial installations. The tactics involve violent combat-type actions, rapid disengagement and swift, deceptive withdrawal or suicide. Raids are often designed to demonstrate strength, destroy and/or damage facilities, kill and/or injure personnel, and to create fear or terror.

Hostage Taking

A final perpetrator tactic, hostage taking, is a high-profile activity designed to capture headlines. Hostage taking may be implemented as a retaliatory activity or to advance ideology. Perpetrators may kill their hostages and even desire to be killed themselves, in order to enhance their organization or message. Negotiations may be futile.

Operation Style

Once a courthouse has been selected for attack and a tactic has been chosen, operation style is considered. The styles to choose from are known as overt or covert. Overt operations are conducted with no attempt made to conceal either the operation or identity of the subjects involved. Overt operations are chosen in order to obtain maximum publicity. Covert operations are designed, planned, and executed in order to conceal the identity of the subjects involved. The operation receives the publicity instead of the perpetrators.

The Mechanics of Planning and Developing a Violent Attack

The actual planning sequence will usually involve the most complete and accurate information that time allows. Timetables are usually controlled by the perpetrator. The offender will often consider the court's location. The location is important for many reasons; for example, urban/suburban areas may generate more incidental or collateral damage, death and/or casualties than a rural target. A rural target may be much easier to infiltrate and exfiltrate than an urban/suburban target due to terrain features and sparse population.

Second, offenders may gather maps, photographs, schedules, brochures, sketches, and blueprints of the targeted courthouse. Maps may include commercial maps, topographical maps, and site-generated maps. Photographs may include air-to-ground shots, ground level stills or camera recorded media cut from courthouse disseminated brochures, newspaper articles, magazine articles, etc. Schedules include advertised tours, meetings, special activities and programs, VIP visits, and daily operating schedules. Brochures disseminated for advertisement or information purposes may be gathered and sketches may be drawn depicting line-of-site areas. Blueprints of buildings and facilities may be obtained from government entities, i.e., federal, state, county, and local sources.

Third, facility power/fuel type may be of interest due to flammable, explosive, and contamination properties. Fourth, the number of employees on-site during regular shifts and off-shifts and work hours/days may be documented. If mass casualties are desired, a perpetrator may attack during peak operational hours or, if infiltration is a priority, off hours may be chosen in order to lessen the chance of discovery.

Fifth, courthouse transportation capabilities may be targeted for initial neutralization along with facilities. Finally, security personnel may be evaluated, specifically focusing on the type, i.e., unarmed, armed, trained, or untrained. Security force strength and work schedules may also be projected. Normal duties/locations and emergency response duties/locations may be plotted. Information concerning physical screening systems, alarm systems, communication systems, and emergency access/response procedures may also be gathered.

Once all of the planning elements are gathered and completed, an appropriate attacking force may be assembled. This force may range from one perpetrator to a number of offenders possessing conventional/unconventional weapons and explosives. Mission scope delineates the attacking strength. Time is required for perpetrators to become motivated, answer critical questions, choose tactics, seek proper training, decide upon operating style, complete planning, and gather equipment and attacking forces. During this time span, judicial facilities may operate in a lackadaisical manner believing "nothing has ever happened here and nothing ever will." This mind set must be avoided at all cost or defending against a determined well-planned attack will surely end in disaster.

Thwarting the Attack

To best thwart perpetrators planning a violent attack, it is imperative that judicial systems and law enforcement officials develop a partnership. Launching and strengthening police/judicial partnerships can positively support court violence prevention actions, spur interest in additional preventative measures, and reduce crime, victimization, and fear. The best reason for working together is the sharing of responsibility for the safety of the courthouse and the community it serves. Emergency procedures can also be agreed upon in advance. Finally, the partnership will often generate mutual goals, bolster more power to persuade others to change and/or to get involved, and provide greater information sources for solutions.

The key partners in this endeavor are the senior judicial officials and senior law enforcement officials. The match should be one-to-one, and the partners should have decision-making authority, even though it is realized that most policies cannot be enacted unilaterally. Senior officials should work together to establish agreements and understandings about policies and procedures, develop both preventative and problem-solving strategies, keep each other informed of activities and issues that touch on security and safety, encourage close communications between supervising agencies, and periodically review progress.

Finally, to begin the partnership, officials should set up a short initial appointment to talk about courthouse safety and security issues, review actions that require policy changes, discuss issues or problems with respect to the facility, identify additional community partners, review elements of collaboration among the cooperating agencies, draw up memorandum of understanding (MOU) covering identified key issues, agree on a regular communication schedule and what data will be shared, and get the partnership moving by initiating some early action steps.

Early action steps may be divided into three areas: policies and procedures, training, and public education and supporting programs. Of course, not all of these ideas will represent a viable option for all courthouses. Policies and procedures may include steps to take upon discovery of a weapon, identifying what data needs to be gathered and shared, and establishing effective communications systems. Finally, training and education may include training courthouse staff and law enforcement officers to work together when handling courthouse emergencies or a crisis.

Chapter 2

INTEGRATED SECURITY SYSTEMS FOR JUDICIAL FACILITIES

Introduction to Integrated Security Systems

Given the recent violence in courthouses, it is easy to understand that drastic steps must be adopted in order to ensure personal and facility security. However, there are a number of questions that need to be answered before any security steps are adopted. For example: What are the ultimate costs to judicial systems, criminal justice professionals, operating budgets, citizens, and personal freedom? Will the costs outweigh the benefits? The implementation of drastic security policies and throwing money in the direction of the latest high-tech hardware will certainly give the public the perception of newfound security, but how much of it will actually provide the best safety and security at the lowest cost? With limited budgets and tremendous pressure to do something, security administrators are facing a crisis never before seen in our society. Security administrators must ultimately ask themselves the question: "What can we afford to protect and how can the task be achieved?" This chapter targets these questions and concerns and endeavors to provide the answers.

Any suggestion that a security administrator is not doing everything possible in the area of courthouse security is certainly a political if not moral time bomb. Thus, the goal is to focus on core security issues and the best, most cost-effective ways to reduce risk. While the installation of the latest high-tech hardware may give everyone a quick fix feeling that "somebody is finally doing something," there is a definite need to go beyond politics, policies, and hardware. To better deal with recent court violence, many courthouses are adopting tighter security controls, more effective security programs and methods. Indeed, courts around the world are testing different security systems, ranging from stand-alone methods to integrated systems.

The author has decided to place an emphasis on integrated security systems due to the fact that courthouses share many characteristics with other types of occupancies that focus on security concerns. Indeed, as the reader looks at semantics, he or she is sure to see a correlation between courthouses and other types of entities. Judicial system districts should consider following the footsteps of corporations that have already learned and embraced the concept of security system integration as a cost-controlling feature, as well as a way of ensuring that the staff and citizens are receiving the highest level of security that technology can offer.

To begin the discussion on integrated security systems, the author has decided to cover some statistics gathered in 1999 by *Access Control & Security Systems Integration* magazine. These statistics will be broken down into the following categories: the best reasons to spend money on security; top four areas of concern facing heads of security; top four areas of concern facing organizations; top five challenges facing security professionals in their efforts to provide security for the organization; top areas of responsibility for security directors; important factors to consider when making security product/service purchasing decisions; preferred security system components; important people involved in the decision-making for security systems; best reasons to integrate security; and the best targets for integration.

The author has decided not to list figures or percentages but instead to focus on security topics. Furthermore, the results will be listed in descending order of importance. For example, the best reasons to spend money on security include lowering the incidence of crime/violence, improving operations, lowering liability and litigation, lessening loss/shrinkage, improving customer and employee confidence levels, achieving a return on investment, meeting mandates, lowering insurance premiums, improving business information, reducing staffing, and employing fewer security guards.

The top four areas of concern facing heads of security include employee theft, workplace violence, asset protection, and theft from outside sources. The top four areas of concern facing organizations include insurance and liability, asset protection, workplace violence, and data and information security. The top five challenges facing security professionals in their efforts to provide security for an organization include issues related to money/budget/costs, management/employee support and education, technology issues/outdated equipment, finding/retaining good employees, and workplace violence/protecting employees.

The top areas of responsibility for security directors include access control, perimeter security, electronic surveillance, fire detection/prevention, budgeting, information and data security, loss/shrinkage, employee tracking, and article identification. The important factors to consider when making security product/service purchasing decisions include product liability, service/sup-

port capabilities, ease of use, expansion/upgrade capabilities, meeting specifications, vendor reliability/experience, ease of servicing, and service costs.
Preferred security system components include CCTV/surveillance, electronic access control, intrusion alarms, fire detection and alarms, electronic locks,
photo ID/badging, perimeter security, contract guard services, intercoms/
communications, and security forces (in house).

The important people involved in the decision-making for security systems
include the security manager/director, facilities manager, president/owner,
human resources manager, other security titles, systems integrator, outside
consultant, design engineer, dealer/distributor, and the outside installer. The
best reasons to integrate security include centralized monitoring controlled by
a central computer network, centralized management, minimized redundant
systems, ease of communications, shared databases and information, and sin-
gle-user interface. Finally, the best targets for integration include electronic
access control, intrusion alarms, electronic locks, fire detection and alarms,
CCTV/surveillance, photo ID/badging, computer network security, perimeter security, energy management, and intercoms/communications.

The broadest definition of security system integration is very simple: to
allow multiple security subsystems to work together making the final master
system more efficient. For example, a commonly integrated system includes
access controls, alarm monitoring, and closed circuit televisions (CCTV); for
example, as an access control is breached, an alarm sounds and a CCTV system monitors and records the act. A key criterion in selecting and designing
an integrated system is flexibility, in other words, developing a system that
meets both current and future needs. Making integrated systems work
requires focusing on the solution, not the technology.

Courthouse administrators and law enforcement agencies should collabo-
rate when deciding what, if any, security technologies should be considered
in the development of safe courthouse strategies. Security technologies
require thoughtful consideration, focusing not only on potential safety benefits, but also on the costs that court systems may incur for capital investments;
courthouse modifications; and additional staffing, training, and equipment
maintenance and repair. The intent of this chapter is not to replace the use of
appropriate expert advice or provide detailed instructions on installing equipment or making cost estimates. The intent is to offer practical guidance that
should enable judicial systems and law enforcement agencies to make better,
more informed decisions on security technology.

Physical security controls are a vital component of a courthouse securi-
ty/protection system; however, these controls are only one element in what
should be a complete integrated protection program. Other measures, both
physical and psychological, must be implemented to provide optimum protection. Indeed, physical controls, from a practical point of view, can be

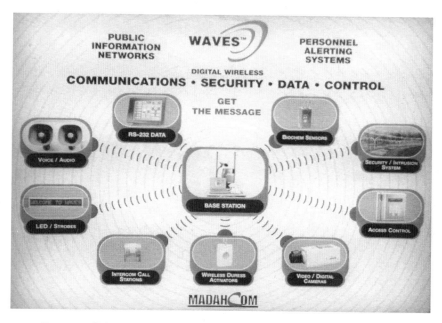

Figure 1. Schematic of MADAHCOM integrated security system.

expected to act as psychological deterrents. Their purpose is to discourage the undetermined offender and delay the determined offender. Physical controls are usually designed to influence the movements, activities, or conduct of everyone entering the courthouse. Finally, the design and use of physical security controls and security personnel should be focused on reinforcing courthouse administration strategies.

Court security is not simple and straightforward. At any particular courthouse, security is effected by funding, facilities, courthouse age and layout, administrators, criminal justice professionals, citizens, courthouse order, operations, policies and procedures, security personnel, local law enforcement, fire codes, local government, politics, the community, and judicial system reputation. Indeed, many courthouses have a number of common inherent problems; for example, courthouses do not usually have the funding for aggressive and complete security programs; courthouses generally lack the ability to procure effective security technology products and services at the lowest bid; many courthouses cannot afford to hire well-trained security personnel; courthouse administrators and their staff rarely have training or experience in security technologies; courthouses have no infrastructure in place for maintaining or upgrading security devices (when something breaks, it is often difficult to have it repaired or replaced), and issues of privacy and potential civil rights lawsuits may prohibit or complicate the use of some available security technologies. Finally, no two courthouses will have identical and successful security programs, meaning that a security solution for one courthouse cannot just be replicated at another courthouse with complete success. The most effective way to find a security system and to develop associated programs which will best fit the needs of a particular courthouse is to perform a security survey.

Security Surveys

Unfortunately, many courthouses operate with little regard to security matters. Usually some security problem must surface before any action is taken to address security matters. The old philosophy arises, "it is cheaper and easier to be reactive in lieu of proactive." Of course, security experts realize the fallacy of this concept that include compromised safety, damage or destruction of property, disruption or destruction of courthouse operations, personnel injury, loss of life, and negative public perception will likely outweigh any current monetary savings.

Quite often, only token security measures, "window dressing," are used in order to give the public the perception that the courthouse is secure (dedicated adversaries will not be fooled by token security measures). In addition to "window dressing," more serious breeches in security arise when novices are placed in charge of security forces and/or other security related operations. Novices may be assigned security management duties through politics and personal favors because many people believe that anyone can be a security officer. This belief is erroneous and leads to poor quality security forces, procedures, and protective measures.

To avoid window dressing, any judicial facility concerned with security must complete a security survey. A security survey is designed to identify, by means of an on-site inspection, all requirements associated with the application of physical security personnel and equipment to counter one or more substantiated or perceived threats. Indeed, a security survey represents a proactive process to prevent and/or minimize the potential for future security incidents. Additional reasons to complete a security survey include regulatory requirements, insurance requirements, activation of a judicial site or facility, significant changes in a courthouse operation or layout, planned courthouse upgrades, increased threat levels, or in response to an actual or attempted courthouse violence crisis or other security incident.

When a security survey is desired, a process must be placed into motion. This process consists of gathering data necessary to conduct a thorough analysis of the physical and operational environment in which the security system must operate and the threat postulated against it. Considerations include the full range of events potentially confronting the courthouse or assets to be protected; the consequences of loss or compromise; and what equipment, personnel, and techniques would be necessary to deter or prevent such events. The scope and complexity of the security survey is flexible and determined on a case-by-case basis.

Factors influencing the scope of the security survey include the size, mission, and complexity of the courthouse; size and complexity of desired security systems; and the desired end results. To obtain specific end results, administrative recommendations may be required; for example, courthouse design changes, security expansion and upgrades, or the complete replacement of existing security systems. The official performing the security survey must remember that desired end results must be decided upon and understood prior to commencement of the security survey.

A security survey should contain the following for each specific courthouse facility: a description of the courthouse to be protected to include any unique operational factors; description and evaluation of any existing security devices; description of any vulnerabilities; details of new protection recommendations; necessary upgrades or structural modifications; estimate of design and construction costs; and an evaluation of security force capabilities.

In-house entities, security equipment suppliers, security consultants, and/or security system integrators can perform security surveys. Each of these options has unique limitations; for example, in-house personnel may possess a great deal of institutional knowledge, but may not have the necessary expertise to conduct a full-scale site survey. Also, it is the author's experience that the purpose of in-house security surveys is almost always defeated by institutional politics; for example, survey personnel may be reluctant to point out problems, especially the ones located in their area of responsibility–how many people fail a self-assessment? Further, cost-saving bonuses may become the in-house goal in lieu of heightened security. To obtain a cost-saving bonus, in-house personnel may select substandard, inadequate, limited security systems that in the long run will perform poorly and require continuous maintenance. Finally, in-house surveys generally work best for small add-ons to existing security systems.

If an organization lacks in-house expertise, outside advice should be sought. Indeed, sometimes the best approach is to seek outside help–as long as there are internal processes in place to monitor and manage that outside assistance. When seeking outside help, planning and a common sense approach are paramount. The selection of a security consultant or firm (vendor) should be based on what the company or person can give back. For example, how far is the person or company prepared to go for knowledge transfer? Does the vendor offer a build, operate, and transfer option? Is the vendor fully conversant with the security market? Will the vendor be around in the future? Finally, does the vendor have a security staff with years of security experience and information?

When preparing to work with an outside vendor, the courthouse administrator should put together a list of requirements and goals intended to fit into courthouse objectives; for example, what is the baseline, what value does the organization place on security, and is security something that will enhance the operation of the organization? These three questions will help determine the emphasis placed on security in the courthouse complex and will help administrators understand exactly what they are trying to achieve.

A baseline review is the start of the process that links security processes and technologies to courthouse objectives. After establishing the baseline, an administrator should clearly see the connection between the security and operating objectives being managed and measured. This marker is an understanding between or requirements within a discipline that supports the courthouse operation including the definition of a target level of security to achieve compliance with organizational needs, integration of these controls to support courthouse objectives, and a structure that provides flexibility for the introduction of new controls when required and a review process to monitor and ensure compliance.

Once the baseline has been determined and the baseline set, the administrator should determine what areas need to be measured in order to achieve desired objectives. The two major factors requiring measurement are security compliance and the risks associated with this compliance. This will result in a better understanding of whether the administrator and organization are security aware and whether security will effectively support courthouse operations. Part of the baseline should also include a review of previously installed technology in order to determine where to go next. The review should include the following questions: what prompted the implementation, was it justified, who signed off on it, dose it conform to policy, is human resource policy supportive, have responsible personnel been adequately trained to understand the technology, and why has it been installed? Guidance should be sought, but a common sense approach will provide the administrator with a quick and realistic view of its security posture and, in turn, a better understanding of where the organization should be headed.

Outside vendors include security system equipment suppliers and security consultants. Security system equipment suppliers generally offer free security surveys to current or potential customers; however, the results often tend to be biased toward the suppliers products. Unnecessary or redundant equipment may also be recommended. This type of security survey should be relegated to current security system add-on work.

Security consultants operating as independent operators can conduct security surveys, but they are only as good as their individual level of expertise.

Security consultants may operate alone, in small teams, or subcontract portions of the security survey to other security consultants. Subcontracting involves one weakness–the dependence on a number of independent operators who may or may not perform to standard. However, efficient subcontracting or teamwork concepts are indicators of quality consulting because few individuals possess all of the knowledge required for optimum performance in every area of a security survey.

Beware of the "know it all-done it all" security consultant. Full-time security consultants are usually a better choice than part-time security consultants because full-time security consultants are building and risking future job opportunities on each and every performance. They know that the security market will not bear many mediocre or even standard results. The best security consultants will have proven track records supported by a list of references. While some part-time security consultants are very good, many are not, since they have other means of support, interest, and obligations that often interfere with security survey mechanics. "Let the buyer beware," many part-time security consultants are in the business for a "quick buck," operating under the philosophy "just give me one big score."

Security system integrators perform security surveys by using a number of security consultants operating in conjunction with a multidisciplined staff capable of delivering a total security survey package. These consultants often specialize in conducting large-scale security surveys, determining requirements, and integrating a wide variety of products and personnel into complete operating systems. The project leader normally chooses a security system integration staff after performing an analysis of presecurity survey data. Like the survey itself, the make-up of the survey team is flexible and dependent on the individual circumstances of each courthouse.

Security surveys should be written in a professional and responsible manner in order to assist in motivating the recipient to take action to minimize security risks; provide an approach or plan that the recipient can use as a framework for taking action; validate or change the opinion of the recipient with regard to the level of threat potential within the surveyed environment; establish a channel of communications between involved parties to include law enforcement agencies and courthouse administrations; and finally, provide the recipient with a benchmark or measuring device by which evaluation of the steps taken in attempting to secure the environment can be measured.

In conclusion, the outside vendor must be security aware, able to demonstrate that it has an understanding of how to measure security, demonstrate a common sense approach, and be able to make sense of security to the administrator as an individual. Look for a vendor that provides real value for the money spent and demonstrates a knowledge that relates to organization requirements. Security is the by-product–look for skill and expertise. Security isn't a product or group of products; it's a process that must fit the individual courthouse complex needs. It shouldn't put up barriers to hinder a courthouse from being productive. Remember, installing technology does not automatically make a courthouse secure. Look for vendors that offer services rather than technology solutions. Technology follows as part of the logical flow.

Initiating the Security Survey

There are generally four major headings in any effective security survey, they include an introduction, identification of the courthouse, elements of the courthouse surveyed, and recommendations. The introduction should include the name, address, and telephone number of the target facility. The dates and times the security survey took place should also be included. The person or persons who conducted the security survey should be identified as well as a briefing-type format stating the reason the security survey was conducted, under what authority the security survey was made, and whether or not the security survey was an initial effort or a follow-up action.

The identification of the courthouse should include the location of the target site by street address, physical directions through the use of a recognizable landmark, and the types of facilities and/or residences located in proximity to the site. Elements of the site surveyed should include the types of risk potential beginning with the boundary and finishing with the interior of the courthouse building(s). Each risk potential should be discussed in the security survey through the use of easy to understand terms.

Specific recommendations should be addressed and discussed in detail after each security element has been addressed. To accomplish this step, two levels of detail may be sought; for example, the site surveyor may describe the minimum steps to be taken to correct security hazards, or second, the site surveyor may recommend the optimum steps to secure the site. Naturally, site surveyor(s) should present findings and recommendations as soon as possible upon completion of the site survey to the individual who requested or authorized the site survey.

Presurvey Planning Phase

The first step in conducting a security survey requires the completion of a presurvey planning phase designed to capture the following information:

1. A master site map depicting all buildings and utilities, roadways, waterways, airstrips, neighboring population location, communication lines, electric lines and substations, and railroad tracks located within

Figure 2. Examples of master site maps.

approximately three miles of the target site. All of these places will be of interest to adversaries and may be used as avenues of approach or escape. Further, these areas will also be of interest to response personnel who may require the delivery of special operations items if a court violence crisis spirals into a protracted problem.

2. A topographic map depicting major terrain features, coastlines, forests, swamps, areas of erosion, creeks, lakes, and rivers. The terrain may assist or complicate site security and adversary activities.

3. Photographs and videotape of the site from as many angles as possible.

4. Information pertaining to important site characteristics.

5. Meteorological data. Are there certain times of the year that produce weather conditions conducive to adversary missions? Weather conditions may also affect response operations.

6. Documentation from prior site surveys. There is no need to completely reinvent the wheel.

7. A prioritized list of assets or high-risk areas that require protection to include a description of their function and sensitivity. Photographs of the asset should include aerial and ground-level photographs plus videotape. Blueprints, drawings, and proposed modifications should also be gathered.

8. All data concerning existing security systems.

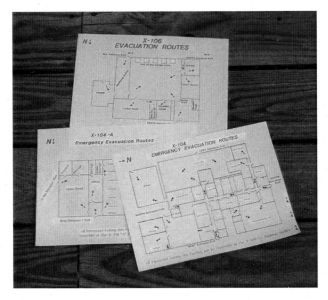

Figure 3. Examples of facility evacuation routes.

9. Current and potential threat data.
10. Copies of all relevant security, safety, and fire regulations to include evacuation routes.
11. Security force data to include response capabilities. This information should be shared with the security staff to create an atmosphere of openness and encourage them to express their opinions. Officers should be reassured that their opinions are welcome and valuable. An existing security force will often be staffed by personnel possessing a tremendous amount of knowledge especially if these individuals have a great number of years of service under a number of courthouse administrations.
12. Site access restrictions such as security identification, prohibited articles, searching requirements, and escort requirements.
13. Courthouse operations description focusing on primary and secondary missions including their sensitivity and criticality.
14. Data concerning planned upgrades or site modifications. These future activities can easily downgrade current security activities and even render them useless.
15. Data concerning the number and type of employees to include background checks.

Conduct of Events

A security survey should be conducted in an organized manner through the use of a defined conduct of events. An effective conduct of events should include an entrance briefing; site tour; validation of presurvey data; survey of specific buildings or areas; survey of safes and vaults; survey of fences and perimeter terrain; evaluation of existing internal defense systems; survey of parking facilities; evaluation of site security forces; evaluation of site interface with local governments and population; survey of adjoining property; evaluation of site access controls; evaluation of lighting systems and requirements; survey of power supply systems; survey of telecommunication systems; and finally, a survey of vulnerability countermeasures. Each one of these surveys or evaluations will now be discussed individually.

Entrance Briefing

The entrance briefing should be conducted on the first day of the survey. A designated team chief should brief applicable courthouse personnel on the objectives of the survey, the information to be gathered, and the procedures to be followed. At this time, the courthouse representative should voice any special concerns, requirements, or restrictions. Finally, logistical support questions should be addressed and resolved.

The Site Tour

The site tour should be conducted immediately after the entrance briefing and before the start of any detailed survey activity. This tour provides a "feel" for the overall courthouse site, layout, and mission. A thorough courthouse site tour should include as many angles and elevations as possible to include air assets, vehicle conveyed and foot propelled activities. Every floor of multi-storied buildings should be walked through as well as all underground areas and rooftops.

Presurvey Data

Identifying any previously unidentified buildings or areas that may also require a survey should be validated in presurvey data. Validation may disclose discrepancies in presurvey data and also identify any changes that may have occurred since the presurvey data was prepared. Officials must remember that presurvey data is very time dependent especially when dealing with rapidly expanding sites.

Performing the Security Survey

When surveying specific buildings, a description of the building, activity, priority, sensitivity, and existing security devices should be recorded. Physical and environmental conditions should also be recorded. Site personnel responsible for the building should be interviewed concerning operational considerations and planned structural modifications. Photographs should be made of the building to include aerial, and ground-level still photographs and videotapes, plus blueprints and drawings should be gathered. A list of supporting utilities such as communication lines, electric lines, and water lines, plus their location should be recorded. The goal will be to identify proposed new security protection and any necessary structural modifications.

When surveying safes and vaults, the type and construction should be evaluated to include locking mechanisms, structure thickness, weight, attachment to the physical structure, suitability for the application of internal defense systems, tamper indication device use, utilization—opened daily, weekly or infrequently, documentation of sign-offs and second party checks and finally security officer checks and audits.

When surveying fence lines, age and condition should be considered. Rust, fabric tension and material should be evaluated. Holes and the interface of the fence fabric to the ground should be noted. Interface should be evaluated by observing anchors, bottom railing, or wire design and the properties of the ground. The ground should be evaluated for washouts or other erosion. Concrete, gravel, and asphalt bases should be evaluated for strength and physical appearance. Fence attachment to support poles should be noted as well as the condition of gates. Top guard type and condition should be evaluated in addition to overall fence stability. Finally, the fence should be evaluated for proper lighting and existing internal defense systems such as sensors.

When surveying the perimeter terrain, the grade should be considered and typed as flat and level, rolling and hilly, or mountainous. The proximity of the perimeter to bodies of water, high vehicle traffic, pedestrian traffic, landing strips, and railways should be evaluated. Ground cover should be considered and typed as defoliated, rock/gravel, paved/asphalt surfaces, grassy, heavily foliated, or forested areas. Finally, soil composition should be broken down by type, compaction, stability, drainage, surface coloration and reflection.

When evaluating internal defense systems, a record should be developed concerning the type, location (internal or external), specific components, age, condition, and effectiveness. Alarm annunciations should be tracked and recorded, paying particular attention to the amount, types, conditions, and results of physical assessments.

Parking facilities should be surveyed by considering the physical location, amount and type of vehicles parked, access requirements, lighting requirements, and existing internal defense systems. Site security forces should be evaluated by considering the size of the force, training level, equipment available, vehicle number and type, employee turnover, overtime worked, absenteeism, and morale.

Courthouse personnel interface with local governments, military entities (military assistance to back-up response forces), general public (focusing on the local populace), local law enforcement agencies (especially the ability of local law enforcement agencies to assist internal response forces), and jurisdictional considerations must be completed and evaluated.

A survey evaluating adjoining property should be conducted focusing on neighboring industries, the economic climate of the surrounding area, and the potential for mutual aid programs with other nearby proprietary security forces.

Site access controls should be surveyed by evaluating badging and identification systems, vehicle access controls, electronic access control systems, the effective channeling of personnel to appropriate access control points, effective manning of access control points and access control point capabilities.

Lighting systems and needs should be surveyed by considering area lighting; building perimeter lighting; fence, gates, and access point lighting; parking lot and other structure lighting; and lighting in support of internal defense systems, especially closed circuit televisions/cameras.

A survey should be conducted focusing on the power supply, distribution systems, and back-up systems. The focus should be placed on on-site power and off-site power generation; power supply capacity; capacity for expansion; condition of power facilities; number, location, capacity, and condition of back-up power systems. Finally, the fuel supply for the power supply should be observed with a consideration placed on type, quantity, security, and location.

A survey should be conducted on existing telecommunication systems to include installation (above or below ground), capacity and potential for expansion, current assignments, condition, and type. A survey of vulnerability countermeasures should also be conducted focusing on barriers—natural, man-made, active or passive, command activated, or intruder activated. Finally, a survey topic should be developed to fit any unusual considerations or sites.

The reader should remember, while many of the aforementioned survey topics are generic, the survey is site specific and should be adjusted accordingly. The end product should contain observed weaknesses and strengths and applicable recommendations for the enhancement of existing or additional internal defense systems, physical protection devices, and protective forces. Upon completion of the various survey topics, the information should be compiled into an appropriate format for presentation to the customer. A condensed oral briefing should also be prepared and presented as required.

In conclusion, security surveys are designed to find vulnerabilities or root causes to be corrected in order to neutralize or, at a minimum, decrease security threats. All courthouse administrators should invest the time and funds required to complete a security survey. It is amazing that many courthouses continue to operate under the false assumption that "nothing has ever happened here and nothing ever will." This false assumption ignores the changing circumstances of politics, demographics, target criticality and vulnerability, and specific facility mission. The costs of major theft, pilferage, sabotage, bombing, arson, assassination and/or kidnapping of key personnel, destruction or disruption of operations, negative public perception, and the resulting embarrassment of these acts easily exceed the time and cost of a security survey.

Arguments Against Security Initiatives

Once a security survey has been completed and security initiatives are chosen to address security problems and/or weaknesses, it is not unusual for a variety of personnel to lodge arguments against proposed security initiatives. Indeed, many courthouse administrators are slow to implement physical security controls. Courthouse administrators may be reluctant to approve any changes they feel would detract from the open and friendly atmosphere of the courthouse and physical security controls may also be perceived as inhibiting the free flow of the courthouse population. However, the numerous types of security devices and reaction systems available today can go a long way in complimenting an open and friendly courthouse atmosphere.

Specific arguments against the implementation of new security controls typically include statements such as: "We've never done it that way before." One can see the fallacy of this statement. Times have changed, especially since September 11, 2001, and will continue to change; thus, courthouse administrators must evolve security strategies in order to keep up with these changing times. "This is a knee jerk reaction." A short-sighted view, many security solutions will be chosen to address immediate threats while longer-term programs are developed and put into place. "Our courthouse will look like a prison." This may be true if security systems are designed in this manner; however, properly designed security systems will generate the look of a well controlled facility. "Citizens rights may be infringed upon." Security operations and citizen rights can exist in harmony. Furthermore, citizens have a right to a safe and secure courthouse environment.

Further arguments include: "People will think we have a bad courthouse." A faulty thought, the courthouse may actually gain the reputation of being a "good courthouse" as people recognize the fact that the courthouse is taking proactive steps in controlling security/safety problems. "We may be sued." In the aftermath of any courthouse violence incident, courthouse officials will more than likely be sued if security systems were not developed and in place. Further, "security controls cost too much"; as a rule of thumb, the cost of any physical security system should be compared to the value of the items being protected. In the case of courthouse security, the highest value is placed on human life, which is priceless.

Additional common arguments include: "There's no way you can secure a courthouse; look at the size of the building(s) and number of doors." This is inexperience talking, the number of security devices and supporting programs that can be implemented can provide a high degree of security even in very large structures. Of course, any security system can be penetrated; however, the idea is to make the courthouse as secure as possible instead of throwing up one's hands and saying that it can't be done. A ludicrous argument, "We're not doing anything different today than we were yesterday." This is pompous to say the least and falls in line with the many people who have said that they recognized and fully addressed courthouse violence prior to the recent rash of court violence. An organization operating under this philosophy will quickly be left behind by changing conditions such as demographics and security threats.

A final argument includes: "It's hands off unless you need us." Courthouses and law enforcement agencies operating under this philosophy will find out that "when you need us" will likely prove to be too late. This philosophy goes back to the age-old reactive law enforcement operation. Further, this philosophy usually means that the courthouse administration and law enforcement agency is not communicating when communications is central to the support of proactive courthouse security efforts.

In conclusion, the challenge is to apply security technologies in courthouses that are effective, affordable, and politically acceptable but still useful within a number of difficult constraints. If a courthouse is perceived as unsafe (it appears that no security authority prevails), the courthouse will often actually become unsafe. Security technologies may be instrumental in reducing crime or violence in courthouses. Indeed, security technologies may diminish a number of security infractions, eliminate or at least make crime and/or violence more difficult to accomplish, and increase the likelihood of perpetrators being caught. Through technology, a courthouse can introduce ways to collect information or enforce security procedures and rules that it would not normally be able to afford or rely on security personnel to perform.

Court Security: A Comprehensive Program

The goal of court security is to create an environment that is perceived to be safe by all citizens and courthouse staff members; however, safety and security technology should only be viewed as one part of a comprehensive program that each courthouse must develop in order to create a safe and secure environment. Indeed, security technologies are not the answer to all courthouse security problems. Thus, courthouse administrators should never totally rely upon one type of physical security device, security/safety program, or security/safety action. One type of proactive measure will typically fall far short of an acceptable level of security (if one lone program fails, the perpetrator has won).

To generate an acceptable level of security, a number of security systems should be placed into what is known as an integrated system. An integrated system ties a number of security devices and physical security operations together, in such a way that if one device or procedure fails, another will be present to act as a back-up. These integrated systems develop a security measure known as defense in depth. Finally, it should be noted that few courthouse facilities can afford a security program that detects and protects personnel against all possible incidents. Here is where the concept of an integrated security system really shines. First, areas are carefully measured for risk by considering valuable assets and/or current threats. Then, using the integrated system concept, high-threat areas may be protected by the most expensive systems while areas of lesser concern are protected by more cost effective security methods. To clarify, security measures are driven by the characteristics of the courthouse and its surroundings.

For example, a courthouse may be experiencing a number of security problems such as outsiders on site, fights, vandalism and other malicious acts, theft, drugs, smoking, alcohol, weapons, parking lot problems, fence climbing, false fire alarms, bomb threats, and citizen safety issues. Outsiders on site may be effectively addressed by fencing-in certain areas to include no trespassing signs, assigning security officers to man a main entry point, placing greeters in strategic locations, requiring visitors and staff to wear identification cards or badges, requiring the display parking stickers on vehicles, locking exterior doors, utilizing a challenging procedure for any suspicious person, placing security cameras in remote locations, and channeling all visitors through the front office.

Fights may be reduced by the use of security cameras, duress alarms and/or whistles. Vandalism may be reduced by the use of graffiti resistant sealers, glass-break sensors, assignment of security officers, eight-foot fencing in certain areas, and the effective use of security lighting. Theft may be reduced by the use of intrusion detection systems, property marking, reinforced windows and doors, elimination of access points up to rooftops, security cameras, doors with hingepins installed on the secure side, bolting down computers and televisions, locating high-value assets in interior rooms, key control programs, and advanced alarm systems.

Drugs may be addressed by using drug detection swipes and other detection methods such as vapor detection devices and drug dogs. Alcohol use on courthouse grounds may be addressed by having breathalyzer and saliva test kits on hand to test suspicious acting personnel. If weapons are a problem, courthouse administrators may institute the use of walk-through metal detectors, hand-held metal detectors, vapor detectors, x-ray inspections, and random searches.

Courthouse officials may address parking lot problems by using security cameras, parking decal registrations, fencing, identification card systems for parking lot entry, parking lot sectioned off for different courthouse schedules, motion sensors in parking lots that should have no access during certain times, walking patrols, and bike patrols. False fire alarms can be controlled by installing sophisticated alarm systems designed to assess alarms (cancel themselves out) before they become audible. Boxes may also be installed over the pull alarm that sounds a local alarm when activated.

Bomb threats may be addressed by installing caller ID on phone systems; offering rewards for information concerning bomb threats; recording all phone calls, complete with a message regarding this fact at the beginning of each incoming call; routing all incoming calls through a district office; contacting the phone company for support; preventing the installment of pay phones inside the courthouse; and developing a policy instituting strict/controlled use of courthouse telephones. Finally, employee safety may be enhanced by issuing or installing duress alarms, instituting roving patrols, leaving office doors open, installing security cameras in high-threat areas, and instituting controlled access to administrative areas.

Of course, other options are certainly available and an integrated security system design is only limited by one's imagination. However, any application of a device, policy, or system should be researched and evaluated by the local legal organization and law enforcement agencies. It may be beneficial to check with other courthouses in the area to see if they have already implemented any of the security measures under consideration. Finally, staff members should be contacted for their opinions. It is true that including these people will likely lengthen the decision-making process; however, invoking their participation may ensure their buy-in and the community will surely hear that the courthouse is taking active security measures to develop a safe and secure environment.

Physical Security Philosophy

There are three basic elements of physical security: control and monitor the access of persons or vehicles; prevent and detect unauthorized intrusions; and safeguard people, assets, and buildings. These elements are achieved by employing physical security controls, systems, processes, and procedures that deny unauthorized access; deter or discourage attempts to gain unauthorized access; delay those who attempt to gain unauthorized access; and detect both criminal and noncriminal threats.

A courthouse facility's protection system may be referred to as a series of perimeters or protective rings that goes far beyond the fringe of the courthouse. Physical security controls are utilized at each of the three main perimeters or rings in an attempt to control or delay entry and in some cases to control and delay exiting. The main perimeters are referred to as the outer, middle, and inner protective rings.

Outer protective rings consist of physical controls such as fences, barriers, lighting, warning signs, and alarms. These controls are generally designed to define the property line, channel personnel and vehicles through specified access points, and enable general surveillance of the activities occurring in these areas. A middle protective ring typically focuses on the exterior of courthouse buildings. This protective ring may include lighting, alarms, locks, window and door bars, warning signs, barriers such as fencing and walls, CCTV, and access control devices. The inner protective ring focuses on the interior of courthouse buildings. Like the middle protective ring, the inner protective ring may include lighting, alarms, locks, window and door bars, warning signs, barriers such as fencing and walls, CCTV, and access control devices.

Physical Barriers

Physical barriers may be used to define a physical area, prevent penetration, and/or control access to specified areas. The correct choice of barrier can enhance security to a significant degree; however, many physical barriers used in the world of high-threat security operations are not suitable for courthouse facilities. Thus, only specific physical barriers deemed appropriate for court security will be discussed. Example physical barriers include walls, barbed wire, fences, obstacle systems, natural barriers, locked/blockaded entrances, and lock systems.

Security walls are generally used in a point protection role and may be used to cover doors, various openings, windows, other walls, and similar areas. Security walls are generally add-ons, meaning they are not part of the structural integrity of the building. Security walls may be constructed in various thickness and heights and from various materials such as wood, concrete, bricks, masonry, metal, rocks, sandbags, and/or plastic, etc.

Barbed wire is available in various designs and forms, for example, wire with knotted barbs; wire with razor-like barbs, string wire, and rolled wire/concertina. The use of barbed wire should be very limited in courthouse environments. Barbed wire will often be viewed as adversarial by a number of people and thus generate negative comments. Plus, there could be liability issues directed toward courthouse officials if a citizen is injured by structures or physical security barriers topped with barbed wire.

Fences represent one of the oldest forms of physical security devices and are typically used to define a particular area, preclude inadvertent or accidental entry into an area, prevent or delay unauthorized entry, and to control pedestrian and vehicle traffic. Fencing is usually less costly than other types of construction materials and can be adapted to fit almost any security application. Fences may be constructed from a number of materials and in different designs and come complete with various means of fence support. There are many types available, for example: flat wood/picket fence; round wooden posts; wooden slats; chain link (metal); chicken wire (metal); iron grill/spiked metal; fabric/rope/material; soils plastic/vinyl, and rollable continuous–plastic expedient fencing. Finally, the protection offered by fencing is in direct proportion to its height. For example, a short fence is basically a psychological deterrent whereas a high fence with barbed wire outriggers is a physical deterrent.

Some general suggestions concerning fences include the following: chain-link fences should be constructed of 16 gauge wire or stronger to avoid being easily cut; fencing should consist of a two-inch opening per link (fine mesh can be hard to see through and wide openings can provide intruders with hand and toe holds for climbing); fences should be eight feet tall or higher with a minimal number of entrances and exits; and fence materials should be installed under the ground and covered to prevent intruders from tunneling or crawling underneath.

Further, barbed wire, concertina wire, or razor ribbon may be attached to the top of the fence to discourage intruders from climbing over the top. Additionally, fences should be positioned where there are no physical or organic obstructions nearby which could afford intruders ways to scale or otherwise breach the fence. Vehicles and machinery should be prohibited from parking or otherwise be located within 10 feet of any fence. These devices may afford an offender the opportunity to scale the vehicle or machinery and jump over the fence. Of course, security personnel should periodically check the fence for damage or signs of unauthorized access.

Additional fencing concerns include the following: gates, alarms, surveillance systems, security personnel, and dogs. Gates should be few in number and placed in strategic, easily observed, well-illuminated locations. Further, gates should be secured with heavy chains, padlocks and/or a closable locking bar, and may be controlled by electronic card-keys, electronic push-button codes, or security guards. Alarms and surveillance systems may be incorporated into fences to serve as additional protection. Finally, fences may be periodically patrolled by security personnel and/or canines.

Obstacle systems accomplish their purpose by providing various types of obstacles and blockades that hinder access to certain areas. Possible types of materials and designs include the following: planted trees; shrubs; bushes; hedges and plants; felled or partially felled trees; wooden, concrete, or metal blocks partially embedded into the ground; bricks, rocks, or stones; and road spikes. For example, trees and shrubs may be used to create physical barriers or to enhance other barriers. Bushes with thorns are an effective physical barrier by themselves or can be planted in front of a wall or fence. While trees and shrubs are used effectively as part of a security protection system, they can create security vulnerabilities. For example, trees and shrubs permitted to grow out of control can conceal persons trying to penetrate the area or provide a convenient place to store contraband or stolen property. Mechanical devices may also be used as obstacles. These mechanical devices are typically vertically or horizontally hinged, and are often capable of being remotely opened to allow traffic, when desired, through a point of entry. Mechanical systems may also include door/gate entry systems.

Natural barriers may be considered in the original plan of design to accomplish various objectives. Essentially, these types of barriers are naturally located in an area; for example, hills, ridges, canyons, valleys, water, forests, plateaus, and plains. Although some of these natural areas are not necessarily barriers in the colloquial sense of the word, such as plateaus or plains, they can enhance the physical security of an area by allowing a greater degree of observability of the surrounding area.

Locked/barricaded entrances often use barriers that can be removed intentionally to allow access and entrance into a certain area. For example, doors and windows which by design are meant to open and close, are included in this category. Courthouse administrators should develop policies mandating that windows remain closed and locked to avoid avenues of accessibility by unauthorized personnel or the introduction of contraband into the building. Further, aside from being locked and closed, entrances must also be designed with sufficient strength to resist forced entry. Forced entry protection may also be required in the following areas: roofs, ceilings, floors, walls, and dividing barriers (expensive locking and alarm systems mean nothing if one can easily enter through one of these areas).

Figure 4. Perimeter fence showing good lighting and a vehicle barrier in the background.

Of course, windows and doors will prove to be the most vulnerable to unauthorized entry so a few additional concerns will be noted. Hinges should be located on the inside of the area protected to prevent an outsider from removing the hinge pins and the entire door. Further, doors and windows may be purchased that have hinges located within the confines of the door/window itself or they may be constructed using a pinless design. Window glass may be protected through the use of impact resistant glazing or the attachment of bars/grills/fences that are secured to the structure itself and then locked in place.

Finally, the strength of many doors and windows is sometimes a function of the strength of the screws that hold them in place. Long, strong screws should be used in these areas. Also, one-way screws may be used to avoid tampering and or removal of screws in areas where screw heads are exposed.

Figure 5. Perimeter fence with vehicle barriers in the background.

One-way screws allow the turning of the screw with a conventional screwdriver only in the tightening direction. A regular screwdriver cannot be used to remove these screws. Of course, where possible, screws should be situated in such a way that they cannot be removed from the outside.

Protective Lighting

Protective lighting provides a means of continuing, during hours of darkness, a degree of protection comparable to that maintained during daylight hours. The major purpose of protective lighting is to enhance safety during operating hours, create a psychological deterrent to intruders, and to enable intruder detection. Generally, protective lighting is the least expensive and perhaps most effective security measure a courthouse can employ. Of course, lighting should be positioned to prevent glare and silhouetting. The placement of lights and the style of lighting fixtures must be considered, if closed circuit television (CCTV) equipment is being used. **Note:** See the full explanation of CCTV and protective lighting concerns described later in this chapter. Additionally, protective lighting enables security systems to continue operations during hours of darkness. Finally, effective protective lighting makes the task of an intruder difficult. Indeed, protective lighting is an essential element of any integrated physical security system.

A number of lighting types are typically in use on courthouse areas, they include: incandescent, fluorescent, and high-intensity discharge. Incandescent lighting in the most expensive to operate and includes the flood or quartz lights that are commonly used for exterior home security applications. Most fluorescent lighting is used indoors for office and work area lighting. High-intensity discharge lighting is the least expensive to operate (more light is produced with less power consumption) and is the most common for commercial exterior lighting applications. High-intensity lighting includes high-pressure sodium and low-pressure sodium lighting. A disadvantage of high-intensity discharge lighting is the restrike time. If a momentary power outage occurs, these lights will go out and can take up to several minutes to return to full brightness. Low-pressure sodium lighting is somewhat more efficient to operate than high-pressure sodium due to its ability to provide a fairly uniform light pattern.

There are generally five basic types of lighting systems: continuous lighting, controlled lighting, area or entry lighting, stationary or portable lighting, and emergency lighting. Continuous lighting is the most common protective lighting system and is used to continuously light a specific area. Standard design usually consist of a light fixture mounted on a pole or building. Controlled lighting is typically used when there is a need to limit the area of illumination, for example, avoiding the illumination of adjoining property.

Area or entry lighting is normally used to illuminate perimeter doors and/or entrance-ways. Stationary or portable lighting is normally used to supplement continuous lighting by using floodlights or searchlights. These light systems are usually moveable and capable of directing a beam of light on a specific area or object. Finally, emergency lighting is primarily used as a back-up lighting source in the event of a power failure that affects a facility's continuous lighting. Emergency lighting can usually be employed to duplicate any lighting system.

Some common types of perimeter lights include floodlights, streetlights, fresnal units, and searchlights. Floodlights form a beam of concentrated light and are often used to illuminate boundaries, structure exteriors, and other areas. Floodlights may be positioned to produce glare for intruders trying to look into certain areas. Streetlights usually cast a diffused, low-intensity light in an even pattern, over a certain area, for example, parking lots and storage areas. Fresnal units provide a long, narrow, horizontal beam of light in areas where glare is undesirable. Finally, searchlights may be used that are either portable or fixed. Searchlights provide a highly focused light beam that can be aimed in any direction. These lights are ideal for emergencies requiring additional lighting in a specific area. All of these lights can be timed, manually operated, motion activated, sound activated, or photoelectric.

There are also several types of lamps used in protective lighting systems. Some of the more common lamps include incandescent, mercury vapor, sodium vapor (high and low pressure), fluorescent, and metal halide. Mercury vapor lamps can be identified by the strong bluish light they emit while sodium vapor lamps cast a soft yellow light. The low-pressure sodium lamp is perhaps the most cost-effective and is an ideal lamp for outside protective lighting.

There are also some nontraditional lighting systems that may be encountered; they include infrared (IR) or near-infrared lighting. The spectrum for this lighting is just below red and is not visible to the human eye. Commercial IR light sources include incandescent and light emitting diodes (LED). The incandescent IR type typically uses a 300–500 watt lamp, a visible light cut filter, and will provide more illumination than an LED type. IR lights are expensive to purchase, operate, and maintain. The LED type emits light in the IR and is also expensive to purchase but uses less power and has a much longer life expectancy than IR lights. With either type of IR light, more light fixtures will be required to illuminate an area than with standard visible lighting.

Lights must be evaluated for effectiveness by observing their functioning at night, noting times of operation, brightness, area covered, and ease of access to wires and bulbs. Lights beams may be designed to overlap one-another in a continuous arc or designed to highlight specific areas. All dark areas should be noted and evaluated for attractiveness as an ingress/egress point. Naturally, possible ingress/egress points should be covered with effective lighting schemes. Lighting systems should also be periodically checked for operation. Any malfunctioning lights should be noted and replaced as soon as possible (perpetrators hate lights and may telegraph intentions by breaking or removing light bulbs a few days prior to an attack). Lights should be evaluated for any interference caused by foliage such as weeds, shrubs, bushes, and trees. Foliage must be trimmed or removed if it is causing shadows or completely blocking light beams.

Finally, any protective lighting installation must take into consideration the vandalism problem associated with light fixtures. Proper design and location of fixtures can reduce the probability of malicious destruction; for example, break-resistant cover guards may be used or the fixture design should be such that the failure of a single lamp will not leave the area unprotected. Of course, periodic inspections should be conducted in order to evaluate lighting efficiency and to discover any malfunctioning lights (discrepancies should be addressed as soon as possible).

Mechanically/Manually Operated Lock Systems

Locks represent one of the oldest forms of security and their function is to deter or deny access from unauthorized personnel. Lock systems come in many shapes, sizes, capabilities, and kinds and may be categorized into two types, mechanically/manually operated and electrically operated. Mechanically/manually operated systems generally entail a locking mechanism with a key and/or manually operated opening and closing mechanism. At times, the locking unit may be spring-actuated allowing an automatic locking capability. Other systems entail a design that has the locking unit being the same as the opening and closing mechanism. Generally, mechanically/manually operated locks are the most common and easy to operate locking systems available.

The following is a list of some common mechanically or manually operated lock and key systems and accompanying components: cylinder locks—barrel bolts, barricade bolts, cylinder straight dead locks, and cylinder guards; key-in-knob locks; mortise locks; night latches; panic hardware; pivot bolts; police bolts/braces; straight bolts; vertical interlocking dead bolts; vertical swing bolt locks; multidirectional door-frame interlocking systems; air lock systems; bar locks; channel locks; hook bolts; and combination locks.

Barrel bolts are an inexpensive type of dead bolt that do not use a key from the exterior. Barrel bolts consist of a cylindrical rod that is free to move in a metal housing attached to a flat plate. These locks are frequently used for fences or gates and are sometimes used on windows. Barricade bolts consist of a massive metal bar that is attached to large strikes on both sides of a door. Barricade bolts are available with locking devices and are completely removed from the door when not in use.

Cylinder straight dead locks consist of a type of dead bolt that is controlled by a key-operated cylinder lock. Essentially, the working mechanism of most of these locks consists of a series of pins which are pushed in some direction by the properly designed key so as to allow the cylinder to turn, thereby allowing the actual locking unit to enter either the locked or open position.

However, there are many cylinder designs, each of which functions in a different way. Some of these designs require straight keys that have grooves cut in them and fit the working mechanism of the particular lock being used; other designs have round cylindrical keys. Some cylinder designs have the grooves cut straight in a vertical fashion, and some have the grooves cut at various angles to the plane of the key. Some keys have no grooves and are magnetically coded.

Some cylinder designs are easy to pick while others are very hard to pick or otherwise defeat; however, any cylinder lock can be defeated when subjected to various types of physical attack if the cylinder is unprotected. For example, the use of cylinder guards prevents the cylinder from being wrenched or pried away from the door. Two examples of cylinder guards consist of a steel plate that is fastened over the cylinder and another is a ring that is mounted around the cylinder. Finally, lock manufacturers have different policies for duplicating keys for certain locks. For example, some manu-

Figure 6. Interior view of a solid wood office door fitted with a barrel bolt just above the doorknob.

facturers allow the use of standard key duplicating equipment found in many hardware stores; others require specialized equipment; and still others require the serial number of the lock be sent to the company so that the manufacturer can provide directly, based on the information on file, keys for the lock.

Key-in-knob locks consist of locks installed in a door as part of the doorknob. These locks are available with spring latch bolts or dead-locking latch bolts. The outside knob is locked against movement when a push-button or thumb-turn located on the inside of the door is actuated. Key-in-knob locks should not be used as the only door lock unless it has a dead locking latch bolt because spring latch bolts can often be moved out of the locking position by physically forcing the bolt.

Mortise locks are inserted into a rectangular cavity cut into the edge of a door or into a cavity fabricated in a metal door at the time of manufacture. These locks are available in a number of operational configurations. Mortise locks should not be used in a wooden door unless the door is specifically designed for such use because the rectangular cavity will severely weaken most wooden doors. Vertical swing bolt locks are a type of mortise lock designed for use in thin doors with small frames. These locks use a bolt designed to swing up from the lock, rather than project horizontally.

Night latches are typically rim locks that are attached to the inside surface of a door and cannot be operated from the outside. The latch is projected into a strike box that is surface mounted to the doorjamb. Some night latches incorporate a dead-locking latch bolt. Many of these locks are unsuitable for serious security efforts.

Panic hardware is often used on doors that are secured from outside entry but provide rapid interior access in case of emergency evacuation. Panic hardware usually consists of a massive lock and strike and a horizontal rod across the door. When the horizontal rod is pushed, the door is unlocked and opened at the same time.

Pivot bolts are keyless locks whose resistance increases as the amount of force against it increases. These bolts consist of a cam that moves in and out of place by swinging on a pivot. Pivot bolts lock automatically when the door is closed and released by manual action from the inside.

Police bolts/braces commonly use bars which are braced between the inside surface of a door and the floor; however, some of these bars are simply wedged beneath the doorknob. Some of these bolts/braces have a key locking mechanism attached to the door allowing the brace to be locked. Straight bolts consist of a metal bar attached to a door that is manually moved into a strike located on the doorjamb.

Vertical interlocking dead bolts are attached to the inside surface of a door in the same manner as the night latch. This lock uses a bolt system in which the strike has two or more metal rings that are aligned vertically and extend out from a metal attaching plate. These rings mesh with similar rings on the edge of the lock when the door is closed. Each lock ring contains a bolt which is basically a vertical rod positioned on the end of a lever. When the unit is locked, the rods are moved vertically into the strike rings. These locks have the advantage of restricting lateral movement, making jimmying efforts more difficult.

Multidirectional doorframe interlocking systems generally consist of a door-mounted key/knob and lock system which, when locked, projects one or more bolts/rods into the doorframe at various locations (top, bottom, center, left, and/or right). This system provides a very powerful door locking capability. Another locking system, known as the air lock system, uses pneumatic and air pressure mechanisms to provide for the locking and unlocking procedures.

Bar locks consist of a rigid bar that is extended between the center edge of a sliding glass door and the opposite jamb. Some bar locks have keyed locking devices, may be permanently mounted on the door, and are often pivoted at one end so the device can be moved out of the way into a stored position when not in use. Another lock, called channel locks are placed so that the device butts against the edge of a sliding glass door or window and fastens to the adjacent channel, or track, where the door or window slides. In some cases, the side of the channel is drilled in a number of places so that the door/window can be either locked or opened to one of these positions, with the lock being bolted through the appropriate channel hole. In other cases, the lock is held in place by being clamped to the channel. Finally, a channel lock may be completely manual or include a keyed lock.

An additional mechanical or manually operated lock to be discussed is called a hook bolt. A hook bolt is often used as the primary lock in sliding glass doors. This lock is mounted inside the doorframe, and can be manually or key operated. The bolt has a hook on its end and swings downward from the inside of the lock front, hooking into the strike hole to prevent the door from being moved laterally.

A final mechanical or manually operated lock to be discussed is called a combination lock (push button and dial) that consists of a number of tumblers which must be matched to open the lock. These locks are often more effective than key-operated locks in the sense that they do not allow intruders the opportunity to gain access into the inner workings of the lock. These locks do have the disadvantage of requiring a number of operators to memorize a code in order to operate the lock.

Electrically Operated Lock Systems

Electrically operated systems may use the same basic locking mechanism designs as the mechanically or manually operated systems. However, their opening and/or closing mechanisms are connected to electrical sensing systems. The following is a list of some common electrically and/or electronically related locking systems: card reader locking mechanisms, electric strikes, fingerprint access mechanisms, physical attribute access mechanisms, and push-button locking mechanisms.

Card reader locking mechanisms open a lock when an authorized card is inserted into the card reader. Cards are scanned either optically or magnetically and some systems will retain unauthorized cards and/or sound an alarm. Some computer-operated systems allow authorization codes to be changed as required. Another type of card reader, called a proximity reader, scans cards with radio waves, infrared waves, through magnetic means and/or use other noncontact methods.

Another system, called electric strikes, uses a button to electrically move the strike away from the locking mechanism so that the door can be opened. The door is also capable of being operated in a normal fashion with a key. Electric strike systems may be used in conjunction with an intercom (voice identification), by line-of-sight (visual identification), or closed circuit television cameras (visual electronic identification).

Fingerprint access mechanisms use holographic (three-dimensional photographic) techniques to examine fingerprints by comparing a fingerprint stored on an access card with a control system or an actual fingerprint may be compared with a file stored in a control system. Another system operating along these lines is the physical attribute access mechanism. These mechanisms control access by comparing an individual's physical attributes (hand shape, retinal signature, voice signature, palm print, written signature, body weight, and similar aspects) with measurements stored on file in the system. These biometric devices will be covered in detail later in this book.

A final electrically operated locking system to be discussed is called a push-button locking mechanism (also known as cipher locks). These devices employ a keyboard or push buttons mounted in a protected housing adjacent to the locked door. When the buttons are pushed in the proper coded sequence, the electronic circuit actuates the door bolt or electronic strike to permit access. These devices may also operate on a mechanical basis to allow for manually opening the locking mechanism and manually locking it, when desired.

In conclusion, there are many different types of locking systems that provide various levels of security oriented design. The combination of properties needed or desired should be properly analyzed so that the optimum design is chosen and implemented. Finally, any lock and key system will only be as good as an accompanying control system. Indeed, each court facility should have a key control plan designed to cover the entire courthouse facility.

For example, all keys should be assigned to specific personnel and should be accounted for during periodic security inspections, personnel should be prohibited from loaning their keys to anyone, all personnel should be prohibited from making copies of keys, lost keys should be reported immediately, and compromised locks should be replaced. Finally, a master key (a key that will fit all of the locks of a specific type) should be provided to a responsible law enforcement official.

A master key will quicken law enforcement response (enable key entry without fumbling around with numerous keys) and lessen damage (ramming doors or breaking down doors or breaking windows) to the building during crisis response missions. Some facilities use what is known as a "Knox Box"—a steel container accessible by a special key. The Knox Box is mounted in a strategic location and contains a master key that operates through an encoder and decoder system. Using this system, the master key is irretrievable until a dispatcher or other authorized person enters a release code.

Seals and Seal Presses

Locked or otherwise secured areas may be enhanced by the use of seals and/or seal presses also known as Tamper Indicating Devices (TID). TID may be color coded for specific security area use and/or display a serial number or other identity method. Seals are primarily used to identify whether an area, building, or other protected area has been entered or exited. Seals may be constructed from steel, brass, lead, wire, plastic, paper, or other materials. Steel seals are also called railroad seals and the author recommends using this device only as a last resort. These seals are expensive and present a safety hazard to the user because they have sharp cutting edges. The author has witnessed several people cutting their hands and fingers on these seals; some required stitches. When affixing seals, security personnel must correctly thread the seal through the object to be sealed and connect the seal, insuring that the integral locking mechanism engages; the seal should then be physically inspected for correct affixing.

To clarify the use of seals, the following description is provided: a locked door would have a seal affixed through the locking mechanism, and once an alarm or periodic inspection takes place, the broken or unbroken seal will visually flag the responding officer as to whether the door had been opened. If the seal is intact, the door has not been used; if the seal is broken, the door has been accessed and unauthorized ingress or egress has taken place. Of course, a broken seal may also mean security systems have been circumvented and contraband has been passed into the courthouse. For ultimate protection, seal issue and use must be controlled and recorded by security personnel.

Security System Technologies

Like physical barriers, security screening technologies are numerous, varied, and have many different applications. A comprehensive discussion concerning each technology would be beyond the intent of this book. However,

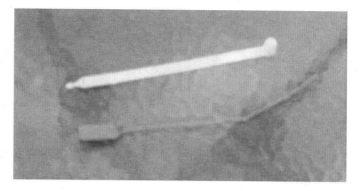

Figure 7. Examples of plastic tamper indicating devices (TISs).

in order to fully present the reader with a general knowledge base concerning these technologies, a large number of security systems will be discussed in an overview fashion. Next, a number of security systems deemed as particularly applicable to courthouse security will be discussed in detail. The intent is to provide the reader with enough information to streamline research efforts when considering security systems/devices for the needs of any particular courthouse. The discussion will begin with alarms and accompanying reaction systems will be discussed at the end of the next section.

Alarms

The function of an alarm is to provide notification of physical condition changes. Alarm systems may be implemented in courthouses to detect unauthorized entry or exit, breaking and entering, smoke, fire, water spillage, equipment malfunctions, changes in temperature (hot or cold), humidity, and the presence of various substances (toxins, for example) in a room or area.

Security personnel must be thoroughly familiar with alarm locations, operations, and procedures at the courthouse they are assigned to protect before their efforts will be efficient and effective. The following is, in part, a listing and discussion of some of the sensing, detector, triggering components, and reaction systems. For example, alarm glass (detector) consists of glass containing small wires (sensing) molded in the glass which triggers an alarm if the glass is broken or cut. Sensing mechanisms may use point (such as the alarm glass described above), area (a doorway), or volume sensors (a large room) that sense a triggering occurrence either at specific points or in large encompassing areas.

Generally there are four types of alarm systems: local alarms consisting of units which produce a loud audible sound intended to alert nearby individuals that a breach or attempted breach of security has or is occurring; proprietary alarms focusing on in-house operations using alarm boxes; on-site central station alarms monitored by contracting security agencies; and off-site police connection systems which are monitored at police stations.

The devices to be discussed include alarm glass, alarm screens, capacitance proximity detectors, duress buttons/switches/alarms, metallic foil, photoelectric controls, photoelectric detectors, pressure mat switches, pull/trip trap switches, stress detectors, and switch sensors. Vibration detectors; infrared motion detectors; microwave motion detectors; sound monitoring systems; sound sensing units; ultrasonic motion detectors; video motion detectors; laser system detectors; personal alarm transmitters; door/window alarms—self-contained; portable audible alarm devices; vehicle alarms; and wafer switches will also be discussed.

Alarm glass typically includes small wires molded into the glass that triggers an alarm if the glass is cut or broken. Alarm screens are usually placed in front of windows or other areas and contain thin metal wires that activate an alarm if the screen is cut or broken. Capacitance proximity detectors respond to a change in the electrical capacitance of a protected metallic item or area caused by the approach of an intruder. They can be used in conjunction with metallic screens, doors, safes, and similar items. Emergency buttons/switches/bars are activated manually and can alert security personnel to a particular situation or trigger a reaction such as the locking of ingress/egress points.

Metallic foil may be used on glass or other breakable materials. The thin foil is designed to break with the glass or other breakable material thereby activating an alarm. Photoelectric controls sense a change in available light and may be used to turn lights on or off or to detect any individual, vehicle, or object coming between the light source and the sensor, thereby triggering an alarm. Photoelectric sensors consist of a light beam, often an invisible infrared light beam, and a corresponding receiving unit. The detector is triggered when an object or person interrupts the beam by passing through it.

Pressure mat switches are often placed under carpets or similar materials and are triggered when pressure is placed on the device, for example, stepping or setting an item on the device. Pull/trip trap switches are mechanical switches that respond to the pulling of wire connected to the device. Typically, the thin wire is placed across a particular area and as an intruder walks into the wire or otherwise pulls the wire, an alarm is sounded. Stress detectors are very sensitive instruments which are usually connected to a floor area, steps, or other structural components. These devices activate an alarm upon sensing stress placed on the particular structural component.

Switch sensors are normally used to detect the opening of doors or windows. The switch itself detects the actual movement and in turn activates an

Figure 8. A Door contact alarm is shown to the left on the wall. The sensor contact switch, the small circular object located in the doorjamb, is designed to mate with a sensor contact switch built into the doorframe. If contact between the two is interrupted, the alarm will sound.

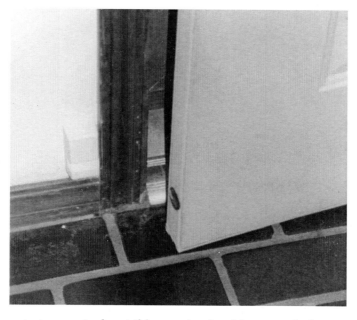

Figure 9. A contact sensor is also visible as a circular object near the bottom of the door.

Figure 10. Ceiling mounted sound/impact monitor. This device will sound an alarm when a window is impacted and broken.

Figure 11. Security alarm system master board.

alarm. Switch sensors are usually found in one of three types: magnetic switches–the switch opens and closes in response to movement; mechanical switches–the switch opens and closes by spring action; and mercury switches–the switch open and closes when moved or tilted.

Vibration detectors detect the vibration of structural components of a building, wall, or other structure caused by the force of an attempted forced entry. Infrared motion detectors sense a source of heat that has moved into the field of sensitivity. Microwave motion detectors use microwaves such as radar waves to detect motion within a given area. Sound monitoring devices automatically respond to unusual, unwarranted, or different sounds or noises typically associated with a break-in. Some of these units incorporate a device that allows various noises (such as equipment starting or running) to proceed without triggering the alarm system. Also, various combinations of sound sensors and sound monitoring systems are possible.

Ultrasonic motion detectors generate a high-frequency sound that is above the normal hearing range of humans. A microphone monitors the sound and triggers an alarm response if motion within the protected area modifies the constant sound the device has been set to receive. Video motion detectors monitor a stationary scene on the video transmission field/sector/screen. Any change in the transmission field caused by motion will be detected, implementing a response system. Laser system detectors are similar to photoelectric detectors (described above) except that these devices use laser beams in lieu of regular light.

Personal alarm transmitters are actually portable panic switches. These devices are low-power radio transmitters that allow a person carrying one to actuate an alarm by pushing a button or pulling a lanyard. The response system reacts to the received radio signal and implements whatever response has been previously arranged. Further, these devices operate on batteries and, depending on the power available, have varied ranges and capabilities.

Self-contained door/window alarms are usually battery powered and include an integral audible alarm. Generally, they can be controlled only from inside the protected area; however, some systems include a radio signal and accompanying control box which allows the device to be turned on or off from outside the protected area. These devices are typically used on doors and windows or other entrances and sense the opening of the supporting structure, sounding the alarm.

Portable audible alarm devices are self-contained and are carried by a person. When activated, they emit a loud alarm that can be used at any location to summon assistance or to deter a transgressor. Portable alarms are typically powered by compressed air, compressed gas, and/or conventional batteries. Vehicle alarms are designed to sound an alarm if someone tries to gain unauthorized access into a courthouse vehicle. These devices are normally powered by the vehicle's own power supply; however, back-up power units are available.

Most systems provide only a local audible alarm, some systems may provide only a remote signal alarm, and some systems may provide both types of alarms. Some vehicle alarms sense the opening of various entrance points through mechanical means or through a change in a vehicle's electrical system equilibrium. Finally, some vehicle alarms sense any significant movement of the vehicle including the shaking or vibrating of the vehicle in one or more directions.

Wafer switches are essentially miniature pressure switches. However, instead of signaling an alarm when pressure is applied, these switches operate when the pressure is released. For example, when an item of a certain weight is placed on the switch, the contacts close completing the alarm circuit. When the item is removed, the contacts open and the alarm system is activated. For example, these switches are easily concealed and do not interfere with the attractiveness of a display.

Reaction Systems

Reaction systems are tied into alarms and serve the purpose of visually or audibly notifying personnel that a security situation is or has occurred. Like alarm systems, reaction systems are numerous, varied, and have many different applications. Various reaction systems include sirens; horns; buzzers; bells; flashing lights; strobe lights; continuous beam lights; mechanical spraying of water, dyes, or other materials; camera activation; telephone dialer units; automatic locking of certain ingress/egress points; and central alarm station notification. The reactions may be local (within the vicinity of the triggering occurrence) or remote (notification of a central monitoring station) or a combination of the two (local and remote). Reaction systems should be chosen to meet various individual courthouse requirements.

Audible reaction systems (sirens, horns, buzzers, or bells) may be chosen for two reasons: first, to shock an intruder with the noise of the alarm and with the fact that the intrusion did not go unnoticed; and second, to alert various individuals that an intrusion or attempted intrusion has occurred. Visible/light alarms also known as alerting annunciator lights (flashing lights—colored or standard beam, strobe lights, and continuous beam lights) may be used in addition to and/or instead of audible reaction systems. Visible/light alarms usually employ sudden flashes or continuous beams of light to deter the intruder and to alert personnel in the area that an intrusion or attempted intrusion has occurred. These units may be particularly useful in noisy areas where it might be difficult to differentiate the noise produced by a local audible alarm from that of surrounding sounds.

Telephone dialer units, upon activation by an alarm unit, automatically dial one or more telephone numbers and relay a recorded message to those on the other side of the line. They may be used to dial the police, security personnel, courthouse administrators, and/or others. The mechanical spraying of water, dyes, or other materials; camera activation; and the automatic locking of certain ingress/egress points are examples of other response mechanisms. Of course, there are a vast number of response mechanisms that could be added to this list.

Finally, central alarm station notification involves contacting proprietary security personnel that an intrusion or attempted intrusion has occurred. These units are basically receivers of data, captured either through wireless transmissions, telephone line transmissions, or cable transmissions. The data received is then coded or identified in a manner that relates to the particular location of the triggered alarm. Upon notification, the personnel attending the central alarm station employ their specific alarm response procedures.

Popular Courthouse Security Systems

For the purpose of this book, the following security systems are deemed as particularly applicable to courthouse security and will be discussed in detail: hand-held and walk-through metal detectors, explosives/narcotics detectors, video surveillance, blast mitigation systems, intrusion detection systems, x-ray devices, duress alarms, and robotic devices.

Handheld Metal Detectors

Metal detection is not an exact science and no guarantee has been or can be made as to the results obtained when using these devices. The success of metal detection will depend upon speed of movement, the distance the metal detector is from the metal object, and other factors. A metal detector actually detects any conductive material (anything that will conduct an electrical current). Counter to popular belief, the mass of a particular object is not significant in metal detection. The size, shape, electrical conductivity, and magnetic properties are the important aspects. Indeed, metal detectors are considered a mature technology and can accurately detect the presence of most types of firearms and knives. When a questionable item or material is detected by these devices, the detector produces an alarm signal which may be audible, visible (lights), or both audible and visual.

Handheld metal detectors are usually battery operated (9-volt or rechargeable Nicad) and are moved around a person's body in a set pattern to search for conductive materials (metal) on or in a person's body. When a suspect object is discovered, the detector will sound an alarm, display a light, or sound an alarm and display a light at the same time. Unfortunately, a metal detector alone cannot distinguish between a firearm and a large metal belt buckle. Thus, trained personnel are required to make these determinations. However, metal detectors work poorly if the operator is untrained or lacks attention to detail. Indeed, a metal detector is only as good as the operator

Figure 12. Garrett handheld metal detector.

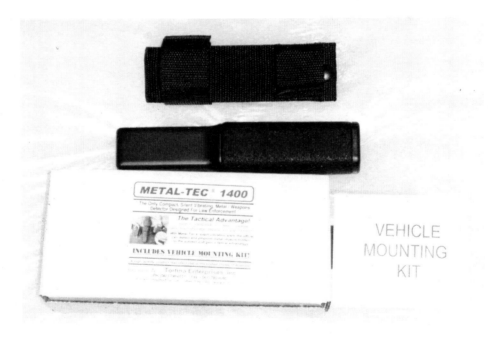

Figure 13. Metal-Tec 1400 handheld metal detector.

Figure 14. Control screening handheld metal detector.

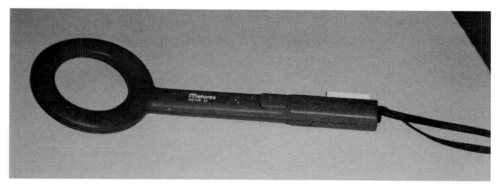

Figure 15. Metorex handheld metal detector.

overseeing its use. Further, metal detectors are usually not effective when used on purses, briefcases, or other hand-carried items due to the large number of different conductive items they contain or the materials used in their construction. These items will typically require a physical hands-on inspection.

Handheld metal detectors should have the following desirable features: a long detection paddle (at least 10 inches long in order to reduce the amount of passes necessary across a person's body); a warning light or beeping system (distinguishable from the alarm tone) that warns the operator that the battery is running low; and an audible feedback alarm that alarms louder or changes alarm pitch for larger suspicious items and softer for less suspicious items. If not accidentally or intentionally abused, most handheld detectors will require no maintenance. The only in-house maintenance that is required is to provide for the replacement or recharging of batteries each night (a new or freshly recharged battery will last for approximately one hour of constant screening). Therefore, handheld metal detectors should be turned off when not in use. A supply of fresh batteries should always be on hand. Handheld metal detectors should have a useful lifespan of about five years and much longer if used infrequently. Finally, smaller compact metal detectors may be purchased and carried on the belt of specific personnel at all times in order to supplement the metal detection program.

Furthermore, handheld metal detectors require less space and are not as sensitive to their surrounding as walk-through metal detectors. However, there are space requirements such a waiting area, a 6' x 6' scanning area, and space for a table used to support hand-carried items and people as they lift their feet for scanning. Finally, the area should be in plain view of everyone in order to avoid possible misconduct, accusations of misconduct, or a confrontation with a citizen. The exception to this rule may occur if a citizen is suspected of hiding some type of contraband on or in a private area of the body.

Though hand-held metal detectors are affordable, it would be unusual for a courthouse of any size to effectively scan people for contraband by solely using hand-operated metal detectors. Manpower would be the major cost of such an endeavor. Plus, using a through-put (scanning) rate of approximately two people per minute, a courthouse would need one operator for a full hour for every 120 citizens entering the facility. Of course, this example through-put rate assumes the citizen arrival rate is evenly spread across a one-hour time period, which is not likely. (Note: The through-put rate will be discussed at greater length in the walk-through metal detector section.) Indeed, handheld detectors are most frequently used in conjunction with walk-through metal detectors. For example, handheld scanners are usually required for use on people who have triggered an alarm while walking through a portal type detector and the operator cannot determine what object has caused the alarm.

Although handheld metal detectors work well, when properly operated, written procedures will need to be developed, followed, and enforced to maintain an acceptable level of performance. A disinterested or unmotivated operator can negate much of the benefit that could be derived from a courthouse's metal detection program. While it is not difficult to learn to use a handheld metal detector correctly, security administrators should not underestimate the value of periodic training for their operators. Training sessions should also include selected members of the courthouse staff who may be called upon to serve as back-up or supplemental operators.

To support any metal detection program, standard operating procedures (SOPs) should be written to describe operating procedures and to support the use of metal detectors. For example, it must be clearly established in written form that in order to ensure the integrity of any metal detection program, everyone must be subjected to the screening process. This SOP should include judges, lawyers, elected officials, courthouse support staff, courthouse administrators, and visitors. This SOP may grant an exception to law enforcement personnel who are armed and emergency response personnel who are responding to an emergency. However, granting an excessive number of exceptions will prove counterproductive, may be viewed as prejudicial, and will generate the opportunity for breaches of security to increase.

Guidelines should also be developed for procedures concerning how many times a person may try to pass through the walk-through portal, when handheld metal detectors and other support scanning devices will be used, procedures in response to discovered contraband, and processes for calling local law enforcement support. A courthouse administrator may also consider having both male and female operators to perform scans on citizens of both genders as the handheld process is a bit more personal than other scanning methods. An option to this procedure is to perform the handheld scan in front of a recording CCTV system. Further, it may be a good idea to post signs notifying people that metal detectors are in use and the fact that if anyone refuses to be screened, he or she will be denied access to the courthouse. This sign may also include a list of items designated as contraband within the courthouse.

While these metal detectors are seen nearly every day, there have been advances in technology which are worth noting. For example, many handheld metal detectors can now be adjusted for sensitivity by external switches and/or internal adjustments. This allows a security entity to adjust screening efforts to fit current threat levels. Some detectors now provide proportional audible and visual alarms in reference to the size, distance, and location of an object. Another new feature is the ability to use earplugs or headphones; these help the operator hear and prevent an alarm annunciation from being heard by the subject being scanned. Other new features concern good-battery/low-battery indicators and operating strengths calibrated to avoid endangering pacemaker wearers or damaging magnetic tapes. Finally, handheld metal detectors are becoming smaller and lighter (8.6 oz. or less), enabling security personnel to easily carry the detector through the use of built-in belt clips.

For example, two compact handheld metal detectors include the Metal-Tec 1400 and the Garrett Enforcer G-2. The Metal-Tec 1400 is designed to be used as an extension of an officer's hand during searches and is not intended to be used as the sole means of searching for weapons. The Metal-Tec 1400 is designed to be used in close contact with the subject and should be used in conjunction with the officer's hands, while conducting a search for weapons.

METAL-TEC 1400. The Metal-Tec 1400 is designed as an enhancement of the officer's hand during searches. Furthermore, the Metal-Tec 1400 requires only one hand for operation, leaving the other hand available for more important tasks. For example, this device can be held between the forefinger and the thumb, freeing up the other fingers so that they can be used during a search or frisking of the subject. The Metal-Tec 1400 can find a metal object and pinpoint its location without the need for a constant sweeping motion. Once detected, the operator can easily determine the object's size by the vibration signature. This pinpoint accuracy capability is very important for discovering metal objects which may be otherwise overlooked when using other metal detectors.

The Metal-Tec 1400 has two advanced features: (1) A vibration signature which can reportedly determine the approximate physical shape (length and width) of a metal object being detected. This is done by turning the Metal-Tec 1400 on end to observe where the vibration starts and ends while moving the unit over a suspicious object. (2) A density discrimination capability which can help the officer determine the threat level of an object based upon its size. For example, large objects such as handguns can be detected approximately three to four inches away, smaller objects such as razor blades can be detected approximately one to two inches away, and metal foil (which may contain drugs) can be detected approximately one-eighth inch to one inch away based on the amount of foil. The Metal-Tec 1400 contains a triaxial sensor that detects in all directions simultaneously regardless of the position relative to the subject.

The Metal-Tec 1400 has only one switch, the power push-on/push-off switch that is embedded in the handle and protected by a water resistant non-slip metal grip. The Metal-Tec 1400 is reportedly the only unit on the market with "silent vibration" which gives the operator a tactical advantage by not warning the subject when metal is detected. The Metal-Tec 1400 can be used in up to 2,000 searches using one nine-volt battery and includes a low-battery indicator designed to notify the user that the battery has been depleted to a level which no longer meets operating specifications. The low-battery indicator causes the unit to constantly vibrate which notifies the user to replace the battery. This feature removes the possibility of the unit being used with a weak battery that may give incorrect detection results. Furthermore, the battery is housed in a separate water-tight compartment and can be inserted into the unit in either direction (a nonpolarity capability) making battery replacement in the field easy and uncomplicated.

The Metal-Tec 1400 is a single piece design and is constructed of high-impact ABS plastic that has a tensile strength of 6,800 PSI for maximum durability. The Metal-Tec 1400 is 7.9 inches long, 1.75 inches wide, 1.30 inches high, and weighs approximately 8.8 ounces. The device is factory set for sensitivity and should never need adjustment in the field. The unit is self-calibrating and will automatically adjust itself for temperature changes between -15 to +30 degrees F.

The unit comes complete with a heavy Nylon web holster that includes a Velcro® strap for easy device deployment. The holster also includes a metal snap, to allow easy removal of the holster from the duty belt, and also serves as a trigger to indicate if the unit is left on when it is returned to the holster (the device will start to vibrate in the holster). Finally, there are five other holster types which may be chosen to match existing gear and a vehicle mounting unit for those personnel who do not want to constantly wear the device.

GARRETT ENFORCER G-2. The Garrett Enforcer G-2 operates by using a transmitter/receiver with automatic instant retune (no adjustments are necessary). The Garrett Enforcer G-2 is 6.3 inches long, 3.25 inches wide, 1.1 inches thick, weighs 8 ounces and is powered by a standard nine-volt battery. A speaker in the unit automatically sounds an audible alert when metal is detected. The sound can be heard in the ambient atmosphere or directed through an optional earphone assembly. The alert tone can also be used to indicate battery condition (when approximately 10% battery life remains, the sound emitted when metal is detected changes from a warble to a steady tone).

The Garrett Enforcer G-2 also has a red light located atop the unit that illuminates whenever metal is detected. This light appears whether the earplug is in place or the detector's speaker is sounding. When the power control switch is depressed and held, the unit will detect metal, when the switch is released, the unit automatically ceases to operate.

Walk-Through Metal Detectors

The typical pulsed-field walk-through metal detector generates electromagnetic pulses that produce very small electrical currents in conductive metal objects within the portal archway that, in turn, generate their own magnetic field. The receiver portion of a portal metal detector can detect this rapidly decaying magnetic field during the time between the transmitted pulses. This detection method is called "active" because it generates a magnetic field that actively looks for suspicious materials or objects.

Some people fear the use of metal detectors on themselves because of the possible side effects of being subjected to the magnetic field. This fear has proven to be unfounded; metal detectors emit an extremely weak magnetic

Figure 16. Control Screening walk-through metal detector.

field that need be of no concern to anyone, including heart patients who are using pacemaker-type devices. For comparison, an electric hair dryer subjects the user to a much stronger field than would be received by a person walking through a metal detection device.

The portal metal detector, perhaps better known as a walk-through detector, is a stand-alone structure that resembles a deep doorframe. These devices will typically take up a space on the floor about 3 feet across, 2 feet deep, and 7 feet high. Weight can vary from approximately 60 pounds to 150 pounds. Portals are generally freestanding and are rarely attached to the floor or a surrounding structure. Power requirements are generally a one-plug system leading to a 110-volt wall outlet.

Figure 17. Metorex walk-through metal detector.

One of the problems associated with walk-through detectors located in courthouses is the fact that the bulk of the courthouse population will arrive to be monitored over a short period of time. Thus, courthouse administrators must decide how many detectors will be required to scan the courthouse population plus the anticipated visitor population. The logistics concerned here may prove problematic; for example, most screening processes will occur indoors so space will be required for people waiting to be scanned (court-house personnel will have to monitor this area to control foot traffic and prevent any potential problems from occurring as numerous people mill about in a constricted area); each device will require one operator; at least one other person will have to be available to hand-scan people who fail to pass the portal scan, and at least one other person may be required to physically search hand-carried items or operate other types of scanning equipment.

Furthermore, to avoid sending conflicting signals to the detector, the person waiting in line to use the portal should be kept back at least three feet from the current user walking through the portal. Additionally, operators of the equipment and people who have already walked through the device need to be at least three feet from the portal in all directions before the next person enters. Further, if more than one portal metal detector is being used, each device needs to be located at least 10 feet from the other device unless the devices have been professionally synchronized.

Finally, it is very important that there be neither space nor opportunity for people to walk around the detection system. Definite boundaries must be established to prevent circumvention of the system and prevent the pass-back of contraband (handing prohibited items from outside the screening area to those who have already successfully cleared the scanning process). Of course, some of these problems may be alleviated by staggering employee reporting times, staggering court times, locating the staging/scanning area further within the courthouse facility, or by developing several multiple entry setups.

Some courthouses have experimented with random spot checks in lieu of a full-scale, every-morning, every-person effort. However, it is very difficult to perform truly random checks with any hope of locating weapons. There is almost always a small but distinct group of citizens that a courthouse administration is most concerned about possibly carrying a weapon. These high-risk citizens often object when they are searched more frequently than other citizens and once this pattern is set, they may solicit help or force another citizen to carry their weapon into the courthouse. Perhaps, a more successful approach to the random spot check is for the courthouse administration to choose an entire room(s) at a time and scan every person in the room.

A well-trained and motivated operator should be able to process between 15 and 25 people per minute through a portal type metal detector; however, this does not include investigation of alarms or intentional/unintentional delays generated by citizens. Thus, the through-put (scanning rate) is generally driven by several circumstances: the number of metal detectors in use; the rate at which people arrive; the motivation of the citizens to cooperate and move through the system quickly; the breakdown and subsequent troubleshooting of equipment; the familiarity and training of personnel operating the equipment, and the arrival of citizens not familiar with the scanning process. **Note:** To address these issues, courthouse administrators may purchase back-up equipment, borrow or rent back-up equipment from a vendor, or enter into a pooling arrangement where spare equipment is shared within a certain judicial district. Indeed, the pooling of equipment will often generate a mass purchase of equipment that will in turn lower the cost per unit.

In general, for a complete, full-scale metal detection program to be conducted every morning, for every person entering a courthouse, approximately one to two weeks will be needed for courthouse employees and frequent visitors to acclimate themselves to the screening process. The first week of any metal-detection program will likely be chaotic. However, as frequent visitors and courthouse personnel become familiar with the scanning process, they will avoid taking prohibited items with them into the facility, avoid taking items with them that will sound an alarm, avoid wearing clothing that is suspect, and add an additional few minutes to their schedule in order to clear the process in time to adhere to their schedules. Courthouse employees and frequent visitors may be assisted in learning the scanning procedure by being issued handouts and attending verbal presentations describing required steps. Signs may also be posted at entry areas that provide proper scanning instructions.

In designing the layout of the metal detection system, the composition of surrounding walls, furniture, flooring, near-by electromagnetic equipment (such as an elevator), near-by plumbing in the walls, and even metal trashcans must be taken into account. Indeed, the optimal effectiveness of a portal metal detector can be downgraded by a poor location.

Like handheld metal detectors, walk-through metal detectors are seen nearly every day, and there have also been advances in this technology which are worth noting. To effectively organize this discussion, walk-through metal detectors will be placed into categories; for example, base-level, high-sensitivity types; multi-zone types, weatherproof types; and high-discrimination types.

High-sensitivity, walk-through metal detectors offer uniform detection sensitivity over the entire walk-through area from top to bottom. Magnetic fields are now capable of detecting all metal objects regardless of orientation in the detector. New technology has coupled high sensitivity with lower false alarm rates that enhances security efforts while generating an optimum traffic flow. New technology includes the following list of advances:

1. Microprocessor technology possessing multiple programs and the ability to select 100 or more sensitivity levels.
2. Uncomplicated mechanical construction.
3. Self-diagnostics used to continuously monitor unit operation.
4. Automatic sensitivity for easy calibration.

5. Programmable reset times.
6. External noise displays complete with volume and tone controls.
7. Visual displays which indicate the area of alarm.
8. Adjacent detector identification through the use of variable tones.
9. Manual and automatic reset capabilities.
10. Easy maintenance procedures.
11. Portability enhancing the ready use of spare/reserve units, the building of integrated systems, and the ability to move the device at will.
12. Finally, these metal detectors are designed to be safe for the monitoring of cardiac pacemaker wearers and magnetic recording materials.

Multizone-type, walk-trough metal detectors possess many of the same technological advances listed above; however, these detectors have numerous additional unique characteristics, for example:

1. Uniform detection can be provided by eight or more separate overlapping detectors that eliminate weak points found in older models.
2. The ability to recognize the presence of several innocuous metal items without combining them into a single item causing subsequent false alarm responses.
3. The ability to display all metal detected at each designated level whenever the signal exceeds the threshold level for that particular zone.
4. The ability to use the metal detector above a metal floor or near other areas of local disturbance by adjusting the sensitivity to provide uniform performance.
5. The availability of integrated construction systems that afford easy installation and dismantlement.
6. Enhanced maintenance abilities assisted by self-testing diagnostics.
7. The ability to detect all metals including mixed alloys.
8. The development of continuously active capabilities meaning that at no time is it possible to toss, pass or slide a weapon through the system without detection.
9. The development of enhanced throughput capabilities made available through the use of fast reset functions.
10. Finally, the availability of adjustable speed responses designed to cover a wide range of velocities or object speed.

Weatherproof walk-through metal detectors also possess many of the same technological advances listed above; however, these detectors possess unique characteristics designed to offer full weatherproofing, protecting the unit in harsh climates ranging from severe winter conditions to tropical environments. Finally, high-discrimination, walk-through metal detectors also possess many of the same technological advances listed above; however, these detectors have some additional unique characteristics designed to offer high-discrimination factors. These include, for example, improved discrimination of metal objects reducing false alarm rates to less than 5 percent; improved interference rejection; enhanced uniformity of detection in high-traffic areas; improved reset speeds for optimum traffic flow and minimum alarm times; and the availability of preset programs designed to meet the requirements set by leading security organizations.

An additional technological development concerning walk-through metal detectors can be found in the area of monitoring networks. These computerized networks provide for the development of remote security monitoring systems. For example, one central PC can be programmed to monitor and adjust numerous walk-through detectors in an instant. Various preset security levels can be applied at any single detector, group of detectors, or a whole network of detectors. Indeed, a specified detector can be set independently of existing security levels, if required. These networks control the detectors' settings and alarms, if deviations arise. In case of emergency situations or detector malfunctioning, both a signal and a printed message are sent to the PC operator. Furthermore, the operator will also receive a message if a detector's setting is altered at its physical location. Finally, the network is protected by multilevel passwords in order to prevent unauthorized access.

In conclusion, to make any metal detection program effective, courthouse access during the rest of the operational day, during off-hours, and during special activities needs to be tightly controlled. A motivated perpetrator can defeat a lax system. Lax systems, improperly operated systems, or poorly designed systems will be a waste of precious security resources and courthouse funds. Finally, a successful metal detection program cannot be poorly funded or run by a courthouse administration that is reticent to make major changes to courthouse policies and procedures.

Intrusion Detection Systems (IDS)

Exterior security at many courthouse facilities, especially the perimeter, is often given only cursory consideration. This lapse of security can often be attributed to an unfamiliarity concerning basic perimeter security systems. The root cause of this unfamiliarity can often be traced to the lack of a basic understanding of the principles of sensor technology and confusion involving the real threat compared to a perceived threat. To begin any satisfactory discussion concerning exterior security, the four parts of an effective security system (detection, delay, assessment, and response) must be considered. To clarify, effective exterior alarm systems must detect an intrusion, provide a delaying effect while the intruder(s) attempt to defeat the system, allow time for both remote and on-the-ground assessments, and provide security forces with the information needed to choose an appropriate response. It must be understood that no intrusion detection system (IDS) is 100 percent perfect, some degree of successful penetration is inherent in all security systems. Thus, it is important to study an applicable intruder profile in order to choose an IDS barrier that has the highest probability of defeating or thwarting the efforts of the profiled intruder.

Designing an IDS

To design an exterior IDS, the following aspects must be considered: the physical configuration, the site, the sensors, probability of detection, nuisance alarm rates, and vulnerability to defeat. Proper physical configurations generally consist of the following three parts: a sector, a detection zone, and a clear zone or isolation zone. A sector is defined as a segment of a perimeter sensor system with a specified length, usually 100 meters. A detection zone is defined as the volume of space in which an intrusion sensor is expected to detect the presence of an intruder. A clear zone or isolation zone is usually defined by two parallel fences between which all obstructions to visibility have been removed. These three configurations are required for the generation of perimeter intrusion detection goals—detection, delay, assessment, and response.

When evaluating the site, particular attention must be focused upon the condition of existing physical barriers, for example, walls or fences, etc. A solid physical barrier is critical because it acts as an initial deterrent against human intrusion, protects sensors from environmentally-caused nuisance alarms (wind blown debris or stray animals), and the barrier may be chosen as a platform for a sensor system. Of course, the perimeter must be well illuminated, visible (free of obstacles and vegetation), and well maintained. Remember, the perimeter is only as strong as its weakest point (areas that might afford an easy means of system bypass; for example, storm culverts, overhead utilities, adjacent light poles or trees, close building structures, equipment parked next to the perimeter, etc.).

Today's exterior IDS sensors have improved greatly over the past several years and are reliable if they are properly applied according to the installation recommendations of the manufacturer. However, it must be understood that exterior IDS sensors have a lower probability of detecting intruders and a higher false alarm rate than their internal counterparts. This is attributed largely to many uncontrollable factors such as wind, rain, ice, standing water, blowing debris, stray animals, random human activity, vehicle traffic, and other sources to include electronic interference. Keeping these factors in mind, IDS sensors must be evaluated by considering three standards: probability of detection, nuisance alarm rate, and their vulnerability to defeat (all discussed in detail below). Of course, sensors must be adequately maintained and routinely tested.

IDS Types

There are a great number of security intrusion detection systems on the market today. Some are applicable to interior applications only, exterior applications only, and a combination of the two applications. The reader will soon understand that a complete description of each IDS is far beyond the scope of this book thus, in the interest of brevity, a listing of technology available has been compiled minus extensive technological descriptions. IDS sensors include microwave, bi-static and monostatic microwave, exterior active infrared, dual-technology passive infrared/microwave, fence vibration, electric field, capacitance, strain sensitive cable, fiber optic fence, taut wire, in-ground fiber optic, ported coax buried line, balanced buried pressure, buried geophone, video motion detection, radar, and acoustic detection (air turbulence). Additional IDS fall into a category other than sensors which include CCTV, night vision surveillance systems, and wide area thermal imaging systems. Even this list is not inclusive of all exterior IDS due to the plethora of new or improved equipment being continually developed and introduced into the market place.

IDS Sensors

Sensors are generally classified into five different types: passive or active, covert or visible, line of sight or terrain following, volumetric, or line detection. Passive sensors are non-radiating and detect some type of energy that radiates from the target, or change in a natural field caused by the movement of the target; for example, passive infrared, seismic or magnetic, fence disturbance, sensor fences, or video motion detection. One advantage of a passive sensor is its difficulty of being intruder-identified. Active sensors use a radiated energy to create a detection field that is disturbed by the intruder; examples include microwave, active infrared, and RF buried or surface mounted sensors. Active sensors have the advantage of offering more data for advanced signal processing and are more difficult to defeat by spoofing.

Covert or visible sensors include the plethora of IDS listed above. Visible sensors may act as good intruder deterrents while at the same time offering easier installation and maintenance. Covert sensors do not reveal (to the layman) any form of IDS on the perimeter; however, covert systems are much more expensive to install and more difficult to maintain than visible sensors.

Line of sight sensors require an unobstructed view from the origin of detection field to its termination point; examples include bi-static (an active intrusion detection sensor in which the transmitting and receiving devices have separate locations) and monostatic (an active intrusion detection sensor in which the transmitter and the receiver devices are either the same or in the same location) microwave, and active and passive infrared. Line of sight sensors are easy to install and service but may require a great deal of site preparation. Furthermore, detection zones are readily identified by potential intruders. Terrain-following sensors are mounted on platforms conforming to the existing terrain—up and down, twists and turns, etc. While terrain following sensors solve the problem of site preparation, they are often more expensive to purchase, maintain, and install. Examples of terrain following sensors include buried sensors, sensor fences, fence-mounted sensors, and RF electric field sensors.

Volumetric sensors have a three-dimensional detection field, or a wide area of detection (the wider the detection pattern, the more difficult the system is to defeat). Examples of volumetric sensors include microwave, passive infrared, electric field, video motion, and buried ported coax. These sensors offer a high degree of probability of detection plus require a great deal of real estate. Line detection sensors detect along a finite line or point. These sensors require less real estate, require a great deal of maintenance, and are easy to defeat by bypassing efforts since they require physical contact by an intruder. Examples of line detectors include fence-mounted sensors, strain sensitive sensors, and sensor fences.

Probability of Detection

The probability of detection may be broken down into the following six factors: amount and pattern of emitted energy (the more definitive the energy pattern the better); size of the object (the larger the object, the greater the chance of detection); distance to the object (the shorter the distance to the sensor the greater the probability of detection); speed of the object (the faster the movement of an object the greater the probability of detection); direction of movement (lateral movement has a higher probability of detection than straight-on movement); and reflection/absorption characteristics of the energy waves by the intruder and the environment (the greater the contrast between an object and the overall reflection/characteristics of the area under surveillance, the greater the probability of detection).

False Alarms/Nuisance Alarms

For the purpose of this book, the term false alarm rate will encompass both false alarms and nuisance alarms. False alarms may be defined as an alarm where the cause is unknown and an intrusion is therefore possible, but a determination after the fact indicates no intrusion was attempted. Nuisance alarms may be defined as an alarm event where the reason is known or suspected (e.g., animal movement/electric disturbance) and therefore probably not caused by an intruder. False alarm rates are of great concern, multiple false IDS alarms equate to multiple assessments and responses which, after awhile, may be ignored and/or generate inadequate responses. Remember, many intruders don't intend to defeat security sensors, but attack poorly designed assessment and response procedures. Therefore, a system without effective assessment and response is dangerous and at the very least almost worthless. To effectively address false alarm rates, a maximum number of false alarms should be established; once this number is reached, delineated compensatory measures, recording and reporting procedures, and maintenance guidelines should be initiated.

Any discussion of alarm types would not be complete without covering two additional alarms—intrusion alarms and tamper alarms. Intrusion alarms are defined as alarms that are actually caused by an intruder(s). Tamper alarms are defined as alarms generated when access doors to sensor electronics or wire connections are opened or when the sensor detects a spoofing attempt.

Vulnerability to Defeat

Vulnerability to defeat is accomplished by either bypassing the system or by spoofing (causing numerous repeated alarms at various places along the perimeter over short periods of time). Spoofing generates assessment methodology frustration, security force confusion, and overloads alarm monitoring personnel and equipment. Vulnerability to defeat can be reduced by designing sensor coverage using multiple units of the same sensor, and/or co-locating more than one type of sensor to provide mutual sensor protection and overlapping coverage (defense-in-depth) of the area. The major goal of a security planner is to choose and field an integrated IDS that exhibits a low false alarm rate, possesses a high probability of detection, and is not susceptible to defeat. Technology will certainly make these goals more achievable in the future, as sensors become "smarter" through the use of advanced digital signaling processing.

Explosives/Narcotics Detection

There are a variety of new explosives/narcotics detection devices available which will certainly prove valuable in many integrated security systems. Indeed, chemical trace detection and identification systems may provide substantial improvement in security against the threat of explosives or the introduction of contraband drugs into courthouse facilities. These systems strengthen essential elements of physical security programs such as access control points and enable the development of more efficient preplanned responses to suspected or actual explosives/illegal drug discovery.

However, it should be noted that any system is not foolproof. For example, it has been reported that books and fruitcake can be too dense for bomb-detection machines to read through and will often set off an alarm. Further, food items like cheese or chocolate can also be mistaken by bomb-detection machines for explosives, and generate a "false positive."

Intelligent Detection Systems

Some of the newest explosive/drug detection systems operate around the principle of trace detection devices manufactured by Intelligent Detection Systems (IDS). IDS allows the operator to detect what can't be seen by the human eye, for example, minute traces of organic compounds. This trace detection technology incorporates both gas chromatography (GC) and ion mobility spectrometry (IMS). This resulting GC/IMS dual technology enables operators to simultaneously sample and analyze vapors and particles generated from explosives and narcotics. This compounding of technology reportedly delivers the highest level of chemical accuracy (a combination of high probability of detection coupled with low false alarm rates) available on the market today.

Future IDS systems will likely be built into walk-through explosives detectors. Presently, walk-through explosive detectors look similar to walk-through metal detectors, except that these devices are much larger and include electronic voice instructions; digital cameras to shoot a picture of personnel passing through the system; puffers, blowers or suction nozzles that collect particle samples off a person walking through the system; and chemical trace analyzers. All of these components are stored in immense side cabinets as big as the portal itself. Present models are very expensive; however, the goal of manufacturers is to drop the price to approximately $100,000 per unit, which would still be four to 10 times the cost of typical walk-through metal detectors.

Walk-through explosives detectors are presently being made by Barringer Instruments, Ion Track Instruments, Thermo Detection, and Sandia National

Figure 18. Ion Track handheld detection system.

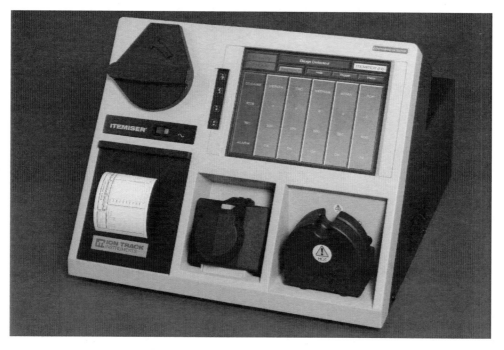

Figure 19. Ion Track detection systems control panel.

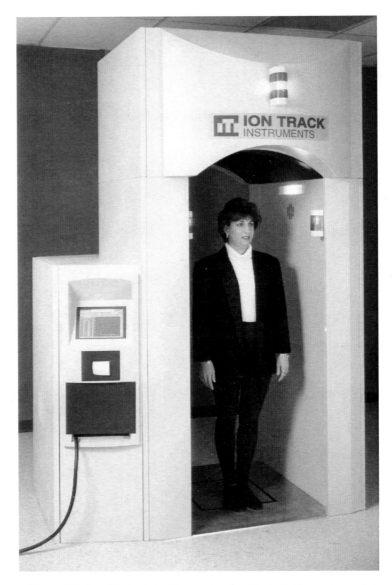

Figure 20. Ion Track detection systems with walk-through model.

Laboratories. Each device basically works the same way: first, an electronic display or voice directs a person to step into the portal; next, the person is directed to turn sideways and a digital camera takes a photograph (photographs are only retained if the device silently alerts); third, the person is enveloped by puffs of air; finally, the person steps through the portal and awaits direction from the operator monitoring a digital display board (a green display means no chemicals have been detected and a red display means the device has alerted). The entire process only takes about 6 seconds.

Chemical Trace Detection Systems

Cutting edge chemical trace detection systems should deliver accuracy, plus effectiveness and enable the following critical system aspects to be realized: high throughput, sensitivity, low false alarms, ease of use, portability, integration, adaptability, low maintenance, and be cost-of-ownership effective. High throughput capabilities means trace detection scanning can be effectively performed in high-volume areas. Sensitivity focuses on the ability of the system to detect minute traces of organic compounds (nanograms to picograms for particles and parts per million for vapors) and the ability to detect and identify specific compounds among varying background levels of other substances.

Low false alarm rates (about four of every 10,000 people will set off a device) are possible due to dual technology use (false alarm rates enhance operator confidence that alarms are real and actionable). Ease of use is especially important for new personnel who are inexperienced and have minimal training. These individuals must be able to learn to use the equipment and be able to interpret test results quickly and efficiently. The system must be user friendly in order to facilitate its use at facilities with high personnel turnover. Portability (lightweight, handheld devices to stationary yet mobile devices) is often important for effective field operations. Integration is important to achieve efficient security-in-depth operations, for example, chemical trace detection systems integrated with x-ray tomography and/or K-9 units.

Adaptability is necessary for application engineers to tailor chemical trace detection systems to the users' needs, specifications, and operations. Low maintenance and cost-effectiveness can be enhanced by a well-designed support program. Indeed, a support program should be negotiated in any contract and should include technological advice and guidance given online, by telephone, and through on-site visits. Support programs should also include full documentation of related activities and the training of operators. All of the aforementioned chemical trace detection system aspects are necessary for fast, accurate, clear, and dependable results, while being safe, cost-effective, and convenient to use.

IDS

There are a variety of chemical trace detection systems on the market today. One of the most comprehensive lines is offered by IDS; an example is the Orion system, an automated, stand-alone, one-step, sampling and analysis explosives detection system. The OrionPlus explosives detection system simultaneously detects explosives and ICAO-mandated taggants. The Ariel stand-alone stationary system detects a wide range of drugs, including cocaine, heroin, amphetamines, and hallucinogens. The Sirius system, which is reportedly the only commercially available system in the world capable of simultaneously detecting both explosives and drugs, and the Northstar one-step, lightweight, hand-held GC/IMS drug detection system are also available. IDS also offers some custom systems such as the Orion walk-through system and V-BEDS–fully automated systems designed respectively to inspect personnel and vehicle traffic based on the OrionPlus architecture.

Ion Track Instruments

Another line of chemical trace detection systems is available from Ion Track Instruments (ITI). ITI manufacturers the ITEMISER and the Vapor-Tracer. The ITEMISER desktop contraband detector is a dual function detection and identification system, ideally suited for detecting trace quantities of narcotics and explosives. For example, the ITEMISER is designed to detect all common explosives such as C4, RDX, PETN, TNT, EGDN/NG, Dynamite, Semtex, and Ammonium Nitrate. Furthermore, the ITEMISER is also designed to detect all common narcotics such as heroin, speed, THC, LSD, morphine, amphetamines, PCP, and cocaine. The ITEMISER can be easily programmed to screen and search for approximately 40 types of narcotics and explosives.

The ITEMISER can be used to successfully screen and search for the trace quantities of contraband that inevitably contaminate the surfaces of baggage, vehicles, cargo pallets, and all types of containers in which contraband may be hidden. Any surface where contraband has been present, including walls and floors, furniture, and even people, can be tested. The ITEMISER switches instantly from a narcotics detector to an explosives detector making the system ideal for circumstances where the search mission concentrates on both substances.

The ITEMISER works by first trapping traces of vapors or particles given off or left behind by explosives and/or narcotics. These trapped samples are evaporated and drawn into the detection system where they are analyzed by a new technology detection system which provides almost one hundred times more sensitivity than any previous detector (as reported by ITI). The detection technique is known as Ion Trap Mobility Spectrometry (ITMS) and operates by ionizing the target vapors and then subsequently measuring the mobility of the ions in an electric field. The mobility of each target ion differs sufficiently so that each is uniquely identified. The whole detection process can take less than three seconds to complete.

Sample collection is accomplished either by wiping a surface with a paper filter (sample trap) or by the use of a battery-operated hand vacuum that uses a sample trap. In either case, the trap containing the sample is simply dropped into the ITEMISER sample inlet automatically triggering the analysis. The ITEMISER confirms the presence or absence of the contraband within five seconds, allowing numerous samples to be processed each day. When contraband is detected, the ITEMISER's alarm panel flashes, the substance is identified, and an audible alarm sounds. A bar graph display changes colors to indicate the strength of the alarm, or for a more detailed analysis, an ion signature spectrum known as a plasmagram can be selected. The ITEMISER can be set to automatically print out the plasmagram or alarm, or it can be stored on computer disk. The stored data, which includes the time and date of the alarm and any notes entered at the time of the alarm, may be recalled for printout or display at any time.

Ion Track Instruments (ITI) also markets a portable contraband detector called the Ion Trap Mobility Spectrometer–ITMS VaporTracer Portable Contraband Detector. The Vapor Tracer is a battery-powered (110/220 current, 90 minute fast recharge battery or a six hour battery pack) portable device which uses ITEMISER (see above) technology. This instrument is 16 inches long, 5 inches wide, 9 inches tall, weighs 7 pounds, and is capable of detecting and identifying extremely small quantities of narcotics or explosives. The system works by drawing a sample of the vapor into the detector where it is heated, ionized, and then identified by its unique plasmagram. Furthermore, this device is easy to operate through the use of a five-button keypad and LCD display. Indeed, the instrument requires little operator training, and is internally calibrated with the touch of a single button. Finally, the VaporTracer can be connected to the ITEMISER contraband detector for analysis and access to the touch screen display and on-board printer.

Concealed Weapon Detection System

The National Institute of Justice has teamed up with the Federal Aviation Administration to develop a system (presently called a NIST device) to reveal concealed weapons in a crowd of people. This technology involves a radar-like apparatus which would illuminate a group with low-level electromagnetic waves. Clothing is transparent to the waves, but objects concealed beneath the clothing are not. Images of guns, knives, and plastic explosives are reflected back to the NIST device, then directed through a set of optics which focuses radiation onto an array of eight centimeter (three-inch) silicon wafers with millimeter-wave antennas attached. The antennas are so tiny that 120 can fit onto a single wafer. An electrical package converts the concentrated electromagnetic radiation into images, and these are projected into a laptop computer screen.

Ventilation Protection

Guidelines should be developed for protecting ventilation, airflow and filtration systems from chemical, biological, and radiological attacks. The idea is to reduce the likelihood of a contaminate attack and to minimize the impact if one occurs. The Centers for Disease Control and Prevention's (CDC) and National Institute for Occupational Safety and Health (NIOSH) has published the following information concerning ventilation protection: prevent access to outdoor intakes; prevent public access to mechanical areas and the building's roof, implement guards, alarms, and cameras around sensitive areas; and restrict access to the building's operational information.

Video Surveillance Systems (CCTV)

When practicable, closed-circuit video surveillance should include the court facility, parking areas, entrances to the court facility, court lobby, courtrooms, and all other public areas of the court facility. Perhaps the best thing about cameras is the deterrence factor they introduce to outsiders who do not belong on courthouse grounds and to visitors and employees who do belong on courthouse grounds. An important aspect of security and response involves knowledge of what's happening or what has happened around or in a specific area. One of the most efficient methods to obtain this information is through the use of cameras. There are many types available each serving a particular need. Closed circuit television (CCTV) has two basic security uses, access control and general surveillance. These systems are very useful in observing perpetrators in the act allowing real time intervention or for recording evidence on tape. From a cost standpoint, the use of CCTV frees up manpower. Finally, the solid documentation that a video recording provides can be invaluable in situations involving liability claims.

Of course, CCTV systems are not without a down side. CCTV systems may be very expensive to install and logistically difficult to service. Additionally, choosing the correct camera equipment requires some technical knowledge. Typically, a single camera is often limited to viewing smaller areas than originally expected. Thus, areas may actually require a number of cameras and supporting equipment and may ultimately raise cost. Further, cameras can be stolen or vandalized and ongoing maintenance and/or operational support are often required. Some applications or areas will not avail themselves to CCTV use and some individuals or even communities will challenge the legality of using cameras. Additionally, CCTV may be circumvented or once the location of cameras becomes common knowledge, people may move their misbehavior to uncovered areas. Finally, someone has to monitor the cameras; if not, who will see the crime happen and take action to stop the action? Otherwise all the courthouse has is a recording of a crime that has already happened.

The hard evidence made available in the form of a video recording can more than make up for the cost of a recording system. Indeed, quite often, when a suspect is shown a recording of himself/herself, he or she is likely to admit to a role in the incident even though there may not be enough detail on tape for a positive identification. Ease of prosecution and the likely prevention of future incidents are additional benefits. Further, color cameras are probably more helpful for most courthouse applications than black-and-white cameras. While color cameras are more expensive, require brighter and more evenly distributed lighting, and are not as defined as black-and-white cameras, they typically produce much more information concerning the scene (color of hair, clothes, and color of car) than black-and-white cameras.

Two types of camera configurations are available on the market: the fixed camera and the pan-tilt-zoom camera. Fixed cameras are mounted in a stationary position and will view the same scene until they are physically relocated. Of course, these cameras may be mounted on a mobile platform such as a patrol car. The scene is typically recorded but may also be viewed simultaneously on a monitor by security personnel.

Some courthouses are using remote viewing services provided by emergency services with the intent of achieving immediate response to a real-time crises. However, the real-time viewing of video monitors has typically produced inconsequential results. Security studies reveal that after 20 minutes of watching and evaluating monitor screens, the attention of most individuals degenerates well below acceptable levels. Indeed, monitoring video screens is both boring and mesmerizing due to a lack of intellectually engaging stimuli. The task of trying to watch multiple monitors will generally exacerbate the situation. A practical real-time security application concerning fixed cameras is to point them at a specific target (a locked door) and tie in a video alarm that will sound if the area is disturbed. Of course, the use of cameras and a real-time display unit without the benefit of a recorder is not recommended. Finally, new technology may achieve a heightened measure of real-time response as computer-operated CCTV systems enable operators to control live video and live audio (two-way conversation may be possible).

Pan-tilt-zoom cameras can operate in one of two modes. The mode for which these cameras are most useful allows the scene that is viewed to be controlled by an operator sitting at a video monitor. The operator controls the direction and angle of the camera as necessary and the zoom option allows the operator to focus in on parts of a scene. The second mode is an automatic mode. The automatic mode allows the camera to automatically scan back and forth over a certain range. Normally, these cameras are protected and shielded from view by opaque enclosures such as domes so that it is difficult for a would-be perpetrator to ascertain where the camera is actually pointed. Pan-tilt-zoom cameras may be effective if they are employed during a fixed portion of the day (lunch periods), if an operator is available to watch and track suspects with this type of camera. Finally, a few pan-tilt-zoom cameras may be placed in certain areas in order to supplement fixed cameras and foster a defense-in-depth posture.

However, most applications in courthouses are better served by fixed cameras. One consideration is that pan-tilt-zoom cameras costs much more than fixed cameras. More important, is the fact that pan-tilt-zoom cameras, when run by an operator, consume the time of a security staff member that may be better spent on roving patrol. When run on the automatic mode, the chance of a pan-tilt-zoom camera looking and recording in the direction where an incident is occurring is much less likely than the chance that it will be looking in the wrong direction. Pan-tilt-zoom cameras also introduce a mechanical component to the system that will require additional maintenance. Finally, it will normally be more cost effective and more reliable to capture incidents using multiple fixed cameras looking in different areas from a single point than to use a single pan-tilt-zoom camera.

Whatever the choice, CCTV cameras should include dome enclosures. Domes are inexpensive, virtually indestructible, protect the camera from the elements, and keep people guessing because they cannot see which way the camera is facing. Domes are also available in different colors to make surveillance units more discreet.

CCTV Terminology and Operating Requirements

Before purchasing a CCTV security system, courthouse administrators should become familiar with basic terminology and operating requirements. This information is important in selecting a CCTV system that will provide the most efficient and effective security requirements for the money spent. Courthouse administrators cannot afford to waste precious funds on non-essential or inadequate CCTV equipment.

A basic CCTV system consists of four elements or subsystems and functions in the following manner: the camera lens collects light and forms an image on a sensitized camera chip; this image is then electrically transmitted

Figure 21. Extreme CCTV Surveillance Systems dome.

over a transmission link to a monitor which translates the signal back to a visible image. A fifth subsystem would be to incorporate a recording device, otherwise known as a video tape recorder (VTR), for preserving the image.

Basic terminology and operating requirements include formats, resolution, pixels, lens focal length, field of view, lighting, shadowing, camera aiming, and camera sensitivity. Formats, resolution, pixels, and lens focal length are the camera-specific part of what determines if a camera scene will be useful for a particular security application. Camera format relates to the size of the cameras imaging device. The sizes may be 2, 1/3, 2/3, or 1/4 inch. The current trend is to make camera formats smaller as picture element densities increase.

Resolution is the ability to resolve or see small details in an image. Resolution is usually specified in terms of horizontal lines per inch. Higher resolution equates to higher image quality. Typical color security cameras produce approximately 300 to 400 lines of horizontal resolution while black-and-white cameras range from 500 to 700 lines of resolution. Higher resolution cameras can be used to distinguish objects farther away than a lower resolution camera. Typically, fewer higher resolution cameras will be needed than low-resolution cameras in some interior and many exterior applications. Of course, higher resolution cameras will typically cost more than lower resolution cameras.

Pixels refer to active picture elements and are directly related to horizontal lines of resolution. Pixels are the actual number of light sensitive elements that are in the camera imaging device. Pixels are expressed in a horizontal number and a vertical number. For example, a camera specified with 768H by 494V picture elements has 494 rows of picture elements vertically, with each row having 768 elements horizontally.

The lens focal length describes the relative magnification of the lens. Similar to the camera imager format, there is a formal size for lenses. The most common sizes are 4.8mm, 5.6mm, 8mm, 12mm, 16mm, 25mm, and 35mm. A 35mm lens has the longest range with the narrowest field of view (the size of the area that a camera will see at a specific distance from the camera). The 4.8mm lens can see much shorter distances but will have a much wider field of view. Most lens sizes can be used in exterior applications, depending on the view desired. However, shorter focal length lenses are typical for interior applications due to the shorter distances involved. Further, the lens format size should be matched to the camera image format size. Mismatched format sizes can result in the focused image being too large or too small for the camera imaging device.

Lighting, shadowing, camera aiming, and camera sensitivity will correspond to the effects of blooming, streaking, and glare that will wash out the video image. Exterior cameras should be mounted below lighting sources and aimed downward to shun direct sunlight, especially that occurring during sunrise and sunset. Most courthouses generally will not attempt to use exterior CCTV cameras at night due to the high levels of lighting that are required. Important items to consider for nighttime camera lighting are illumination level, camera sensitivity, lens type, light-to-dark ratios, area of illumination in the camera field of view, and lighting position.

Illumination level must be high enough for the camera to produce a useable image. The light level required depend on camera sensitivity and lens type and quality. Black-and-white cameras generally have more light sensitivity than color cameras and are thus recommended for most nighttime applications. The light-to-dark ratio is generally set at six to one (as measured on a horizontal plane one foot off the ground). This ratio applies to the entire area of interest that the camera is viewing. The idea is to prevent areas that are so dark or so bright that a person or object would be obscured. Furthermore, a minimum illumination of 70 percent of the camera field of view is normally recommended. A camera is an averaging device (if too little of the field of view is illuminated, the camera will average between the illuminated areas and the non-illuminated areas, resulting in blooming and loss of picture detail in the illuminated area).

The position of lighting in relation to the camera field of view is also important. As much as possible, lighting sources must be kept out of the camera's field of view. Lights that are illuminating a camera scene should be mounted higher than the cameras. Of course, extraneous light sources (other structure or area lights that will be in the cameras view) must be considered since they may cause blooming or streaking. **Note:** Distant light sources that are relatively dim are usually not a problem.

There are a few special lights that may be used with security cameras; these include infrared (IR) or near infrared and light-emitting diodes (LED). The spectrum for this lighting is just below red and is not visible to the human eye. Most black-and-white cameras have sensitivity into the infrared range; however, security cameras must be specifically designed to make use of IR lighting.

Additionally, there are a few types of security cameras that can see at night without the use of artificial lights; they include intensified cameras and thermal cameras. Intensified cameras can produce a picture in conditions ranging from moonlight to starlight. Thermal cameras use the thermal energy radiated by objects in order to produce a picture. Like the lights mentioned above, these cameras are mentioned for information purposes only because they are probably cost prohibitive for most courthouse systems.

Cameras should always be mounted on solid surfaces to prevent movement caused by the wind and vibrations. Furthermore, in the interior environment, cameras cannot be mounted higher than the ceiling so it may be easy for an intruder out of view of the camera to vandalize or otherwise tamper with it. This situation may be mitigated if the scene viewed by two cameras includes the other camera; for example, cameras mounted at each end of a hallway or room should be aimed to include a view of the other camera.

Covert Cameras

There is a special purpose camera that should be discussed due to the fact that they may be used in specific instances. These special cameras are known as covert cameras that are designed to be used when it is suspected or known that unlawful events or security lapses are occurring in a certain area. However, laws concerning privacy issues and civil rights may vary widely, so before any electronic surveillance program is initiated, legal council should be sought. One generality concerning electronic surveillance that is fairly consistent across the country maintains the position that cameras may not be used in any area where there is a reasonable expectation of privacy (bathrooms, changing areas, and some private offices).

Normally courthouse security cameras are mounted in plain view; however, covert cameras are hidden from view. Of course, conventional size cameras may be installed in a hidden location such as behind an air duct, but covert cameras are very tiny and may be placed virtually anywhere. Covert cameras may even be disguised as nearly any common object and are available with a wide range of lenses and capabilities such as infrared operation.

Further, covert cameras come in black and white or colors and often include microphones (caution must be exercised, when using microphones, due to state laws intended to protect private conversations). Audio recording is often considered to be a greater legal concern than video recordings in most states. The recording of conversations is viewed as more of an invasion of privacy, as conversations often take place where the participants do not expect to be overheard. Finally, while the use of covert cameras can be extremely effective in providing evidence for prosecution, most courthouse administrators are more interested in deterrence. Thus, not all courthouse administrators will support the us of covert cameras.

Dummy Cameras

Some courthouses have been known to use dummy cameras in an attempt to fool people into thinking they are under electronic surveillance. This is generally not a good idea because some states have ruled that a person may be misled into believing they will be rescued if attacked. While fake or dummy cameras can create a temporary deterrent to some security incidents, the potential liability it creates due to a victim's impression of being rescued quickly is considered unacceptable.

In conclusion, a camera scene is useful only if an object can be distinguished in the scene. Camera resolution, camera format size, lens focal length, lighting, shadowing, camera aiming, and camera sensitivity all play a role in being able to distinguish objects. Resolution and performance of other components such as TV monitors, recorders, and signal transmission equipment must also be considered.

Video Recording Equipment (VCR)

The video cassette recorder (VCR) is considered to be the weakest link in electronic surveillance systems due to their mechanical nature. VCRs, which typically operate at temperatures between 32 degrees Fahrenheit and 104 degrees Fahrenheit, need to be placed indoors in a well ventilated area where the relative humidity is less than 80 percent and the air is free of noncondensing moisture. If a video recorder must be placed in a dirty environment, a housing complete with a fan, vent holes, and filters should be used.

Further, probably the most ignored maintenance task in most courthouse security departments is the regular servicing and cleaning of VCRs. A maintenance schedule should be developed to include the cleaning of the VCR heads after every 100 hours of use (about every four days of constant recording). The entire VCR unit should be serviced every 2,400 hours, or about every three months of constant use. If well-serviced, a typical VCR will last about four to five years with constant use.

Finally, the VCR should be set up in a secure, protected area. VCRs are attractive targets for thieves, but even more importantly, tapes can be stolen or destroyed if there is an illegal incident to be covered up. VCRs should be placed in a strong lockable cabinet within a locked room. Only the courthouse administrator and appropriate security personnel should have the keys to the cabinet.

Multiplexers

Multiplexers can be used to combine two or more individual video camera signals and send them to a single recorder. This is often referred to as time-share multiplexing and allows up to 16 video camera signals to be recorded on a single half-inch videocassette simultaneously and played back as individual pictures or combinations of pictures upon command. A multiplexer can either be a simplex multiplexer or a duplex multiplexer. The simplex multiplexer can only display a full-screen image of one selected camera or a sequence of selected cameras while recording. A duplex multiplexer can also display multiscreen images while still recording. Essentially, a multiscreen display consists of a split screen that allows for the viewing of all camera images on the system simultaneously.

A duplex multiplexer costs more than a simplex multiplexer and is best utilized when someone is watching or operating the system while it is recording. A more cost-effective simplex multiplexer is best used in courthouse applications where the system is unmanned. Most multiplexers feature camera titling for recording and a permanent time/date stamp on each frame of recorded video. Another feature is compensation for camera synchronization. Multiplexers are equipped with an alarm input for each camera. When activated, these can be used to generate an output to the VCR to place both the multiplexer and VCR into the two-hour recording mode (real time) for a predetermined period of time. Some multiplexers allow only images from the alarm camera to be recorded, but others allow a choice of interleaving (every other field). On-screen programming of the multiplexer allows for simpler programming and review of settings. Programming features should display VCR tables because it is important to synchronize the multiplexer to the particular model and brand of VCR to avoid missing crucial information.

Time-Lapse Recorders

There are also time-lapse recorders that have the ability to incrementally record at specific time intervals, recording a single field or frame of video information with each increment. In other words, a time-lapse recorder can provide a continuous flow of recorded information that can span long periods of time in a very small, storable format.

Event Recorders

Another recorder choice includes event recorders. Event recorders may be designed to interface (viewing the area where an alarm is occurring) with intrusion detection systems or other types of alarms. Upon alarm, this interface signals the recorder to turn itself on to record the alarm event. This feature allows a tape to be used for very long periods of time as no recording is being done during uneventful times. Additionally, event-recorders are generally cheaper than time-lapse recorders.

Digital Recorders

Digital recorders are capable of recording full-motion video. Digital storing and recording have many advantages over a time-lapse or event recorder. The most important advantage is probably the fact that digital recorders require no human intervention, which means no maintenance and no cleaning. This technology is new and is continuing to advance; however, its cost will preclude most courthouse security departments from using this technology for the foreseeable future.

VCR Tapes and Recording Plans

Premium quality VCR tapes are recommended for the constant use experienced by most courthouse applications. Their expected quality lifespan is about 25 recordings. Recording over the same tape indefinitely is not recommended because this practice introduces several logistical problems. For example, some incidents are reported several days after they occur, thus the video of the incident has already been recorded over. A good recording plan should be developed and should include six new tapes every fall and spring (by replacing the tapes every spring and fall, the tape quality is not compromised). Tapes should be labeled Monday through Friday, and weekend. Each morning, the appropriate tape is put into the VCR and when an incident occurs, that particular tape should be pulled and labeled as "removed," along with the date it was last used. A new tape labeled with that day of the week should replace the original. This recording plan should be adequate for most courthouse complexes.

CCTV Warning Signs

It is recommended that the installment of CCTV systems also include the posting of very visible and hard-to-miss signs at the entrances to a courthouse grounds and at major entrances leading into courthouse buildings. These signs may provide an effective frontline deterrence informing the public and courthouse occupants that certain security measures are in force. Additionally, liability issues may be avoided or minimized through the use of signs. Further, public notification that every judicial proceeding is under surveillance may dissuade those who have intentions of disrupting a hearing. Finally, covert approaches to security can sometimes be open to contention, especially by someone who is caught in this way. Thus, signs may reduce contention.

Soliciting Bids for CCTV Systems

Courthouse administrators should follow a number of common sense approaches, when soliciting bids for purchasing any security system. For the purpose of this book and the avoidance of providing redundant information, the bidding process will be discussed in terms of selecting a CCTV system. First, courthouse administrators should identify an acceptance criteria very clearly in the request for proposal (RFP). Second, courthouse administrators should not accept or pay for a CCTV system until it has been installed and is demonstrated to operate according to the RFP specifications. Third, it is often beneficial to request two different camera layouts and their associated costs. One layout should provide the exact capability requested to meet courthouse requirements and the second layout would include the best possible configuration within a specified dollar amount. These two layouts may then be used by the courthouse administrator to approach the approving entity in order to request the funding necessary to meet the goals of the required security system. This is especially important if set funding requires the installation of a security system that will perform substantially below courthouse requirements.

Finally, courthouse administrators should pay particular attention to factory and/or installer warranty language and time lines. A person should be assigned the responsibility of regularly checking equipment functioning and immediately remove any failing components in order to return them to the manufacturer within the warranty period. Of course, it is best for the installing vendor to respond to problems in a reasonable amount of time. Indeed, a maintenance contract is an attractive option and should, if possible, be included in the RFP.

Video Intercom Systems

Video intercom systems are finding extensive applications in courthouse security systems because they offer advantages far beyond typical intercom systems. First, the CCTV capability allows individuals within the protected area to observe individuals outside the protected area. Second, these systems allow the entry door to an area to remain locked at all times and allows operators to selectively grant access onto the premises. Finally, the intercom allows communication from the entry door to the control unit inside the premises. Multiple video intercom systems allow for multiple door coverage, multiple interior stations, and communications between both door to interior station as well as between interior stations. Video intercom systems range from simple door answering units to sophisticated video entry security systems using complex microprocessor-based commercial systems.

Blast Mitigation

Courthouses are often subjected to bomb threats and there is a distinct possibility that perpetrators may use conventional or unconventional explosive devices during a courthouse violence crisis. Due to this possibility and the fact that most injuries and death attributed to explosive devices come from fragmentation (normally glass), courthouse administrators should consider blast mitigation efforts. Courthouse administrators generally have three choices: requiring new structures to have blast-resistant windows, replacing in-use windows with new blast-resistant windows, or requiring the use of blast curtains or blast coating. Naturally, choosing new blast-resistant windows is the best choice. However, many courthouses will not be able to pursue this option. With this thought in mind, only blast curtains and blast coatings will be discussed.

Blast curtains come in a variety of materials, shapes, and designs. Some are easily identified as blast curtains while others are more subdued, having the appearance of conventional curtains. Basically, blast curtains work by capturing blast propelled glass into a special material that bunches these secondary projectiles together, slows their velocity, and drops the pieces directly to the floor. In many cases, blast curtains may be seen as too "adversarial or high profile" for many courthouses. Plus, the number of blast-mitigating curtains a courthouse may require will generally be very expensive. Additionally, blast curtains may interfere with law enforcement officers' attempts to surveil the inside of an area during a courthouse violence crisis response operation. Of course, courthouse administrators may decide only select areas require this type of protection.

Blast coating is typically a 15 mil. thick maximum security film which is custom installed right over the existing window glass. This security film is actually a specially blended, biaxially oriented, polyester laminate capable of providing a measure of protection from bomb blast, severe storm damage, smash and grab crimes, and some bullets. The security film is coated on one side with a resilient, scratch-resistant substance and the other side is covered with an acrylic adhesive so powerful that it reportedly forms a molecular bond with the glass. The film may be transparent or ordered in bronze, gray, or silver tinting. When a window treated with this security film is subjected to a heavy impact, instead of merely breaking as in the case of a normal window pane, the treated glass cracks similar to a shatterproof car windshield, preventing secondary glass projectiles from sailing into a room. If hit hard enough, the coated glass may simply part from the window frame and fall in a contained lump to the floor.

Blast coating may be the best choice for many courthouses for a number of reasons. First, the coating is undetectable until needed. Second, blast coating is cost effective (approximately $6.00 per square foot installed) when numerous windows require this type of protection. Third, the coating is quickly installed and standard size windows can be protected in just a few minutes. Fourth, any size window can be custom fitted with the coating material. Finally, the treated glass may be cleaned in the same manner as conventional window glass.

Window Protection

Over 50 percent of all break-ins are said to occur through glass windows. A number of glass and plastic products have security applications designed to reduce this vulnerability. Some of the most commonly used products include laminated glass, bullet-resisting glass, wired glass, acrylic glazing material, and polycarbonate glazing material.

Laminated glass is composed of two sheets of ordinary glass bonded to an intervening layer of resilient plastic material and is often strong enough to withstand the force of repeated blows. Bullet-resisting glass is also made of laminated glass and typically consists of multiple plies of glass and plastic in a variety of thicknesses ranging from 3/4 inch to 3 inches. Wired glass consists of glass containing wire mesh and is designed to provide resistance to the impact of large objects. However, wired glass has a limited applicability for aesthetic reasons.

Glazing materials are designed to strengthen glass and may be added to standard glass panes at any time. For example, acrylic glazing materials are actually clear plastics which are 17 times more resistant to breakage than glass. Finally, polycarbonate glazing materials are usually blue- or gray-tinted plastics having 300 times the impact resistance of glass and 20 to 30 times more impact resistance than acrylics.

Security Robots

Technology has reached the point that robots are now being used by a number of blue-chip corporations and government agencies to provide physical security in certain areas. Some judicial systems that have a large tax base or that have been successful in obtaining a number of the larger government grants may also be interested in procuring this exciting security technology.

These robots are used in conjunction with computers and video cameras to provide a unique form of security in depth. This technology is moving forward at such a pace that the U.S. Army predicts fully operational security robots such as the Mobile Detection Assessment Response Systems (MDARS) to be in use by the latter part of 2000. Many robots such as Cybermotions Cyberguard SR2/ESP, SR3/ESP, NavMaster III, Cybermotion CyberGuard Security Robot, CyberClean Vacuming Robot, and the ARIES Nuclear Waste Inspection Robot are currently being fielded.

Most robots are designed around two major components: a navigational system designed to enhance movement, and an array of sensors designed to detect a range of hazards. For example, ultrasonic intrusion detectors, intrusion threat assessment logic, optical flame detectors, passive infrared arrays, microwave intrusion radar, smoke sensors, gas sensors, temperature sensors, humidity sensors, ambient light sensors, video transmitters, oxygen sensors, optical pyrometers, inventory tag readers, and high-speed automatic cameras complete with zoom lenses, to name just a few.

The typical robot will operate on its own "random patrol" chosen from a library of pre-established path segments during computer programmed periods—hours of darkness or during the close of business, etc., unless an intruder, fire, chemical spills or imbalances, radiation releases, or other unusual event is encountered. Under these circumstances, an audio/visual alarm is registered in the control room; officers manning the control room may choose to observe the robot as it automatically follows preselected routes to the alarmed area or dispatch the robot using destination commands. Control room officers may even direct the robot to follow perpetrators anywhere in

Figure 22. Cybermotion robot on patrol.

the protected facility, even if an intruder(s) attempts to evade on foot. Furthermore, control room operators can issue verbal challenges or other commands through the robot. Thus, alarms can be immediately assessed and

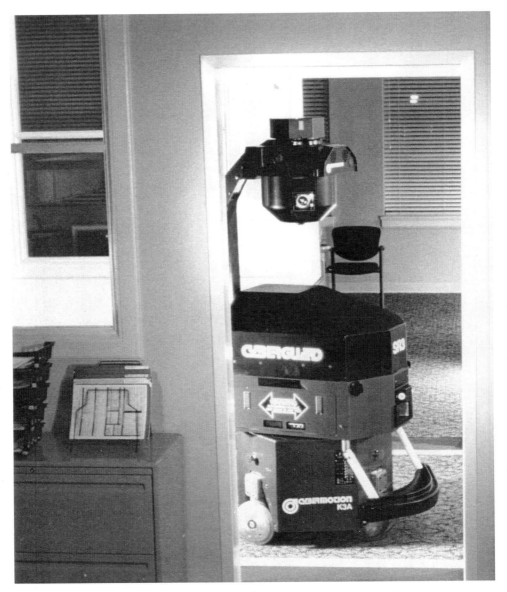

Figure 23. Cybermotion robot on patrol.

some adversary contact can be initiated with no physical risk to security personnel. Most robots are capable of operating from eight to 20 hours and may cover more then 50 miles before requiring recharging.

Some robots also have the ability to conduct an inventory of more than 60,000 specified items while on patrol. This inventory is conducted as the robot reads inexpensive radio frequency (RF) tags affixed to selected controlled items, high-dollar items, sensitive items, easily pilfered items, or special-interest items, etc. Using their RF tag reading capabilities in combination with their navigation system, these robots offer near real-time notification of the presence (or absence) of RF tagged items and their respective locations. Inventory data can be downloaded at the end of the robots' patrol or immediately reported, if desired.

Many robots are equipped with low-light cameras designed to maintain surveillance of an area in total darkness. Some robots have an active near-infrared light source which illuminates the area at an optical wave length that humans can't see but which the robots' camera can see. This is an important concept; by providing real-time surveillance, security personnel will no longer have to take the risk of entering dangerous situations blindly. Control room officers may monitor the robots' camera and then feed responding officers information by radio. Security officers may also enter these situations wearing night vision devices (NVD) that will pick up the robots near-infrared light source in areas that normally would have been too dark for some NVD to operate. These security robots can even be used in conjunction with traditional security forces for searching facilities for intruders or for setting up passive blocking positions.

While moving, some robots use sophisticated sensors to check their current location and to make necessary course adjustments. All autonomous robots have collision avoidance systems consisting of navigation sensors that will detect an imminent collision with an obstacle, even if the unit is being operated by tele-operation. In such cases, the robot will take over the navigation mechanics and either stop or maneuver around the obstacle. If the robot cannot plan and execute a path around an obstacle, it will notify the operating console and request instructions. The controlling officer then has the option of tele-operating the robot around the obstacle. Today's indoor security robots ride on platforms propelled by wheels engineered to deal with rough surfaces, minimize slippage, and climb very low obstacles. Older systems and systems designed for bomb disposal or outdoor activities are propelled by high maintenance tracks. Treaded operation is designed to overcome very rough terrain, climb obstacles, or even push down obstacles; thus, these robots can be very destructive indoors.

During traditional duty hours robots may be stationed at an ingress/egress point to monitor pedestrian traffic through the use of the closed circuit camera and/or monitor the movement of RF tagged items. Typically, robots used in static locations record data for approximately one hour, erase video tape if that period was uneventful, then continue recording for another hour, and start the process again. Of course, there are time-lapse tapes available that provide 48 hours of recording time and these tapes are excellent tools for organizations requiring the archiving of events (remember, events may not seem important at the time of occurrence, only future investigations may reveal the importance of an event). Robots may even be programmed to monitor certain employee identification badges in order to ascertain authorization to certain areas. To reiterate, there is no need to be concerned that robots will run into personnel or equipment as many of these robots track nearby personnel or objects to avoid collisions, plus possess wall navigation and circumnavigation instructions.

A robot's strong points are as follows: robots do not suffer from human foibles and therefore perform duties with exacting consistency, accuracy, and completeness. Furthermore, robots often come complete with a team of experts who work with the purchaser to define the robot's responsibilities and duties; configure the robot to the purchaser's specifications; test and verify the robot's operation; train security personnel to program the robot's functions; provide troubleshooting services; and provide maintenance and service programs. Finally, robots do not require a vacation, pay increases or benefits, and never go on strike. Indeed, robots will often pay for themselves in a short period of time (operating costs may be as low as $1.50 an hour). The author believes that security robots are a viable addition to the sound security principle of strengthening security in depth.

Security efforts will surely be revolutionized as technological advances are applied to future robots. In the future, security robots may be armed with a variety of weapons which range from lethal platforms to less-than-lethal devices. Presently, robots represent excellent systems for providing enhanced security and product assessment within warehouses, educational facilities, office buildings, hospitals, prisons, courthouses, and other enclosed structures where people or property need protection.

Mobile and Static X-Ray Equipment

X-ray equipment best suited for courthouse applications is known as single-energy units. Single-energy units use a vacuum tube to emit x-rays on and through hand carried items. These X-rays come from inside the top of the unit and scan downward in a pencil-thin beam of radiation that generally moves back-and-forth across hand-carried items that are automatically moved through the equipment. Sensors collect the magnitude of the signals that make it through scanned items. For example, items made of a low Z-number material allow more energy through scanned items and material with a high Z-number allow less energy through scanned items. The resulting images are transferred to a TV monitor (black-and-white or color), where an operator carefully examines each image for evidence of firearms or knives. Infrared (IR) beams automatically start and stop the x-ray beam source so that the X-rays are not operational when there is not a hand-carried item located in the imaging position. Shielding has also been added to X-ray machines to protect the operator and the general public. Indeed, today's X-ray machines are safe and are of negligible health risk. About the only potential health risk from an x-ray baggage screening machine would be if someone rode the conveyor belt through the equipment, which would still result in substantially less radiation exposure than would be gained from a medical x-ray.

X-ray equipment offers a valued addition to any metal detection program and is ideal for scanning book bags, purses, briefcases, and other hand-carried items. However, X-ray equipment will require a space of four feet by four feet plus an eight-foot conveyor belt which will add about two feet on either side of the detector itself. Smaller desktop X-ray units are available, but these are used primarily for screening letters and mailed parcels. Unlike walk-through metal detectors, X-ray scanners are not sensitive to their surroundings so virtually no clearance is required around other types of equipment or utilities.

The expected throughput of an X-ray scanner will normally depend upon two things: the efficiency of the operator and the amount of clutter in a typical hand-carried bag. Clutter can also affect the speed of the operator. Purses and briefcases may contain many high Z-material items such as metal rulers, screwdrivers or other tools, foil-wrapped items, etc., which can significantly slow down an operator who is examining each piece of baggage. This clutter may necessitate the bag being pulled from the conveyer and manually searched. Generally, 10 to 20 items can be scanned per minute and as many as 30 items may be scanned if they contain predominantly benign items.

Adequately staffing an X-ray machine may be a problem for many courthouses. These devices require a number of tasks that may require distribution among a number of personnel; for example, placement of bags on the conveyor belt, operating machine controls, viewing the monitor, making a judgment regarding each bag, and performing physical searches of parcels. Of course, security personnel may be assisted by using trained courthouse staff members. The challenging part of operating X-ray equipment is knowing what to look for such as the recognition of contraband or dangerous items.

Most X-ray scanners will last 10 years or more. Indeed, technological advancements are more likely than device failure to render X-ray machines less useful. Thus, there is little regular maintenance required for this equipment.

Great efforts have been made, all over the world, to develop a system or process designed to automatically and reliably detect weapons, explosives, or drugs hidden in mail, luggage, freight, or vehicles. The nearest systems, to date, which begin to achieve these lofty goals concern the use of mobile and static X-rays machines. Indeed, present technological advances have been made which enable X-ray machines to perform a 100 percent noninvasive inspection of parcels, freight or cargo, and vehicles to a degree unheard of in the past.

X-ray inspection systems are now designed to meet a list of essential requirements; for example:

1. The system should be compact and reliable, while at the same time be affordable and economic to operate.
2. Allow integration into existing logistical requirements and security systems.
3. Optimize image representation by furnishing all information relevant to security operations.
4. Maximize inspection quality while expending minimum inspection time.
5. Possess a very high image resolution in order to distinguish very fine structures and differences in density so that wires or hidden items in manipulated luggage or other containers can be easily recognized.
6. Possess image recall capabilities and image manipulation functions for review purposes.
7. Possess loss-free digital recording capabilities for playback requirements.
8. Have the capability to penetrate up to 25mm of steel.
9. Finally, be completely harmless to system operators and personnel located in the immediate area (the X-ray source should generate extremely low radiation dose "integrated exposure" levels outside the direct source beam, allowing operation in confined spaces with insignificant radiation exposure).

Granted, it can be difficult for operators to recognize certain types and configurations of explosives or drugs, especially when using some of the more antiquated systems on the market today. The author considers two of the greatest improvements in X-ray technology today to be the ability of X-ray machines to code material information by means of pseudocolor or color mapping such as the system developed by Heimann Systems, and the ability of some systems to visually highlight drugs and explosives.

Pseudocolor representation works by placing different materials on a continuous color scale according to the atomic number Z of the elements. The color scale comprises colors from orange for elements of low atomic number ($Z<10$); i.e., elements which can be found in organic material, to green for elements of medium atomic number ($10<Z<18$), and up to blue for elements of higher atomic number ($Z>18$). The information concerning material thickness, respectively, the absorption factor is furnished by means of the brightness degree of the color signal so that items composed of the same material which are, however, different in thickness, show the same color while differing in brightness. Material which cannot be classified because of too much thickness is represented in gray. The advantage of a continuous color scale becomes evident when considering overlapping materials: in systems with abrupt color switch-over between organic and nonorganic materials, even thin layers of overlapping materials such as steel, copper, or plastic will lead to organic materials being classified incorrectly as nonorganic materials. The continuous color scale provides a mixed color representation depending on the degree of the mixture of materials that can be distinguished from the color of the overlapping materials. In conclusion, ergonomic color representation presents the operator with additional material information, does not overtax the operator, and supports the operator in making a decision by reducing the confusion many older black/white systems generate.

Perhaps one of the most exciting developments in x-ray inspection systems can be found in Heimann Systems X-ACT inspection technology. X-ACT provides real-time image evaluation functions by marking drugs or explosives with a red frame for explosives or a green frame for drugs—the red or green frame will appear at the same time the image is produced. Thus, the operator is instantly presented with the data required to make a decision without any additional manipulation of the image.

There are a few X-ray inspection systems that are very portable such as the RTR-4 portable digital X-ray imaging system designed and manufactured by Science Applications International Corporation (SAIC). The RTR-4 is a rugged, portable, fully digital X-ray imaging system that can be used by explosive ordnance personnel, law enforcement, security personnel, postal inspection personnel, and industrial quality assurance inspectors in a variety of situations. The flexibility of this system can be seen by considering the RTR-4's ability to penetrate a wide variety of materials from woods and plastics to concrete and steel, while still retaining the ability to detect the thinnest of wires. For example, ordnance disposal personnel may use the RTR-4 to evaluate unexploded ordnance, in order to determine a fusing type, function, or condition. It can also be used by a corporate security staff to perform mail room inspections or point-of-ingress examination of personal belongings. Customs personnel use the RTR-4 for investigation of vehicle panels and tires, when searching for hidden contraband, and even quality assurance inspectors may use the RTR-4 for evaluating manufacturing process control standards.

The RTR-4 was specifically designed to facilitate rapid image acquisition, and provide image enhancement and measurement tools for the evaluation of the content of small objects or packages. The system, powered by 110 or 220 volt AC internal battery or 12 volt DC vehicle battery, is easy to assemble and operate (by one person in less than five minutes), and requires minimal maintenance. The compact size of the X-ray source and imager make it possible for the system to be installed around a fixed target, or situated so that the objects can be placed in front of the imager's screen. Once the system has been assembled, images can be acquired and viewed immediately. Operators may acquire and evaluate images from several hundred feet away by using wireless connections. RTR-4 images are achieved digitally and can be transmitted via modem or floppy disk to other computers for off-site evaluation. Furthermore, these stored images can be used to compile a database for consultation, future comparison, and evidence for prosecution.

Field deployment of the RTR-4 is simplified and made convenient by a variety of custom features. The self-contained control unit, which is housed in a lightweight aluminum case, is designed to operate over broad temperature and humidity ranges. For added protection, the entire system is stored and transported in two foam lined, weatherproof transport cases constructed to withstand the roughest abuse.

Other types of inspection equipment include cargo screening systems such as SAIC's VACIS vehicle inspection system. The VACIS system uses a highly penetrative gamma ray to non-intrusively inspect freight contained on pallets and in trucks, cargo containers, rail cars, and passenger vehicles. Operators viewing the gamma-ray images on a video monitor can quickly and efficiently identify voids, false walls or ceilings, and other secret compartments typically associated with the transportation of drugs, explosives, and weapons. Operators searching for stolen or smuggled goods can use the images to determine whether the cargo is consistent with the declared manifest.

The VACIS gamma-ray based system eliminates the large accelerator-based X-ray source, its accompanying power and control systems, and the conveyor system for the truck or container. This makes the gamma-ray systems far smaller than their X-ray counterparts. The VACIS system can be disassembled, transported, and reassembled in one to three days depending on the configuration. SAIC representatives report that their VACIS-II, Stolen Vehicle Recovery System (STAR) SENTRY-Auto, truck & Cargo Inspection system, Sentinel-Railroad Inspection System, and Recon-Mobile Inspection System packages are faster, safer, more reliable, and simpler to operate than other X-ray systems.

Of course, some of these cargo X-ray inspection systems are static and quite large due to their mission; e.g., full cargo X-rays. For example, some cargo X-ray systems designed by EG&G and SAIC allow a fast, detailed inspection of fully loaded trucks–20-foot and 40-foot containers may be effectively searched without opening the container. This is an important concept especially for organizations that forbid security personnel from breaking seals on containers during routine security inspections. In addition to the cargo, the vehicle structure, cab and engine compartment are seen in great detail. Images are obtained less than three minutes after each vehicle enters the system. Such a detailed inspection by manual methods would take many hours for just one truck or container, possibly causing damage to the contents. False compartments and smuggled goods, such as arms, ammunition, drugs, and fraudulently manifested goods (to avoid payment of duty) are readily revealed, even if hidden in dense cargo. Various image processing functions, which are quick and easy to use, make the examination completely effective. With a minimum amount of training, many of these systems can be operated by customs officers or security personnel.

Like other security systems, X-ray inspection systems are only as effective as the operator–thus, many x-ray inspection system manufacturers offer operator training courses. Any agency intending to purchase or which has already fielded an X-ray inspection system(s) should consider this training for all system operators.

In conclusion, X-ray machines enable a high degree of security to be obtained. X-ray machines make 100 percent visual security check of parcels, freight or cargo, and vehicles to a degree unheard of in the past; offer a broad field of application, for example, enable image evaluation to be carried out in a centralized manner; and finally, offer high throughput capabilities which enable airports and other high security areas to automatically inspect while simultaneously helping to improve operational efficiency. Indeed, X-ray inspection systems protect against a complete range of threats including explosives, weapons, and contraband. Finally, X-ray inspection systems provide a valuable security service designed to enhance security at government buildings, courthouses, corporate offices, and many other high-profile or sensitive areas or facilities.

Entry Control Philosophy

The goal of any entry control program is to ensure safe and secure work areas and to protect against inappropriate interaction between judicial officers including referees and magistrates, and participants in the judicial process. The general public should not be permitted in the area that houses office space for judges and court personnel. The security of the office space housing judges and court personnel must be maintained. Unlimited access to these areas is dangerous and unnecessary. The general public should not be permitted to wander through these areas for any reason.

Figure 24. Vehicle X-rays.

Figure 25. PerkinElmer vehicle X-ray machine.

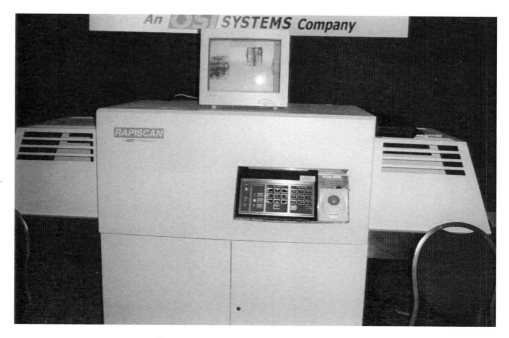

Figure 26. Rapiscan X-ray machine.

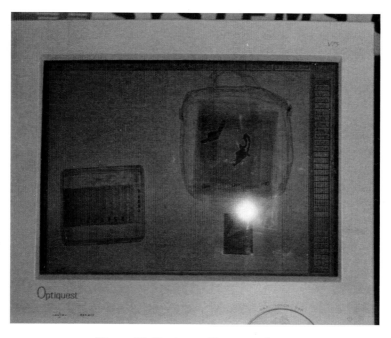

Figure 27. Optiquest X-ray machine.

Figure 28. ViewSonic X-ray machine.

A number of security technologies and procedures are valuable for preventing unauthorized personnel from accessing courthouse buildings and areas such as the judge's chambers and the office spaces of court personnel. In other words, these technologies and procedures should focus on controlling who enters a facility, when people enter a facility, what items individuals take into a facility, who exits a facility, and what items individuals take out of a facility.

Logically, entry control methods and equipment should focus to a large extent on the discovery of contraband items. Further, it is very important for officers to recognize contraband articles and take necessary actions when they are discovered. Of course, certain types of prohibited articles pose no danger to the courthouse population and these items may be confiscated and held for administrative investigation, or released to the owner for subsequent removal from the courthouse. Theses items are varied and are deemed contraband in direct correlation to courthouse rules and regulations, for example, radios, handheld televisions, handheld video games, telephone pagers, cigarette lighters, headphones, and cell phones, etc.

In instances where dangerous or illegal prohibited articles are found, the officer must be able to recognize the articles and handle the item according to courthouse procedures. Certain prohibited articles do pose a danger to the courthouse population and immediate action must be taken to prevent an accident or threat to courthouse inhabitants. Illegal prohibited articles will normally require confiscation and the probable involvement of law enforcement and/or medical personnel. These items include firearms, ammunition, explosives, incendiary devices, alcohol, controlled substances, illegal drugs, and related paraphernalia, etc.

Officers must remain alert to potential danger and/or threat and use all of the detection equipment at their disposal. Officers must apply knowledge, skill, and ability to control the situation and follow post orders, procedures, safety rules, and regulations. When confiscating and holding prohibited articles for evidence, officers must follow chain-of-custody procedures. Finally, officers must complete a full written report concerning any actual or attempted security breach.

Entry Control Operations

Public and private enterprises are becoming more aware of the need for security systems and policies that address entry control. To begin any discussion, the term entry control should be defined. Entry control is the process of managing the flow of people into, throughout, and out of facilities and is best achieved through a layered approach depending on a facility's needs. Comprehensive entry control is comprised of a number of facets all layered together into a succinct program through policy and procedure. The goal of any access control system is to let authorized people, not just their credentials, into specific areas. True access control requires the ability to do several things: identify the person, grant or deny access, and monitor alarms.

Entry control solutions begin with determining specific requirements. If site-specific requirements are ignored, systems may be chosen which do not meet the needs of the courthouse; thus money, resources, and time will often be wasted. As the reader has already observed and will continue to observe, courthouses share many characteristics with other type occupancies; however, they are also, in many ways, unique. Entry control can be tailored to "report personnel who get in that belong in and/or report the ones who get in who belong out." It should be noted that a number of studies have been made focusing on the length of delay people will tolerate when trying to enter an area. Most people will accept a six-second delay to establish their identity; after that, some disgruntlement will arise. Of course, different areas with different levels of security will often require more time, effort, and patience.

Entry control may be broken down into four levels of security: open areas, controlled areas, limited areas, and exclusion areas. Open areas are areas where there is no control over who enters (e.g., perimeter grounds). A controlled area is an area with a minimum amount of control over who enters (e.g., an area where individuals must sign in to gain access or sign out when departing). A limited area is an area where only certain classifications of individuals are allowed to enter (e.g., judges). Finally, an exclusion area is an area where only a few individuals may have access (e.g., administrators). Of course, each of these areas requires different levels of security personnel and devices corresponding to their classification. **Note:** Some courthouse facilities are broken down into three "circulation zones" consisting of a public zone, private zone, and secured zone.

A courthouse facility should have a program for sign utilization that harmonizes with the security or circulation zones of the facility. The signs should be attractive, contemporary, legible, directional, informational, multilingual when appropriate, and incorporated into the interior design of all public areas where they can be easily seen. Furthermore, the sign system should meet all nationally recognized standards, guidelines, codes, and regulations.

There are a number of entry-control technologies in use today and some are more technical than others. Of course, advanced technology does not necessarily equate to high security and lesser technology does not necessarily equate to low security. The best technology in the world will not help anyone if it is not used. Thus, it is imperative that access control systems be easy to use, reliable, economical, unobtrusive, fail-safe, multifunctional, and require low maintenance.

Some of the lesser technological approaches to deterring unauthorized entry include posted signs warning that trespassers are subject to arrest; signs that inform all visitors that vehicles brought onto courthouse grounds are subject to search by officers checking identification at the main entrance gate to the courthouse; the development of written protocol for after hours building entry; and vehicle parking stickers used to identify unauthorized vehicles which are in turn ticketed and towed (this would not include a monitored visitor lot).

Badge systems are an extremely valuable entry control process. A personnel badge identification system is typically used to control access to a courthouse as well as access to specific areas within the courthouse area. Badges may be color coded, numerically or alphabetically designated, contain a number of area specific identifiers, and/or contain individual photographs. A number of safeguards such as personal information, modification/reproduction safeguards, custom transparent images, magnetic strips, bar codes, optical stripes, overlaminates, signature blocks, and holograhics may be utilized.

Every person desiring admittance to a courthouse facility should be required to wear an identification badge; this includes all courthouse officials, visitors, and vendors. ID's may be physically checked as personnel drive their personal vehicle up to a main entry point controlled by an officer, or checked for admittance to courthouse buildings. Identification badges should be worn on the outermost garment above the waist on the torso.

Temporary badge systems developed for visitors, vendors, or for personnel who are awaiting the issuance of a permanent badge are important. However, these systems may generate a possible security breech if they are not administered correctly. A good system (the badge exchange system) requires anyone who receives a temporary badge to exchange an identification depicting the individual's photograph (such as a drivers license) in return for a temporary badge. When the person leaves the courthouse the temporary badge is exchanged for the original identification. It is vital for badging officials to account for all temporary badges at the end of the duty day. No one should leave the area with a temporary badge or the system will be compromised.

Some temporary badges have a time-lapse system that visually displays the fact that a temporary badge has expired. For example, Temtec, Inc. makes a number of time-dependent (TD) self-expiring badges. This system uses a two-part badge (a front part–obverse and rear part–reverse). The reverse part is pre-printed in red migrating ink and the obverse part contains an adhesive. When the two parts are pressed together, the timing process begins. The rate of expiration is determined by the obverse and occurs in two-hours, one-day, one-week, or one-month time periods. These badges can be customized or are available in a generic format displaying the words "temporary, contractor, or visitor." This system solves the problem of lost or uncollected badges, provides a clear visual alert of expiration up to 50 feet away, prevents unauthorized re-use of temporary ID's, requires no hardware or electronics, and offers a simple low cost improvement to a badging system instantly. Finally, time tokens and time spots (small adhesive panels or dots) can be temporarily adhered to existing laminated temporary badges or standard badges. This choice allows an organization to use existing temporary badges or these devices may be used on permanent badges to give a person access to a certain area for a limited amount of time.

All courthouse officials should challenge any person failing to properly display a badge. All personnel, including courthouse officials, must release their badge for physical inspection when entering the courthouse or when challenged. A physical inspection includes taking the badge and comparing the face of the individual with the face on the badge; checking other identification such as markings, area access numbers, expiration date, etc. located on the badge; the composition, weight, condition and facility markings should also be examined to determine counterfeiting efforts. Personnel with broken or damaged badges should be directed or escorted to the badge office for a new badge. Further, if a picture does not reflect current appearance (changes in the length of hair, beards, mustaches, scars, disfigurements, etc.), officers or courthouse administrators should direct or escort the individual to the badging office for a new badge.

Figure 29. Temtec self-expiring badges. The top two images show the obverse and reverse of the badges. The middle image represents an example of a different formatted visitor badge. The bottom two images show an expired visitor badge (left) and an adhesive round sticker used for existing permanent in-house badges.

Personnel who do not have a badge (missing, forgotten, or lost) must be escorted to the badging office for positive identification. A disciplinary program should be developed to address individuals who constantly improperly wear, lose, forget, tamper with, or damage their badge. Lost or stolen badges must be reported to security personnel immediately. Finally, any employee or vendor who is banned from entry to the courthouse should have his or her badge confiscated and his or her photo should be distributed to all security personnel. These photos are typically housed in a do-not-admit book that is subsequently located at courthouse entry points.

A technology now being used in conjunction with badges and biometric systems is known as smart cards, key fobs, key rings, tokens, or similar small objects. The basic attributes of a smart card include computing power, ability to exchange information, and the ability to extract or add data. A computer chip (the smart cards brain) is either surface mounted or imbedded in the card. Some cards can be passed through a card reader while others can be

Figure 30. Temtec badges.

"read" from a distance. Smart cards should be controlled by setting and resetting time parameters, designating when cards are accepted. Finally, smart cards are designed to provide the following unique features: physical and digital identity; secure physical identification; physical authentication; digital identification; digital authentication; authenticated and authorized information access; offline verification; electronic signatures; information storage; read and write capabilities; multiple applications; multiple services; and contact-less capability. Smart card technology is advancing rapidly and a prospective buyer should research the previously listed features fully. Not all of these features will be required or even desirable in certain buildings or areas.

Limiting entry/exit points is an important aspect of current security needs. Indeed, to best control a courthouse, the number of entryways into the building or onto the courthouse grounds must be severely limited. The concept is simple: every opening in an area is a likely avenue of approach and should be considered a weakness. The more openings there are, the more vulnerable the area will be. Further, restricting normal entrance to only one or two locations can greatly reduce the number of security personnel or security devices that must be supported.

A logging in and out procedure may be established at entry/exit points to include parking areas. All visitors, vendors and personnel requesting admittance after specified hours may be required to sign in/out on a daily log containing the following information: name and address of the individual requesting admittance; destination; contact person to include their telephone number; reason for admittance; time in; and time out. The courthouse administrator may also require a printed name and signature of the person requiring admittance, the person conducting the logging procedure, and the escort or person being visited, if applicable. Finally, the person requesting admittance may be required to remain in a specified waiting area while the contact individual is notified and verification of the visiting person's need to enter and identification is ascertained. The visitor may now be permitted to enter, wait for the physical presence of the contact person, or be escorted to the desired destination by a security officer or other designated official. All visitor logs should be turned in to security at the end of the day and filed for at least one year in case future investigations are required.

Some courthouses, especially those located directly on a street, may need to use fences to control entry onto the courthouse grounds. Fencing does not have to be unattractive and razor tape or barbed wire are rarely appropriate for a courthouse setting. Wrought iron fencing may be used to discourage unauthorized admittance while at the same time being attractive. Chain link fencing is common and less expensive than wrought iron and provides an excellent barrier. However, chain link fencing should be at least 8 foot high and have a small mesh (1-inch to 11/20inch) to thwart a person trying to pull their body upward or from gaining a toehold. A robust fence defines property boundaries and forces a person to consciously trespass rather than allowing idle wandering onto a courthouse grounds that have no fencing. The goal of fencing is to deter the casual or unmotivated trespasser. No fence can keep out someone determined to enter the courthouse or who is motivated and comes prepared to breach the fence.

Once entrances to a courthouse are limited in number, the process of allowing or denying access is generally accomplished through one of four approaches. The first is manpower intensive, and the remaining three employ technology devices. These four approaches include: an officer controlled entry point; a special ID card/badge with automatic readers; a personal identification number (PIN) use in conjunction with a keyboard; and a biometric device for feature recognition. Officer control is self-explanatory. However, if officers become bored or complacent, they may easily miss properly identifying a person or may miss the identification of bogus or modified identification cards. Finally, while an officer can do far more than check ID cards, in the long run, they cost far more than technology systems.

ID cards or "dumb cards" using automatic readers require the identification to be validated by an electronic reader before a lock will be electronically opened. For example, an access control card may be used with elevator systems so that employees and visitors must "swipe" a card in the elevator in order to gain access to designated floors and areas. If employees or visitors try to go to an authorized floor, the elevator automatically takes them to the basement, where alerted security personnel are waiting. Viable card technologies for courthouse areas include bar codes or magnetic strips used in conjunction with card-swipe devices. Some courthouse administrators may choose active radio frequency (RF) cards in conjunction with proximity readers. These card readers may be attractive since no manpower is required; however, in some circumstances, more than one person can enter upon one tripping of the lock (called cabusing) if the authorized operator is acting under duress or possible collusion. Finally, the cost of these devices, including installation, maintenance, and support systems, may be too expensive for many courthouse administrators to purchase.

Personal identification numbers (PIN) are normally used in conjunction with an ID card and accompanying reader. Using a PIN system in a stand-alone fashion is usually weak due to the fact that onlookers can easily gain knowledge of the pin code. When used in conjunction with a card reader, one can easily understand the importance of redundant or back-up security systems. Some high-end PIN systems use scramble keypads that allow only the user to view the cipher numbers. Of course, these devices cost more.

A new entry control system that is designed to answer the question "Is this person who he or she claims to be?" is known as biometrics. Biometrics is viewed as a new technique designed to tighten security while at the same time being cost effective (less labor intensive) and faster than other identification methods. Indeed, biometrics is widely becoming accepted across all security applications dealing with entry control technologies. Prices are lower; for example, the newest portion of this technology, the data processing capabilities of both hardware and software, is needed to make biometrics work at an affordable cost especially in noninvasive modes. Finally, accuracy is established and the benefit of increased security and convenience is now being realized.

Biometric techniques identify or verify the identity of individuals by measuring their unique psychological or behavioral characteristics. Perhaps no other conventional entry control technology is able to deliver the same level of information about an individual as biometrics. Biometrics involves a 1:1 matching of biometric features against those stored on a template. Biometric technologies use an electronic device to verify the identification of a person through the use of a personal attribute such as signature verification, key stroke dynamics, hand or finger shape (hand geometry), facial features (comparing three-dimensional features of the human face), fingerprint, vein patterns, DNA, voiceprint, signature dynamics, retinal pattern, or iris pattern. In lieu of describing each biometric technology, hand geometry, fingerprints, and voice recognition devices will be explained as representative technologies.

Most hand geometry devices measure up to 96 separate hand features including hand length, width, thickness, and surface area. This information is compared to data contained on a stored template. When the reader looks at the hand, any changes to the hand will be noticed, but small changes such as cuts or bandages typically will interfere with the accuracy of only one measurement. Other measurements can still accurately identify a match. If a significant change has occurred and/or verification cannot be completed, security personnel can then be called to individually verify access. To enter a facility with a hand reader, a person either enters a PIN number or presents a proximity card. Then, a person slides his or her hand into the reader. This technology is very forgiving and perfect placement is never required. In approximately one second, if authorized, the person is granted access.

Fingerprints are proving to be an extremely popular biometric identifier because the technology is simple, low-cost, easy-to-use, accepted by the general public, and features excellent verification capabilities. The advantage of fingerprint technology is that it provides a simplified touch-and-go security option for authentication. Biometric fingerprint sensors fall into two technology categories: surface and subsurface. Surface-based technologies are the weaker of the two technologies because they are only capable of imaging the surface of the finger. Thus, surface technologies have inherent issues with difficult skin types such as dry or moist skin. Environmental issues like worn, calloused, or damaged skin and everyday skin contaminates such as dirt, grease, or paint also pose challenges for surface technologies. Subsurface technologies are more effective than surface technologies because these devices capture the image below the surface layer of the skin to the live layer and thus are not affected by worn, dirty, dry, oily, or moist fingers.

The voice recognition process begins when a person picks up a telephone adjacent to a secured area and dials an automated security line. A recorded voice will typically ask: Who is this? The person states his or her name and speech recognition software checks the name in the employee database. After finding the person's voiceprint in the verification database, the system compares the phrase just spoken to a stored voiceprint, which is on file for every employee. The system then generates a "score." If a score is above a certain threshold, the system considers the speaker a valid employee, and then passes the door number and the employee's card number via standard telephone touch-tones to the access control system. It then commands the access control module to unlock the door, and the details of each event are logged. If after 20 seconds, a door is left open an alarm will sound and a speech processor installed near the door will annunciate "please close the door." If the door is not closed after another 20 seconds, an alarm is automatically sent to security headquarters or an outside agency.

If the score falls in mid-range, the system will ask a few more questions, such as office phone number and birth date, before verifying the employee and contacting the access control system to open the door. If the voice score is low, the system tells the person "I can't verify your voice print." And loops back to give the employee another chance to say his or her name.

Some of these voice recognition systems also use "exception processing" for employees who wish to use a cell phone in lieu of the wall-mounted phone. In this case, the automated voice will also ask "Which door do you want to open?" The employee then states the name of the door or request that a list of doors be read before choosing the desired door. Finally these systems can also be accessed remotely to unlock doors for immediate vendor delivery.

Because no one technology is ideal for every application, it is critical to capture multiple biometrics data. Biometric identification devices are very accurate, identification methods cannot be loaned, lock and key control programs may be reduced, and there is nothing for a person to remember such as an ID card or PIN number.

Biometric devices are not without problems: they may not be user friendly; are subject to vandalism; may be very expensive to use; possess privacy concerns; suffer from the absence of industry consensus standards; suffer from consumer awareness; and have application limits. Further, each biometric technology has its advantages and disadvantages based on the application. For example, while some biometric systems may not be suited for large-scale applications, it doesn't mean that same technology would not be an ideal solution for a small courthouse complex.

However, the use of biometric technologies will likely increase in the coming years. The benefits for employers, and employees are significant and will continue to grow as costs fall, and while ease-of-use, accuracy, and acceptance rise. Perhaps the most critical factor in the success of a biometric system is user acceptance.

Finally, one of the most often overlooked access control strategies is the mechanical key system. A security department needs to know how many doors are locked and how many people carry keys. A key issue book should be developed to capture the following information: exactly who has been issued keys, what doors do the keys fit, when the keys were issued, and when the keys were turned in. If there is an event, a simple theft, robbery, or serious crime; ascertaining who has access may prove critical.

An audit of this key issue book should be conducted on a daily basis. If keys are lost or otherwise unaccounted for, the building or area should be considered compromised. This compromise may require the replacement of all of the locks a particular key will fit. This may be very expensive if the key is a master key fitting all of the locks in a building. Some agencies hold the individual who lost the key responsible for lock replacement costs. Unknown contractors and maintenance workers should not be issued keys. A permanent employee can easily let these people into secured areas as required. Finally, if possible, all keys should be marked "do not duplicate."

In conclusion, the acceptance of any entry control operation will hinge upon proper implementation. Generally, five areas must be considered for proper implementation; they include: acceptability, ease of use, functionality, throughtput, and enrollment. Acceptability should focus on fully explaining the system(s) and answering any concerns users may express. If people are afraid to use a device, they most likely will not use it properly and that may result in access not being granted to them. People like things that are simple and intuitive, in other words, easy to use. The larger the courthouse population, the more critical this factor becomes. How well a system works (functionality) will determine if it stays on the job. Throughput—the total time it takes for a person to use a device is a logistical issue and must be considered carefully. Finally, as many personnel as possible must be enrolled in the system. If too many people cannot be enrolled, the technology simply can't be used.

Duress Alarm Devices

Judges and court personnel must have a signal system upon which to rely in emergency situations; thus, all courtrooms and hearing rooms should be equipped with a duress alarm connected to a central security station. Duress alarms should be located on the judge's, referee's, and magistrate's benches, and at the work stations of the bailiff, receptionist, secretary, and other officers. It is important that the duress alarm be a type which includes an audible alarm at a central security station; however, the system should not include an audible alarm at the activation site. The duress alarm system should quickly summon additional help from the county sheriff's department or the nearest police jurisdiction when needed.

Modern duress alarms are generally electronic devices found in one of three types. The first type is the panic-button alarm (a push-button mounted in a fixed location). The second type is the identification alarm (a portable device that identifies the owner of the device), and the third is an identification/location alarm (a portable device that identifies, locates, and tracks the person who activated the duress alarm).

The panic button is by far the more common type of duress alarm presently found in courthouses. The simplest application uses a strategically placed button that, when initiated, forwards a signal through a dedicated telephone line. A prerecorded message specifying the courthouse, its location, and the urgency is sent to several locations, such as the police department. Some push-button duress devices are designed to use wiring that transmits a signal (flagging the alarm location) to a location where a visible and/or audio alarm is activated. A final push-button duress system includes the use of public address (PA) systems. When initiated, the PA system speakers can be used in a two-way communication mode. In conclusion, while push button duress systems are cost effective and valuable in many ways, they suffer from some weaknesses. For example, the person in duress may be separated from the area where the push-button is located, mischievous personnel may trigger the alarm, and the alarm does not identify the person in distress—only the location of the alarm may be ascertained.

The second type of duress alarm, the identification alarm, is a portable device that identifies the owner of the device. These systems incorporate a pager-like device that is worn by courthouse personnel. When the built in panic button is pushed, a wireless alarm signal is sent to the closest installed wireless sensing unit that then sends the signal on to an alarm console. The console operator will receive a coded number that corresponds to a specific person. A major limiting factor for this system is the fact that the device must have a clear line of sight to the nearest sensing unit for an accurate transmission. Walls, glass, roofs, floors, etc. will degenerate the transmitted signal that decreases the precision of identifying the individual under duress. An improved version of this system incorporates a two-way radio into the pager device that allows communication between the console operator and person under duress.

The third and final type of duress alarm, the identification/location alarm, is a smarter version of the identification duress alarm described above. This type of duress alarm operates in essentially the same manner as the identification alarm but has the added capability of identifying, locating, and tracking the person who activated the duress alarm.

New Courthouse Designs

Most courthouses in the United States have been constructed to achieve an inviting and open-to-the-community feeling, using multiple buildings with large windows, multiple entrances and exits, and many opportunities for privacy. These layouts are not conducive to many security requirements. Building a new courthouse from the ground up presents opportunities not present in existing or retrofit projects.

Building a new courthouse should involve the input of numerous interested parties, for example, judges, county commissioners, department heads involved in security, the district attorney, and the bar association. One of the main goals when building a new courthouse should be to minimize security vulnerabilities. Tours of numerous new facilities will help in determining good secure building designs and consulting architectural firms that specialize in buildings that incorporate good security principles is a good start. Security-conscious designs can actually help compensate in the long term for tight security budgets, fewer security personnel, and less sophisticated security equipment.

Some security-oriented suggestions to be incorporated into the building of new courthouses include the following: limit the number of buildings (one building is best); minimize the number of entrances to buildings; allow enough room at the main entry point for a security screening area and accompanying security equipment; alarm all exits and relegate them for emergency use only; and minimize the line of sight into traditional courthouse gathering areas from off-site areas. A great deal of emphasis should be placed on circulation patterns that govern the movement of judges, court personnel, and prisoners. For example, circulation patterns should consist of separate routes to and from courtrooms and the avoidance of public areas. The goal of a secure circulation pattern is to separate judges, juries, court personnel, and prisoners from the public.

Also, design parking lots conducive to the posting of security personnel who may effectively challenge each vehicle (one lane ingress and egress is best); provide a drop off/pickup lane for public transit only; minimize the number of driveways or parking lots that citizens will have to walk across to get to the courthouse.

Additionally, build a number of single-stall restrooms to mitigate restroom confrontations and other problems; use fences to enclose the entire courthouse area; design the courthouse building and interior areas so that they can be closed and locked during off-duty hours. Further, minimize secluded hiding places; reduce the number of windows and place them in strategic locations (secure skylights may be used to let light in while being less vulnerable then traditional buildings); maximize the line of sight within buildings; and use large wide spaces especially in hallways and commons areas.

Numerous receivers and transmitters should be installed throughout the structure to allow for dependable two-way radio and cellular phone use in order to defeat dead space; and buildings should be constructed at least 50 feet away from streets, driveways, and parking areas. Furthermore, a basic security alarm system should be installed throughout all hallways, administrative offices, and rooms containing high-value property, such as computers, VCRs, and evidence. Finally, ample lighting should be sufficient to cover all areas of concern.

Security Guards

Security may be defined as, "A stable, relatively predictable environment in which an individual or group may pursue its ends without disruption or harm, and without fear of such disturbance or injury." Thus, in relation to courthouse security, security guards may be tasked with providing the sum total of those preventative and protective efforts designed to generate security as defined above.

There are two types of security services, known as proprietary security and contract security. Proprietary security is in-house, directly hired and controlled by the courthouse administrator. Contract security is provided by outside individuals or organizations. Either of these security services should be directed to provide a broad spectrum of activities designed to eliminate or reduce a full range of potential hazards. These activities include, but are not limited to, the following: personnel protection; building and perimeter protection; intrusion and access control; alarm and surveillance systems; fire prevention and control; emergency and disaster planning; prevention of theft; accident prevention and safety; and enforcement of courthouse rules, regulations, and policies.

Further, there are three main categories of security personnel tasking, they include stationary, patrolling, and alert-response security officers. Stationary security officers usually have a basic function of guarding a particular location. Aside from screening people and materials, or observing various areas, these personnel may be used to provide other services such as providing information and directions, and locating in-house personnel when needed.

Effective patrol is the backbone of any good security and safety program. This tasking affords the opportunity to monitor the entire environment, prevent problems from occurring, correct problems as they emerge, and generate a feeling of personal safety on the part of the staff and visitors. There are several different ways or methods to patrol a courthouse and they can be used in conjunction with each other. Patrolling methods include foot patrol, vehicle patrol (automobile, bicycle, moped, motorcycle and/or golf cart), conspicuous patrol, inconspicuous patrol, general patrol, selective patrol, stake out, indoor patrol, and outdoor patrol.

Roving or patrolling security officers may be used to prevent, deter, and repress crime; prevent accidents; detect and apprehend perpetrators; regulate noncriminal conduct; recover property; and perform miscellaneous services. Miscellaneous services include: checking the condition of various ingress and egress points; performing security checks in certain areas; accomplishing routine and surprise security inspections; and responding to alarms and alerts or other emergency situations.

Some security forces need to have their movements (namely patrol tasks) monitored. Poor security forces may just sit in an office and not perform required patrol tasks. To counter this poor performance, there is a device called the Deggy Control Guard System that tracks each guard's movements. To use this system, the guard carries a Deggy Pen and uses it each time he or she walks by a predesignated checkpoint. Upon each contact made between the pen and the checkpoint button, a date and time is recorded along with checkpoint information. If the guard wishes to report a security infraction such as a broken window, this information can also be recorded in the Deggy pen and later downloaded into a Deggy Download Computer Station. The Deggy Pen can hold 11,000 transactions.

The third tasking, known as alert-response, may require security officers to be dedicated to the function of being ready and available to respond to all alert, alarm, and emergency situations as practical. Their responsibilities may be geared toward a particular type of security category or more interdisciplinary targeting functions involving various security categories.

One of the main problems associated with security personnel is a lack of training. Thus, there is a gap between commissioned law enforcement officers who have typically received many hours of training and the security officer who may not have received any training. This lack of training is amazing when one considers the fact that these personnel are dealing with civil and criminal law not to mention the weight of their duties in protecting personnel. Another interesting fact was reported in a National Institute for Occupational Safety and Health study of on-the-job homicides covering the period of 1980 to 1989. This study listed security guards as having the fifth riskiest job in the country with a homicide rate of 3.6 per 100,000 persons.

Regardless of these facts, many states still do not require security personnel to possess any authorizing authority or registration requirements such as bonding, fingerprinting, criminal record checks, and/or formal training. Training is currently determined by each state. Indeed, state licensing and regulation may not exist (as of 1996, only 23 states required some form of security guard training and out of those 23, only 14 states required any training for unarmed guards). A recent Service Employees International Union (SEIU) survey found that 20 percent of security guards say they have received no training at all from their employers. In this survey, 34 states received an F rating (A being the best and F being the worst). Only South Dakota earned an A for requiring 32 hours of training. Further, the amount of state-mandated training, in 1996, varied between zero and 40 hours, depending on whether the guard is armed or unarmed. Thus, training may be left to the discretion of the security company. In these cases, it is highly unlikely that penurious security companies will spend funds in the furtherance of professionalism.

In many cases, security officers are underpaid, undertrained, and typically stay on the job for just a couple of months. Indeed, many security officers are paid minimum wages (in 2002, the average pay for a security guard was around $7 to $8 per hour), while security companies keep a large part of the fees paid by the customers. Two Rand Corporation Reports, one conducted in 1981 and the other in 1989, revealed that low pay, lack of promotional opportunities, and lack of training attracts marginal security guard personnel, which in turn leads to ineffectual performance and an average annual turnover rate of 121 percent. The context is that historically, security officers have become a completely disregarded work force. Is it any wonder—basically because of low wages—that the majority of security forces are staffed by people who are at the bottom rung of the socioeconomic ladder. It will do little good for a courthouse administrator to purchase expensive security systems and pay installment, maintenance, and service fees, while being operated by underscreened, undertrained, undersupervised, underpaid security personnel.

Security officers must understand the physical control systems used in their facility. Recognizing that a system exists and how that system works will prepare the officer to understand the importance of his or her role in monitoring and supporting the system. The central idea is to use physical security controls to enhance both security and safety for the courthouse occupants and property. Thus, all physical security programs are dependent upon qualified and trained personnel to operate them or these systems will be rendered ineffective.

The responsibilities assumed by security personnel in the protection of courthouse staff, other personnel, equipment, and other physical assets mandates proper and effective training. Indeed, the high level of responsibility that these officers face is often overshadowed by the low esteem in which security officers are held. Security education, training, and self-esteem are vital determinates of job performance. A lack of training will often generate low officer esteem and morale and a lack of professionalism. Further, legal issues demand that the security officer of today remain well versed in the changing laws. Additionally, the problems addressed by security personnel are becoming increasingly complex. Plus, there is a great dependence on technology and information systems. Indeed, security operations will certainly continue to make greater use of innovations and technology. In conclusion, the inadequate protection of personnel and assets plus costly negligence judgments will often be the result of little or no training.

Another topic of vital importance is the proper screening and investigation of the capabilities, character, personality, moral values, allegiance, dedication, and similar factors of candidate security personnel. All security personnel should go through a background check and preemployment screening prior to employment. During preemployment screening, a number of applicants will typically be denied employment due to falsification of applications, poor employment backgrounds, and even felony convictions. Other applicants will require further investigation targeting significant problems that must be clarified, often through investigative techniques, prior to any job offer. This statement can be made in reference to the fact that security personnel are entrusted with the security, protection, and safety of citizens and courthouse staff.

The implied accomplishment of these particular job functions is directly related to the security personnel themselves. Thus, optimum guidelines should be set forth. These guidelines should include proper training designed to meet the requirement of professionalism, proper and respectful modes of conduct and communication, restraint when called for, and appropriate action when needed. Retraining and refresher courses should be given on a regular basis to maintain optimum job performance.

Furthermore, security officers should, at a minimum, be briefed and trained on a clearly delineated code of conduct. This code of conduct should contain the following topics: mission statement (authority and intent), specific duties (job description), special courthouse requirements, job qualifications, standard policies and procedures, security-specific policies and procedures (for example, use-of-force), performance requirements, personal conduct, attendance, working hours, performance appraisals, personnel files, conflicts of interest, safety, release of personal information, sexual harassment, ethics, smoking, uniform and grooming standards, training, and required paper work.

In conclusion, the stereotypes about security officers are often clear and negative. But the fact is that every time there is an emergency situation in a building, the first responders are often private security officers. After September 11, 2001, the demand for professional security guards is soaring due to terrorist threats and high-profile violent incidents. To reiterate, courthouse security efforts will only be as good as the security officers implementing the program.

Police Officers Assigned to the Courthouse

Police officers assigned to the courthouse are sworn law enforcement officers with the same arrest power and duties as other peace officers and are also responsible for the safety and security of the courthouse, staff, and visitors. These officers should attend training specific to the job assignment. This training will typically require 40 to 80 hours to complete. Of course, there is no need to repeat generic law enforcement training, but a number of additional topics should be covered, some examples include:

1. Definition of duties
2. How people are affected by work place violence
3. The causes of violence in courthouses
4. Courthouse security and safety issues
5. Crime prevention
6. Emergency management
7. Legal issues
8. Protective custody
9. Prisoner escort
10. Prisoner security within the court
11. Property management system
12. Arrest procedures
13. Use of force
14. Hostage/barricaded incidents
15. High-risk trial plans
16. Emergency medical plans
17. Bomb threats and disposal
18. Civil disturbance/disaster emergency
19. Emergency evacuation plan
20. Security survey
21. Incident report classification
22. Dealing with the suicidal
23. Job description
24. Assignment and duties
25. Jury trials
26. Code of conduct

An officer assigned to a courthouse must be chosen carefully. This person should be qualified as a police officer and have expertise in the security field. Further, this person must have an interest in and like to interact with citizens including young people. Additionally, it takes a dedicated professional to perform what may be termed as routine security functions. Officer turnover may be great if this person cannot accept performing mundane tasks, finds repetitious tasks boring, or perceives that a courthouse administration has neglected to identify security concerns complete with unwavering enforcement and serious consequences. High turnover rates will eventually make locating qualified people difficult, increase manpower costs, and weaken an otherwise effective courthouse security program.

Canine Operations

Canines often provide a very useful function in a courthouse security program. These functions include patrol/guard duty, explosives sensing, drugs/chemicals sensing, general searching, sound monitoring, and attack/protective modes. When used for patrol/guard duty, canines most often function in coordination with security personnel. However, under certain special circumstances, canines may be left on their own. When used for explosives sensing, canines use their acute sense of smell to pick up vapors emitting from the explosive. Canines are very accurate when searching for explosives and often enhance the safety of personnel who might otherwise be required to manually search for an explosive device. Indeed, dogs have abilities that can't be matched by humans or by scientific instruments. A dog's sense of smell is approximately 3,000 times more sensitive than the average human being. Most dogs have such as acute sense of smell that they can detect minute odors that even sensitive scientific instruments cannot identify. Finally, it has been reported that some dogs can identify 19,000 different compounds.

As with explosives, canines are often used to assist in searching for certain types of drugs, chemicals, or other substances. Dogs may also be used to assist in the task of searching for people. Canines, with their powerful sense of hearing, can also be used to monitor an area for sound and noise, and can be trained to differentiate between various categories of noise. At times, dogs may also be used to supplement security personnel by having the capability to attack. Of course, dogs used in this manner must be highly trained to obey both active and passive commands. Further, there are generally two types of dogs: active and passive. Passive dogs will alert but will not otherwise interact with the subject. Active dogs may bite, scratch, jump, etc. upon alerting and these acts are sometimes considered as a use-of-force. Passive dogs are probably the best overall choice for use in courthouses.

Canines used in scent detection operations typically involve the following: "dog sniffs in public areas are not considered searches and therefore don't require reasonable suspicion, probable cause, or warrants" (U.S. v. Place Supreme Court). Further, dog alerts can be used for probable cause. However, the use of dogs "on people" is very sensitive legally and should be done only if specific affirmative legal advice is obtained.

Integrating a K-9 program into a security force does not come without a price. As with any other specialized unit, there are costs for training, maintenance, and special equipment. Specific costs include purchase of the dog, training dog and handler, food, veterinary care, grooming, vehicle modification, officer compensation, canine protective vests, boarding, and liability insurance. However, canines are well worth the price when one considers the valuable role they play in securing courthouse facilities.

Prisoner Security within the Court

There are three general situations when court security officers handle prisoners. The first situation concerns handling a prisoner in custody who has been brought to the court by a law enforcement officer. The second situation concerns those persons who were not in custody when they first came to court, but who are sentenced or ordered remanded into custody by the court. The third situation concerns a person arrested by a court security officer. Thus, the handling of prisoners is a frequent activity of court security officers.

In order to ensure the safety and security of prisoners, escorting officers, court personnel, and the general public, a number of procedures should be followed. For example, prisoners should only enter and leave the court facility through a designated prisoner holding area (a secure area where law enforcement officers bring prisoners pending a court case). Upon delivery of a prisoner to the prisoner holding area, the court security officer should obtain a positive identification that the prisoner is in fact the defendant and ask the law enforcement officer escorting the prisoner if the person is considered a security hazard. Further, the court security officer should ask the law enforcement officer if the prisoner suffers from a medical condition that could endanger himself, a court officer, or the public. Of course, no prisoner should appear in the court under the influence of alcohol or drugs. If any discrepancies are noted, the court security officer should notify the judge.

Prisoners should always be searched upon arrival at the prisoner holding area. Under no circumstances should a court security officer assume that a prisoner has been searched. A court security officer should always search the prisoner and remove all personal property including any form of tobacco and matches and/or lighter (most courthouses are nonsmoking facilities). Court security officers must assume that the prisoner has had the opportunity to obtain contraband or a weapon anytime he or she is outside the confines of a cell. Thus, prisoners should be searched any time they are removed from their cell and when returned to the cell. If a court security officer feels uncomfortable after any search, the officer should search the prisoner again, ("gut feelings" should always be followed). If any weapons or illegal contraband are found, an appropriate law enforcement agency should be immediately notified and an incident report should be filed. Of course, court security officers should not hand search members of the opposite sex unless exigent circumstances arise.

No visitors should be permitted access to the holding area. Of course, the prisoner's attorney may be permitted in the holding area as long as his or her presence does not interfere with the normal operation of the holding area. However, it is not a good idea to permit an attorney entrance into a cell with his or her client. Additionally, the holding area should be checked no less than three times a day (prior to court, at noon, and at the close of court) to ensure that all prisoners have been removed as scheduled, that there is no damage to the facility, and that there is no contraband in the holding area.

The only area a prisoner should be permitted to enter when out of the holding area is the courtroom, when his or her case is scheduled. It is also a good idea to search the prisoner before leaving the holding area and escort the individual to the defendant's table. The prisoner should not be allowed to engage in conversation with any person except court officials or the defense attorney. Further, the prisoner must not be permitted any physical contact with spectators at any time (physical contact can be a ploy to pass a prisoner a weapon or contraband).

All court facilities should provide secure temporary holding cells containing sufficient fixed benches, washbasins, and toilets. Of course, the holding area (prisoner reception and release area) should be located inside the security perimeter of the courthouse facility and positioned in a way that prisoners can be observed in the secure area by bailiffs or officers on a periodic or continual basis. Holding cells should also provide sight/sound separation of male, female, and juvenile prisoners. It is imperative that every courthouse has provisions to evacuate prisoners in a secure manner in the event of an emergency.

Finally, weapons lockers should be located outside holding areas where prisoners are detained. These lockers should be available to all sworn law enforcement personnel, equipped with individual compartments, and each compartment should have an individual lock and key.

Property Management System

Provisions should be made to secure and store all property belonging to prisoners; for example, a property inventory envelope should be used whenever property is taken from a prisoner. If money is found, it should be counted by the court security officer and recorded by the quantity of each denomination in addition to the total; for example, currency would be listed as 1–twenty, 3–fives, 6–ones, for a total of $41.00. Coins would be listed as 1–quarter, 2–dimes, for a total of 45 cents. Checks or money orders would be listed as 1–$18.96, 1–$329.41, for a total of $348.37. When completed, the property envelope should be placed in a rack attached to the door of a prisoner's cell and the prisoner should be given a written receipt for all property stored by court security officers. Further, provisions should be made to return all property belonging to prisoners when they are released from the jurisdiction of the court after hearings or trials. Finally, each prisoner should sign a receipt for returned property.

Escaped Prisoners

The transportation of prisoners is one of the most dangerous tasks in law enforcement and accounts for several deaths and injuries each year to escorting officers, bystanders, and prisoners. Every prisoner, regardless of age, gender, size, or crime involved, can prove dangerous. Perhaps the most important first step in preparing to transport a prisoner safely is to correctly classify the prisoner as to degree of dangerousness so that proper levels of care, custody, control, and supervision are implemented for each individual prisoner.

Every prisoner is a potential carrier of contraband and is an escape risk; thus, criminal justice officials must make very effort to implement basic practical procedures to provide a reasonable level of security when transporting prisoners. The following guidelines will help prevent prisoner escape:

1. Prisoners should be handcuffed with their hands behind their back and their hands in a back-to-back configuration. The handcuff double lock pins should be engaged once the handcuffs are applied. If a prisoner's arms cannot be physically joined in the back, the hands should be handcuffed in front of the prisoner's body and the handcuffs should be secured to the prisoner's belt or a nylon restraining device. Further, the belt buckle or restraining device's metal clasp should be positioned in the back of the prisoner. Additionally, if a prisoner has other physical limitations, i.e., small wrists, one arm, etc., plastic flex cuffs or a nylon restraining device may be used. Under no circumstances (sick, injured, handicapped, mentally disturbed, very old, very young, infirm and/or incapacitated) should a prisoner be transported without some type of physical restraint attached to their hands. When appropriate, the prisoner should also be secured with leg restraints. Finally, all physical restraint devices should be personally put on the prisoner by the escorting officer and periodically checked for security. Officers must never assume restraints are foolproof.
2. Under normal conditions, one officer should not transport more than one prisoner.

3. When two officers transport one prisoner, the cover officer should be seated in the left rear and the prisoner in the right rear seat.
4. When two officers transport two prisoners, the cover officer should be seated in the left rear seat, one prisoner should be seated in the center area, while the other prisoner should be seated in the right rear seat.
5. Prisoners should also be secured in the transport vehicle by the use of a safety belt.
6. Transport vehicles should be searched prior to and after transporting prisoners to assure that no contraband, weapons, or similar items are present.
7. In those rare circumstances where it is necessary to transport two prisoners, one prisoner should be secured in the right front seat and the other prisoner should be secured in the right rear seat.
8. Officers must never assume that a prisoner will not attempt to flee.

However, if a prisoner escapes while in the custody of the court, the following steps should be immediately implemented:

1. Pursue the prisoner if possible.
2. Notify the appropriate local law enforcement agency and provide the following information about the escapee:
   A. Name
   B. Physical description and date of birth
   C. Description of clothing
   D. Method and direction of travel (if by vehicle, provide a description)
   E. Charge
   F. Social security number
   G. Home address
3. If the escape is attempted in an area equipped with a duress alarm, a staff member should activate the security alarm if the court security officer is involved in a pursuit.
4. It should be the policy of any agency that unless there is a clear and present danger to staff and/or prisoners, every effort should be made to peacefully resolve the situation. Force ranging from the use of restraining devices to deadly, may be employed against a prisoner in defense of life and to protect property, to prevent an escape, or to regain control of a situation or an event. The type of force used will be dictated by situation and will either increase or decrease as the situation or event requires. Force is to be used as a measure of control and should never be used as a means of punishment.
5. Finally, the court security officer should complete an incident report.

Some agencies maintain court security functions and prisoner transportation as two distinct areas of employment and expertise. Indeed, this is a very effective method, however, many agencies cannot afford to specialize due to manpower and other logistical shortages. Thus, officers/deputies will often serve in both capacities and will require cross-training.

Prisoners and Public Areas

Prisoners should not be permitted in the public areas of a court facility when identifiable as prisoners except in case of emergency, i.e., fire, disaster, equipment failure, etc. However, when a separate entrance is not available and public hallways must be used, the following procedures should be followed:

1. A prisoner should be properly restrained. Mechanical restraints should never be used as a means of punishment; about the head or neck of a prisoner; or in any way that causes undue physical pain, restricts blood circulation, or restricts breathing.
2. Court security officers should proceed directly to the destination by the preplanned shortest route. However, the route should be varied in order to be consistent with good security practices.
3. Court security officers should walk holding the prisoner's arm guiding him or her to the final destination. Court security officers should never walk in front of a prisoner.
4. Court security officers should avoid walking the prisoner close to a judge, prosecutor, complainant, or witness.
5. Court security officers should not allow prisoner visits or embraces from family or friends.
6. Court security officers should avoid using public elevators.
7. Court security officers should never pose a prisoner for press photographs or permit prisoner press interviews.
8. The jury should not see the defendant restrained unless so ordered by the trial judge.
9. Prisoners requesting to use the restroom should be returned to the prisoner holding area. A prisoner should not be allowed to use public or private restrooms.
10. Prisoners should not be permitted to smoke while in the custody of the court.
11. When escorting prisoners through public areas, court security officers must be especially alert and ready for the unexpected. Escape attempts, suicide attempts, confrontations with family and friends, and threats to witnesses are not uncommon occurrences.

12. If prisoners cannot be transported through court facility entrances, and separate public entrance must be used, the area should be purged if possible and public movement in the area should be restricted during the time of prisoner transport.

Weapons in Court Facilities

There is no more controversial topic relating to court facility security than whether law enforcement officers should be required to surrender their weapons at the court facility door. Firearms in a courtroom or court facility may increase, not diminish, security risk. For example, many courtrooms have very restricted zones of fire due to the number of persons located within a relatively small area and as the number of weapons increases, so do the chances of a mishap. On the other hand, it is almost universal law enforcement policy that every officer carry a weapon as part of the required duty equipment. Some departments even extend this policy to off-duty hours. These competing views require individual courts to review their needs and formulate a policy based upon these needs and the political realities that exist in a given community.

However, it is undisputed that many acts of violence may occur in court facilities when law enforcement personnel are involved in litigation as a party and not in the capacity of a sworn officer; for example, domestic relations or when an officer has been a victim. Therefore, many court facilities require officers acting outside sworn duties to surrender their weapon, notwithstanding departmental policy. Of course, such a policy should not be viewed as accusatory but merely precautionary.

Hostage/Barricaded Incidents

While the taking of a hostage or an incident of a person barricading him/herself in a court facility is rare, this criminal tactic does occur. Criminals take hostages for a number of reasons; for example, for protection, as a bargaining chip, by accident, or to kill or harm personnel. When a criminal uses a hostage for protection, the hostage is often placed in a strategic position as a human shield. When a criminal uses a hostage as a bargaining chip, the criminal seeks to trade a hostage for something; for example, money, food, transportation, a news broadcast, etc. A criminal may take courthouse personnel hostage by accident when personnel are trapped in an area of the courthouse controlled by the criminal. Finally, when a violent situation erupts, unstable criminals may take hostages in order to harm them later for the sake of revenge, retaliation, or to make a point.

A court facility must adopt policies and procedures designed to prevent such incidents. Of course, prevention is not enough, a plan must also be developed to swiftly and effectively respond to these types of incidents. This plan should focus on the following aspects: obtain the safe release of all hostages; protect the lives of security personnel; protect the lives of hostage takers; apprehend perpetrators; and neutralize the incident as quickly and safely as possible.

First responders have a number of important duties to perform, such as respond immediately to the problem area, determine the nature of the incident, establish an inner-perimeter to contain the incident to the smallest area possible, and begin a dialogue with the perpetrator. Dialogue is vital for slowing the action down in an attempt to de-escalate the incident and allow hostage negotiators time to respond to the scene. Secondary responders should set up an outer perimeter, and evacuate personnel, bystanders, and injured persons.

Guidelines for Hostages

All personnel are vulnerable to being taken hostage so each person should receive hostage survival training. Part of this training should include an understanding of the five stages of the hostage process; these steps include capture, transport, holding, recovery, and readjustment.

The first stage, capture, is the most dangerous time of the hostage-taking process. Capture often occurs at the onset of violence when destruction, violence, and chaos are at their highest levels of intensity. Further, at this point, criminals are generally highly excitable, hostile, confused, emotional, and unpredictable.

The second stage of the captive process is transport. During this stage, hostages are moved from the initial scene to different locations. Further, hostages may be moved numerous times to prevent other staff from learning a hostage's location. Hostages may be stripped of equipment, keys, clothing, and personal possessions, and dressed in the captor's clothing. As personal possessions are removed, hostages often feel dehumanized, powerless, and humiliated. A blindfold may be placed on hostages to prevent the identification of accomplices; prevent the witnessing of additional crimes; confuse a hostage's senses; enhance a hostage's feelings of disorientation, anxiousness, and helplessness; and to conceal physical locations. Multiple hostages may be separated to enhance intimidation and make rescue more difficult.

The third stage of the captive process is holding. During this stage the transport of hostages generally ceases, negotiations begin, a leader often emerges if the situation includes multiple captors, violence decreases, and the safety of hostages increases.

The fourth stage of the captive process is recovery. Recovery occurs when hostages are released or rescued by emergency response teams. If a negotiated release occurs, hostages must remain calm and observant. Hostages may be freed singly or with other hostages. Whatever the case, released hostages should walk calmly to the authorities. Someone will meet captives and guide them to a secure area for a debriefing and medical attention. A debriefing focuses on any information a released hostage has concerning captors and other hostages. This information is important for emergency response teams to safely recover all remaining hostages and for the future prosecution of the captor.

If an assault is made by emergency response teams, hostages should drop to the floor, keep their hands visible, and not resist being handcuffed until proper identification can be made. Hostages should attempt to find protective cover especially when a rescue attempt is in progress. Hostages should try to remain calm, not panic or lose control or captors may try to harm them or use them as a shield. Finally, captives should not run toward the attacking force; they may be mistaken for a captor.

The final stage of the captive process is readjustment. Readjustment includes a feeling of relief and may be accompanied by anger and hostility directed toward the administration and/or captors. During the transition from captivity back to normal life, personnel may decide to return to work immediately, take some time off before returning to work, transfer to another facility, or never work in courthouse institutions again. The type of readjustment chosen depends on one's personality and experiences during captivity.

If taken hostage, a person should seek composure as soon as possible. Composure will allow a person to think clearly and this mental focus may increase survivability chances. Of course, a hostage should never say anything to upset the captor. While heroics may be successful, they are usually unsuccessful and can prove fatal. Court personnel should be briefed on a psychological frame of mind known as the "Stockholm syndrome." The Stockholm syndrome occurs when a hostage develops an association with the captor over time, resulting in the hostage sympathizing with the captor. This association can become so powerful that the hostage starts believing the captor is his or her friend. A hostage may actually believe what the captor says is in fact true and correct. As a result, a hostage may begin to praise the captor and become critical of law enforcement personnel.

In order to survive being held hostage, personnel must depend on common sense, training, experience, preparation, and self-reliance. If a person is taken hostage, the following guidelines will often prove effective in surviving:

1. Remain calm; the way one hostage acts will often affect other hostages and how captors will treat them. A calm appearance will often help reduce panic and fear. Remaining calm is not an easy task. Hostages often experience a rapid pulse, pounding heart, sweating, shaking, and feelings of fear, panic, humiliation, disbelief, isolation, helplessness, guilt, and powerlessness. Emotions must be kept in check. If a calm demeanor and a reduction of stress are not employed, severe exhaustion and anxiety may result. Stress may be reduced by taking deep breaths, concentrating on pleasant memories, and letting muscles relax.

2. Be cooperative. Don't argue. Obey captor's demands without appearing servile, antagonistic, or surrendering dignity or self-esteem.

3. Once a person has been taken hostage, a decision must be made whether or not to resist or comply with a captor's requests or demands. Resistance can take many forms, ranging from a reluctance to follow a captor's instructions to an outright refusal to comply. While resistance may be the best course of action, resistance can also be dangerous, causing captors to kill or injure the resisting hostage and other hostages. Compliant actions may buy a hostage time. The decision on what to do must be made by each hostage.

4. Do not enter into discussions or activities with captors. Do not provoke captors or interfere in their discussions or activities. Be a good listener, and speak only when spoken to. Hostages who bring undue attention may be needlessly hurt or killed.

5. Keep a low profile; look down or away from captors. Avoid the appearance of observing captors. A goal should be to observe everything possible; however, it must appear that a hostage is not watching. Hostages appearing to be consciously observing captors may be considered a witness and thus heighten the danger of injury or death. Captives should try to remember events for later prosecution. It is also important to remember the criminal's location in the facility, number of captors, identities of captors, number and type of weapons seen, and the number and identities of other hostages. These points are important especially when a hostage is released; there will often be a debriefing conducted focusing on these points.

6. Communicate with other hostages, if possible. However, do not attempt to talk to another hostage if captives are excitable and/or hostile.

7. Do not make threats.

8. Be reluctant to give up personal identification and/or clothing. Be especially resistant to exchanges with captors as this could put a person in great danger during a rescue attempt.

9. Try to drink water and eat even when not hungry in order to keep up ones strength.

10. Be cautious of body language that may arouse the hostility of a captor. For example, do not turn your back to captors. Face captors without staring, this is much safer than turning one's back in contempt.

11. Be cautious of making suggestions; captors may hold a hostage accountable if things go wrong.

12. Think of persuasive reasons why you should be kept alive.

13. If a rescue attempt occurs, drop to the floor, keep the hands visible, and do not resist being handcuffed until proper identification can be made. Attempt to find protective cover especially when a rescue attempt is in progress. Remain calm; do not panic or lose control or captors may try to harm you or use you as a shield. Finally, do not run toward the attacking force, they may mistake you for a captor.

14. Attend a debriefing. Hostage situations are very stressful and the opportunity to talk about the incident will help alleviate stress.

15. Request medical help if it is required. Injuries and existing medical conditions should be reported to captors. Captors are usually responsive to injuries and medical conditions because they do not want to be held accountable should a hostage die while in captivity.

16. If taken captive and held in close proximity to the hostage taker, try to keep a maximum amount of distance between the hostage-taker and yourself.

17. All movements should be slow and deliberate.

18. Mentally switch roles from one of authority to one of captivity. Many courthouse positions are staffed by personnel used to being in charge, enforcing rules, and giving orders. When taken hostage, the role changes dramatically. The hostage is no longer in charge or even an authority figure. The captor is now in charge and has all of the authority. While captives must acknowledge this change on the outside for the captor; self-esteem and authority should be maintained on the inside.

19. Be cautious of heroics; heroic actions may cause more harm than good. Do not act foolhardy.

20. A hostage must avoid being too critical of personal actions taken during the takeover or captivity stages. Captives should believe that they will survive the ordeal.

21. If the situation becomes protracted, captives should strive to keep their body and mind occupied at all times. This can be done by mentally writing letters, daydreaming, reflecting on happy memories, reciting poems, and creating or solving math problems, etc.

22. Keep track of time by looking at clocks or listening for other indicators such as noon whistles. Keeping a sense of time will help establish some control over the environment.
23. Exercise if it does not bother captors. Stretches, isometrics, push-ups, and sit-ups can often be performed even in confined spaces. Staying physically fit will help maintain a mental state of well-being.
24. Maintain personal grooming and morale by combing hair and keeping clothing as neat and straight as possible.
25. Remain alert to the possibility of escape. However, escape is extremely risky for the escapee and for the hostages who are left behind. Consider the situation very carefully before attempting an escape.
26. If a negotiated release occurs, remain calm and observant. Hostages may be freed singly or with other hostages. Whatever the case, walk calmly to the authorities. Someone will meet captives and guide them to a secure area for a debriefing and medical attention.

Ways to Save a Judge

The following information was gathered by Judge Richard W. Carter, Retired. This list involves a number of things a judge can do, or avoid doing, that will aid in protecting himself or herself. Many of the suggestions are inexpensive and can be used by prosecutors and other court personnel to improve personal security.

1. Do not reserve a parking space with a sign that says "Judge" or displays a judge's name.
2. Do not use a personalized license plate that says "Judge" on it.
3. Do not drink from glasses or water pitchers that have been left unattended in the courtroom on the bench.
4. Do not have a listed or published telephone number and address.
5. Do not display family photographs in an area where visitors can see them. If a judge must display these items, they should be facing the judge and not the general seating area.
6. Do not publicly announce travel plans of any kind (vacation, school, business, etc.).
7. Do not place a personal residence address on any campaign materials.
8. Do not put any heavy or sharp objects on the bench or desk where others can grab them.
9. Do not answer any door without first ascertaining who is on the other side.
10. Do not use the title "Judge" on personal checks, credit cards, airline tickets, etc.

11. Do not use a street address on personal checks if a post office box can be used.
12. Do not use a formal name on a return address if a residence street address is used and mail should be deposited in outgoing office mail.
13. Do not announce a formal name and phone number on the outgoing message of a home answering machine.
14. Do not volunteer personal information to strangers or identify oneself as "Judge." If asked, use the identity of attorney, government employee, etc.
15. Do not be paranoid, but be aware if someone is staring or appears to be following you in a place other than a courthouse.
16. Do not allow strangers to overhear personal telephone calls.
17. Do not enter a vehicle without first taking a quick examination of the interior and looking for signs of hidden persons or tampering.
18. Do not run into the hallway if gunshots are heard in the courthouse; seek immediate cover and have the judge's chambers and courtroom secured.
19. Do not allow anyone to approach the bench without first asking for and receiving permission.
20. Do not ride in parades unless there are provisions made for security and crowd control.
21. Do not become physically involved in the subduing, chase, or apprehension of disorderly persons or escapees.
22. Do not leave a pistol or other personal protection weapon unsecured in the judge's chambers or on the bench.
23. Do not sit on or behind a bench that is not elevated.
24. Do not sit on a bench that does not have steel plates behind it to stop bullets.
25. Do not use an audible duress alarm that will force a person to quickly "flee or fight." Use a silent alarm.
26. Do not hesitate to request additional security for a high-risk trial or a high-risk defendant.
27. Do not allow public access to the Judge's mail room.
28. Do not issue combination lock codes or building keys without keeping records and periodically changing codes and locks.
29. Do not allow disruptive persons to remain in the courtroom if they can be legally removed.
30. Do not be afraid to visualize court security problems and think about what you can do to reduce the risks and what options are available if an incident occurs.
31. Do not leave file cabinets, desk drawers, briefcases, etc. unlocked when the office is vacated.

32. Do not leave valuable or sensitive papers in sight and unlocked when no one is in the office. This is especially important if building maintenance or cleaning persons will be entering the officer.

33. Do not forget to have a personal and family information sheet secured in the office and also filed with the local law enforcement agency so it can be used in an emergency, hostage or kidnapping situation.

34. Do not be quoted in the news in such a manner as to make the public think you fear violence nor that you think you are at risk. Such quotes can be taken as an invitation or a challenge.

35. Do not run from the bench if shooting starts, instead drop behind the bench and lie flat. Running often exposes a person and may cause the assailant to chase the running person down.

36. Do not try to get up if you have been shot. Either play dead or unconscious. Wait for help. Do not invite another shot.

37. Do not allow the news media to show photographs of your family or residence after there has been an incident of court-related violence.

38. Do not allow the media to learn the names, ages, or schools of your minor children.

39. Do not wear shirts or caps that identify you as a judge while out in public.

40. Do not be reluctant to ask for or demand more money and/or personnel for court security.

41. Do not think just because you have never had court violence that it will never happen.

42. Do not assume that a duress alarm is in working condition. Test it regularly.

43. Do not allow intoxicated persons to enter or remain in the courthouse.

44. Do not allow anyone to close the door to your chamber other than you, your bailiff, or someone you have directed to do so.

45. Do not become intoxicated in public places, therefore, becoming vulnerable.

46. Do not appear at campaign fund-raising events unless you have arranged for security. Consider control of admission by invitations or limited ticket sales or distribution.

47. Do not take magazines to the courthouse until after you have removed any mailing labels containing your name and address.

48. Do not forget to wear your judicial robe in the courtroom. It will normally command respect, and like a police uniform, it will make you more difficult to recognize off the bench when you have removed your robe, i.e., your "uniform."

49. Do not personally post or remove your campaign signs if you can have someone else do it for you.

50. Do not transport your judicial robe in your automobile by hanging it up unless it is covered with colored paper or plastic to disguise it. If not covered, lay it flat in the back seat or trunk.

51. Do not leave the Court Security Manual or security materials where others can access them.

52. Do not campaign door-to-door alone.

53. Do not overdo it with your campaign signs at your residence or bumper stickers on your personal vehicles.

54. Do not tell the news media (and do not publish reports) about what court security you have in place, and/or what weaknesses your court has that need improvement.

55. Do not forget that none of the judges killed or wounded went to work or home thinking they would be attacked. Be aware!

56. Do not hesitate to move a high-risk trial to a high-security courtroom elsewhere.

57. Do not address a party with a tone of anger or sarcasm in your voice.

58. Do not open unlabelled packages or gifts delivered to your home or office.

59. Do not keep or carry a weapon unless it is in proper working condition and you have been trained in the correct use of it.

60. Do not forget to teach your staff and your family what you have learned about judicial security.

61. Do not update any photographs that may be on file with the news media or the government if you can avoid it. An exception is the photograph that should accompany the Personal and Family Information Sheet which is confidentially maintained.

62. Do not let your guard down at home. Practice good security techniques.

63. Do not allow architects to design your courtroom chambers or courthouse without receiving your input.

64. Do not allow budgets to be prepared without providing for court security.

65. Do not operate your court without "Rules of Courtroom Decorum" that are prominently posted and vigorously enforced.

66. Do not discard sensitive materials or information in your home or office trash in a legible form that could be read by scavengers.

67. Do not photocopy sensitive data without accounting for each original and copy.

68. Do not expect privacy when talking on a cellular telephone or a cordless telephone.

69. Do not return officer telephone calls from your residence phone if "Caller I.D." is in operation in your area and if you do not have "Caller

I.D. Blocking." Otherwise, the person you call will obtain a digital readout of your home telephone number.

70. Do not call "800" numbers or make "Collect Calls" unless you want your telephone number to appear on the call recipient's phone bill.

71. Do not use hollow core doors on your chambers.

72. Do not use the same courthouse entrance/exit doors as the public, if you can avoid doing so.

73. Do not allow a crowd in the courtroom to exceed Fire Code limits concerning occupancy numbers. In addition to fire safety, this can be used as to exclude unruly or intimidating spectators.

74. Do not be reluctant to have your staff make a "coded" mark on any case file folder that can indicate a potentially violent or unstable person.

75. Do not hire, appoint, or accept a courtroom bailiff until you have reviewed his or her resume and if possible, personnel file.

76. Do not unreasonably expose yourself to persons with communicable diseases such as HIV, tuberculosis, or hepatitis. Take universal precautions.

In conclusion, it is suggested that this list be periodically reviewed to refresh one's memory. Awareness of the need for court and personal security goes a long way toward improving chances of survival.

Courtroom Security Inspections

A bailiff, court security officer, or deputy should conduct a security inspection of the courtrooms each day before any judicial proceedings begin. The inspection should include, at a minimum, the following areas:

1. Doors
2. Windows
3. Desks
4. Seats/benches
5. Trash cans
6. Locks
7. Cell block areas
8. Walls
9. Ventilation and heating ducts
10. Tunnel entrances or any other entrances

Finally, all courtrooms should be locked and secured at the end of all hearings and trials.

High-Risk Trial Plan

A high-risk trial is one in which its character indicates a serious security threat of which may provoke a strong emotional outbreak by the public, trial participants, or court officials prior to and during the trial. An example of a high-risk trial plan can be seen by referring to the trial of the United States vs. Osama bin Laden which began Monday, February 5, 2001 in New York city. High-risk security actions included the installation of hydraulically operated vehicle barricades on access roads designed to stop trucks loaded to 15,000 pounds and moving up to 80 miles-per-hour. A line of thick, steel posts known as bollards, set four feet into the ground and rising four feet above the ground were installed outside the courthouse. These bollards are capable of stopping a truck loaded to 15,000 pounds and traveling up to 50 miles-per-hour. Heavily armed guards were stationed in steel-encased booths complete with bulletproof windows. Finally, cameras were hidden inside light fixtures or affixed to surrounding buildings, providing a view of the courthouse with lenses so strong they could read a newspaper from a block away.

Under such circumstances, at a minimum of one day prior to the trial, the chief of court security should conduct a briefing with the judge who will preside over the high-risk trial to discuss the security measures to be implemented prior to and during the trial. Specific topics may include the following:

1. The judge should park in a secure area as near as possible to the court facility. The parking space should not be marked or designated with the title or name of the judge.
2. The judge should be escorted to and from court by uniformed and/or nonuniformed court security officers.
3. Travel routes should be established for the movement of the judge from the parking area to the court and from the court to other locations the judge will be traveling within the court facility. When traveling these routes, the judge may be escorted by uniformed and/or nonuniformed court security officers.
4. All changes in the normal routine of the judge should be known and security measures should be modified to meet the changes.
5. Special security measures may be instituted for other court officials.
6. A search of the courtroom, judge's chambers, and the entire court facility should be conducted prior to and following each court session.
7. Routes should be selected for rapid exit for the judge, if disruptive behavior erupts in the court facility. A security officer may be stationed in the bench area, at the entrance to the jury box, and at the witness stand. One security officer should be assigned the responsibility of expediting the exit of the judge through the chamber door or other

alternate secure routes. These additional assignments should be filled with sworn law enforcement officers.

8. Signals and procedures should be developed to respond to unusual or emergency situations.

9. A predetermined limit of disruptive behavior before a security officer intervenes should be established. In the event a person is placed into custody or arrested as a result of disruptive behavior, he or she should immediately be removed from the courtroom and placed in a holding area cell.

10. Court staff should be briefed on a need-to-know basis concerning heightened security measures.

11. The judge should be made aware of any intelligence gathered on the defendant and associates that may interfere with the proceedings.

12. Security measures should be implemented to thwart escapes and prevent harm to any prisoner or defendant.

13. Prisoners should be placed in restraints during any movement within the court facility and may be used in the courtroom.

14. Prisoners should be searched prior to entering the courtroom and upon returning to the holding area.

15. Prisoners should remain in the immediate control of and in visual contact with a court security officer and/or law enforcement officer at all times when out of the holding cell.

16. If multiple prisoners are present, adequate security must be provided for each prisoner. A minimum standard is one officer per prisoner, however, in high-risk situations, this strength formula may be expanded to two officers per one prisoner.

17. It is not a good idea for a prisoner to spend time in the courtroom while other business is being conducted.

18. Prisoner access to evidentiary or other items may pose a security risk and should not be permitted.

19. Privileged conferences between the prisoner and his or her attorney should only occur in the holding cell area.

20. If a defendant is not a prisoner, it may be a good idea to use the holding area for entrance, legal processing, and exit.

21. Witnesses may use a secure sally port as an entrance and exit point.

22. A secure waiting area may be provided to witnesses.

23. A 24-hour witness protection operation may be ordered by the court.

24. Strategically reserved and identified seating may be provided for the defendant, victims, relatives, media representatives, and spectators. Of course, a method must be devised to identify individuals so the court security officer, at the main entrance, can identify these personnel.

25. A policy should also be determined concerning defendant's, victims', relatives', media representatives', and spectators' movements.
26. A policy should be preestablished concerning the allowance of audio and/or video recorders in the courtroom and/or court facility.
27. Screening and searching procedures may require tightening.
28. A news release may be provided; if so, it should be established well ahead of time what will be said and who will provide the release.
29. Jurors may use a secure sally port as an entrance and exit point.
30. Should a jury be sequestered, a meeting should be held between the chief of security, presiding judge, and the chief of police/sheriff to discuss the particulars and gather recommendations.
31. Intelligence on the prisoner should be gathered by contacting the Department of Corrections, Bureau of Criminal Identification and Investigation and other entities to assist in determining the security risk and subsequent measures to be implemented. Photographs of the defendant should also be procured, if possible. Of course, the chief of police/sheriff, bailiffs, security personnel, and resident judge should be advised of any unusual risk uncovered in the intelligence gathering process and advised on a plan of action.
32. It should be determined if firearms will be carried and by whom.
33. It should also be determined if additional equipment will be needed.
34. Finally, at the conclusion of each day of the high-risk trial, the chief of security should conduct a debriefing meeting with all security personnel assigned to the court facility and the presiding judge to determine the effectiveness of the current security measures and to gather any pertinent information concerning the security of the court facility or its occupants. After the debriefing, it will be determined whether security measures need to be changed.

Emergency Medical Plan

The purpose of an emergency medical plan is to ensure the availability of medical assistance and rapid response to medical emergencies within a court facility. If a medical emergency takes place, a court security officer should immediately respond to the location of the emergency; take precautions against blood-borne pathogens; administer first aid; obtain information concerning the victim and direct another person, preferably a courthouse employee, to summons the emergency squad via 911.

There may be a temptation to use duress alarms to signal medical emergencies; however, this is not a good idea. Duress alarms should be used solely for the purpose of communicating a courthouse violence situation. If duress alarms are used for other purposes, security personnel will be responding in a manner different from a courthouse violence incident. This can be deadly for both the officer and person under duress. Thus, medical assistance should be requested by radio, telephone, or word of mouth.

Security and Control Manual

A security and control manual should be developed by courthouse officers to include the following written policies and procedure:

1. Court security duty posts
2. Job description and position responsibilities for each duty post
3. Court liaison duties
4. Courtroom external communications procedures
5. Courthouse population circulation patterns
6. Courthouse facility arrests and placing arrestees into custody
7. Courthouse security guidelines
8. Prisoner control and holding facility procedures
9. Prisoner transportation procedures
10. Weapons control
11. Courtroom search procedures
12. Prisoner escapes
13. Hand-carried article search procedures
14. Screening procedures
15. Facility evacuation plan
16. Court security response
17. Bomb threat procedures
18. Hostage plan
19. Major emergency/disaster plan
20. Special operations/disaster plan
21. Crowd control
22. High-risk trial plan
23. Emergency medical assistance plan
24. Security survey guidelines and procedures
25. Inventory procedures
26. Physical security plan
27. Incident reports
28. Authorized use of electronic immobilization devices (handheld device, belts, and shields)

Detecting Unusual Behavior

In order to discuss unusual or aberrant behavior, a working definition should be developed. One of the first clues to unusual behavior is that there is almost always a change from how the person usually behaves. In other words, any change from the way a person usually behaves is unusual behavior. Of course, not all unusual behavior will require action. The trick is to know which behavior does and which behavior does not require action. At the very least, security personnel need to be alert for possible trouble if anyone is thought to be acting unusual.

Most officers are reluctant to report a fellow officer or employee under any circumstances. Indeed, some officers will bristle at the incorporation of behavior observation programs stating they won't be "rats" or spy on fellow employees. However, it must be understood: there is a clear distinction between spying (going out of one's way to learn something about a fellow employee) and being alert to all of the behavior that is going on around an officer in the everyday courthouse environment.

Officers will generally fall back on a number of reasons why they are reluctant to participate in behavior observation programs; for example, officers may state that they are not confident in their ability to recognize unusual behavior. Additionally, officers may believe if there is trouble generated for the troubled employee there will be trouble generated for the reporting officer. The troubled employee may be a friend; thus, the reporting officer may be concerned that the troubled employee may lose their job as a result of departmental intervention. Furthermore, some officers may believe that courthouse morale will suffer as a result of any ensuing investigation. Finally, some officers may believe the program is really intended to "hang" problem employees. Of course, a poorly designed or operated behavior observation program will be counterproductive and justify the negative observations and concerns of many officers.

A properly designed and implemented behavior observation program will nullify all of the above concerns. A properly designed and operated program should be designed to get help for troubled employees by first identifying the unusual behavior. Second, the program should document the unusual behavior by referring to specific incidents, accurately describe the behaviors observed, and note any discussion with the employee. Third, the program should contain steps for addressing the troubled employee by referring to observed unusual behavior (specific incidents) while at the same time avoiding reference to personal beliefs, moralizing, or diagnosing. The program should also emphasize the employee's value to the courthouse and identify necessary action such as appropriate referrals while maintaining the issue of privacy. Finally, the program should contain follow-up actions as appropriate.

For a behavior observation program to be effective, officers need to know what behaviors reflect mental states, attitudes, or beliefs that could lead to unreliable or dangerous actions. Behaviors can be categorized into three areas: work performance, social interactions, and personal health. The key point in all three observable areas concerns "change." Furthermore, not every change is meaningful. The importance of an observable change should be measured by considering severity, frequency, and/or cumulative effect.

Work performance changes include the following: has the employee's work quality or quantity changed—has there been a change in work speed or level of work involvement? Is the employee making more mistakes or bad judgments than usual—are there numerous incidents, does the employee laugh off errors or reprimands, or does the employee deny mistakes and/or unnecessarily condemn themselves for mistakes? Has the employee's efficiency lessened—does the employee have trouble arriving at decisions, fail to meet deadlines, or need repeated directions for easy tasks? Does the employee have difficulty concentrating—does the employee forget important or obvious things, act without thinking, daydream too much, doodle excessively, or repeat the same actions over and over?

Is the employee absent from the job—late or absent, especially Mondays or Fridays, often takes off half-days, leaves work without notice, falsifies attendance records, takes a lot of sick leave, or gives improbable excuses for absences? Is the employee absent on-the-job—wanders out of his or her assigned area, takes excessively long lunches and breaks, or gets sick while at work? Does the employee ignore courthouse policies and procedures—steals or damages property, disregards or bends rules? Is the employee overcautious—overreacts to normal conditions, freezes or disappears during emergencies, overly concerned about details/accuracy, or double checks work too much? Is the employee overzealous—never takes a break, comes to work extremely early, hangs around after shift, volunteers for excessive amounts of overtime, or suddenly exceeds work expectations? Does the employee engage in a lot of risk taking—drives recklessly, operates equipment carelessly, shows poor judgment when performing dangerous activities, or gambles a lot. Finally, has the employee's cooperation with fellow employees changed—refuses to share equipment or information, refuses to take directions, or refuses to accept help from others.

Social interaction changes include the following: does the employee appear less sociable than before—seems isolated/withdrawn, has shallow friendships, smiles and talks to self, refuses social contact, makes poor eye contact, lacks a sense of humor, seems overly suspicious, holds grudges or sulk? Did the employee become too sociable—talks too much, plays pranks or jokes, monopolizes conversations, displays inappropriate sexual behavior, or flashes money? Are there changes in the employee's choice of friends, especially younger or easily dominated individuals; does the employee have a separate set of friends for drinking or gambling? Are there changes in the way other employees react to him or her–ignore or avoid the employee, get angry with him or her, mistrust the employee, play pranks on him or her, become condescending, or complain or joke about the employee? Does the employee show more anger–seems more impatient, overreacts to real or imagined criticism, becomes irritable, becomes argumentative, physically fights or displays temper outbursts?

Does the employee manipulate others–builds up brownie points, brags, exaggerates, acts naive or innocent, lies, shows off, or borrows money? Is there any change in speech behavior–talks slower or faster, talks more or less, stammers? Has the employee's speech content changed–jumps from topic to topic; talks about a hopeless future, occupied with suicide, disasters, or destruction; occupied with one topic; never chats about family or interests? Does the employee have more complaints about physical ailments, back pain/muscle aches, fellow workers or superiors, being ignored or left out, family or money problems, lack of privileges, or filling out required forms? Has the employee stopped complaining?

Personal health changes include signs of nerves or emotional upset–headaches, startles easily, cries easily, or has a shaky voice. Does the employee use alcohol or drugs differently–drinks too much, displays alcohol on his or her breath, especially during the day; shows preoccupation with alcohol or drugs; gulps drinks, especially the first couple; encourages others to use drugs or drink; or is frequently "on the wagon"? Has the employee had unusual illness–claims large amount of dental, medical, emotional benefits; displays slow recovery from illness; shows preoccupation with death or suddenly become religious; ignores his or her own illness? Has the employee's energy level changed–displayed by yawning, fatigue, restlessness, or fidgeting? Are there any changes in the employee's daily living/working routine such as sleep difficulties, change in after work hobbies or activities, change in amount or pattern of eating, or rigidly following the same pattern without reason? Are there any changes in the employee's general appearance–appears better/more poorly groomed, walks differently (slower/stumbles), or displays changes in posture? Finally, has the employee shown changes in the body or limbs–witnessed by shaky hands; nail biting; weight loss or gain; cold, sweaty hands; twitching or nonseasonal sweating.

In conclusion, everybody knows a lot about an employee after it is too late. Later investigation always reveals that somebody knew or recognized that the employee was troubled after a tragedy occurs. The appearance of unusual behavior(s) listed above should be considered as possible symptoms of a troubled employee. Even though the situation may be delicate (the troubled employee may be a friend or long-time fellow officer), what an officer sees or hears about a fellow employee might prevent trouble if these facts are passed on to someone with the authority to intervene. To place behavior observation programs into perspective, consider how an officer would feel if he or she recognized another employee was troubled, did nothing, and the troubled employee "went off the deep end" and intentionally injured or killed himself or herself, other officers, other employees, or citizens.

Addressing Cost Issues

Yes, it is true that all of these discussed security measures and support programs may be expensive. However, courthouse safety and security is a high-profile political topic. The government is addressing this issue by making funding available for courthouse safety programs. The biggest problem with these programs is the lack of information on where grants are located, the process required for application, and the guidelines for grant award. Of the many courthouse officials the author has contacted in the past two years, few had any idea that grant money was available for courthouse security programs, where the funds were located, and/or how to apply for grant money.

Probably the most effective step in seeking grants concerns involves the inclusion of local, city, and state political leaders in the process. The next important step is to articulate the fact that the grant money will be spent on a formal community-based efforts involving the local law enforcement agency, mental health authority, and other entities. Of course, the more community organizations that are involved, the better the chances that a grant will be awarded to the applicant.

It will also be helpful to understand a few terms connected to the grant process. Readers pursuing grants will find the following terms helpful. There are generally four types of grants: discretionary grants, earmarked funds, formula grants, and initiatives. Discretionary grants are sometimes referred to as "project grants," which are often designed to support research, evaluation, and demonstration projects or service projects. Discretionary funds are awarded for specific periods of time, often covering one to five years.

Earmarked funds are legislative directives in the appropriations laws (as distinct from authorization acts). Earmarked funds normally dictate how to spend certain portions of funds appropriated within larger funding programs. Earmarks may be termed as "hard or soft." Hard earmarks are written into legislation, usually with specific amounts to be spent and the specific recipient of the funding identified. Soft earmarks are based upon conference reports. Earmarks occur in a specific fiscal year and may not be continued to the next fiscal year. Earmarked funds are by far the most likely type of grant process courthouse administrators will encounter. Due to fiscal constraint and the possibility of nonrenewal, courthouse administrators should aggressively apply for these funds at the beginning of the fiscal year.

Formula grants are usually based on population, unemployment levels, census data, or other demographic indicators. Most formula grants go directly to state agencies for on-going services through block grants or categorical programs. Finally, initiatives are special efforts by federal departments and tend to focus on specific issues.

Developing and writing grant proposals is a learned discipline and only the most effectively prepared proposals will generate positive action. Grant writing may be broken down into two parts. The first part concerns preparation, developing an idea for a proposal, community support, identification of funding resources, getting organized to write the proposal, review, and mailing. The second part concerns basic components, an outline of project goals, presenting a credible applicant or organization, stating the purpose at hand, stating project objectives, delineating a plan of action, evaluating a product and process analysis, long-term project planning, and planning a budget.

Preparation begins with researching all pertinent criteria related to the grant. Pertinent information includes a point of contact; the availability of funds; deadlines, if they exist, the process used by the grantor agency for accepting applications; basic requirements; application forms; and any required information and procedures. These topics of pertinent information frequently vary with the federal agency making the grant award. Further, many entities send a specific person to grantmanship workshops to learn the grant writing process and actually staff a grant writing position on a daily or frequent basis.

When developing an idea for a proposal, it is important to determine if the idea has been considered in the applicant's locality or state. A careful check should be made with legislators and area government agencies and related public and private agencies that may currently have grant awards or contracts to do similar work. Federal agencies are required to report funding information as funds are approved, increased, or decreased among projects within a given state. If a similar program already exists, the applicant may need to reconsider submitting the proposed project, particularly if duplication of efforts is perceived. If significant differences, unique circumstances, and/or improvements in the proposed project's goals can be clearly established, it may be worthwhile to pursue federal assistance.

Community support for most proposals is essential. Academic, political, and professional groups; local government organizations; public officials; and lay organizations should be solicited for support of the proposal. Statement of support should be represented in writing if possible. Numerous letters of support, letters of endorsement, and/or affiliation agreements detailing exact areas of project sanction and commitment may be requested as part of a proposal. Even if statements of support are not a requirement, they can be persuasive to a grantor agency. A useful method of generating community support may be to hold meetings with the top decision makers in the community who would be concerned with the subject matter of the proposal. The forum for discussion may include a query into the merits of the proposal, development of a contract of support for the proposal, to generate data in support of the proposal, or development of a strategy to create proposal support from a large number of community groups. Finally, the type and caliber of community support is often critical in the initial and subsequent review phases.

Naturally, the identification of funding resources is a must; however, applicants should also pursue related programs as potential resources. Common sense dictates that the applicant and the grantor agency should have the same interests, intentions, and needs if a proposal is to be considered an acceptable candidate for funding. Furthermore, applicants should review the Federal Budget for the current and fiscal years to determine proposed dollar amounts for particular budget functions.

Once a potential grantor agency is identified, a point of contact (POC) should be located and a grant application kit should be requested, if applicable. The POC should also be used to solicit eligibility requirement suggestions, criticisms, advice, review, and comments concerning the proposed project. If possible, an applicant may conduct a personal visit to the grantor's regional office or headquarters. A visit may establish a favorable face-to-face contact, bring out some essential details concerning the proposal, and/or help secure support literature and references from the agency's library. The more agency personnel know about the proposal, the better the chance of support and of an eventual favorable decision. If the proposal review is unfavorable and differences cannot be resolved, the examining agency POC may be asked to suggest another department or agency that may be interested in the proposal.

The actual development and writing of grant proposals concerns eight basic components: (1) the proposal summary; (2) introduction to organization; (3) the problem statement; (4) project objectives; (5) project methods or design; (6) project evaluation; (7) future funding; and (8) the project budget.

The proposal summary represents an outline of project goals and should appear at the beginning of the proposal. It could be in the form of a cover letter or a separate page, but should definitely be brief—no longer than two or three paragraphs. The summary would be most useful if it were prepared after the proposal has been developed in order to encompass all of the key summary points necessary to communicate the objectives of the project. It is this document that becomes the cornerstone of the proposal, and the initial impression it gives will be critical to the success of the venture. In many cases, the summary will be the first part of the proposal package seen by agency officials and could be the only part of the package that is carefully reviewed before the decision is made to consider the project any further.

The applicant must select a fundable project that can be supported in view of the local need. Alternatives, in the absence of federal support, should be pointed out. The influence of the project both during and after the project period should be explained. The consequences of the project as a result of funding should be highlighted.

The introduction presents a credible applicant or organization. The applicant should gather data about its organization from all available sources. Most proposals require a description of an applicant's organization to include its past and present operations. Some features to consider are a brief biography of board members and key staff members and the organization's goals, philosophy, track record with other grantors, and any success stories. The data should be relevant to the goals of the federal grantor agency and should establish the applicant's credibility.

The problem statement focuses on the purpose at hand. The problem statement (or needs assessment) is a key element of a proposal that makes a clear, concise, and well-supported statement of the problem to be addressed. The best way to collect information about the problem is to conduct and document both a formal and informal needs assessment for a program in the target or service area. The information provided should be both factual and directly related to the problem addressed by the proposal. Areas to document include the purpose for developing the proposal; the beneficiaries—who they are and how they will benefit; the social and economic costs to be affected; the nature of the problem (provide as much hard evidence as possible); how the applicant organization came to realize the problem exists and what is currently being done about the problem; the remaining alternatives available when funding has been exhausted (explain what will happen to the project and the impending implications); and most importantly, a description of the specific manner through which problems might be solved including a review of the resources needed, considering how they will be used and to what end.

There is a considerable body of literature focusing on exact assessment techniques. Any local, regional, or state government planning office, or local university offering course work in planning and evaluation techniques should be able to provide excellent background references. Types of data that may be collected include historical, geographic, quantitative, factual, statistical, and philosophical information, as well as studies completed by colleges, and literature searches from public or university libraries. Local colleges or universities which have a department or section related to the proposal topic may help determine if there is interest in developing a student or faculty project to conduct a needs assessment. It may be helpful to include examples of the findings for highlighting in the proposal.

Project objectives cover goals and desired outcomes referring to specific activities in a proposal. It is necessary to identify all objectives related to the goals to be reached, and the methods to be employed to achieve the stated objectives. Applicants should consider quantities or things measurable and refer to a problem statement and the outcome of proposed activities when developing objectives that will probably be used to evaluate program progress.

Program methods and program design delineate a plan of action. The program design refers to how the project is expected to work and solve the stated problem. Applicants should sketch out the following topics: the activities to occur along with the related resources and staff needed to operate the project (inputs); a flow chart of the organization features of the project; a description of how the parts interrelate; where personnel will be needed, and what they are expected to do; the kinds of facilities, transportation, and support services required; an explanation of what will be the achieved plan for measurable results; and a projection of staff that may be required to produce evidence of program performance through an examination of stated objectives during either a site visit by the federal grantor agency and/or grant reviews which may involve peer review committees.

It may be useful to devise a diagram of the program design; for example, draw a three-column block. Each column is headed by one of the parts (inputs, throughputs and outputs), and on the left (next to the first column), specific program features would be identified (i.e., implementation, staffing, procurement, and systems development). In the grid, specify something about the program design; for example, assume the first column is labeled inputs and the first row is labeled staff. On the grid, one might specify under inputs five officers to operate a central security control unit. The throughput might address a myriad of security monitoring functions; outputs might be to prevent security lapses or respond to actual incidences. This type of procedure will help to conceptualize both the scope and detail of the project.

Wherever possible, applicants should justify, in the narrative, the course of action taken. The most economical method should be used that does not compromise or sacrifice project quality. The financial expenses associated with performance of the project will later become points of negotiation with the federal program staff. If everything is not carefully justified in writing, in the proposal, after negotiation with the federal grantor agencies, the approved project may resemble less of the original concept. Carefully consider the pressures of the proposed implementation, that is, the time and money needed to acquire each part of the plan. A Program Evaluation and Review Technique (PERT) chart could be useful and supportive in justifying some proposals.

Applicants should also highlight the innovative features of the proposal that could be considered distinct from other proposals under consideration. Finally, applicants should, whenever possible, use appendices to provide details, supplementary data, references, and information requiring in-depth analysis. These types of data, although supportive of the proposal, if included in the body of the design, could detract from its readability. Appendices provide the proposal reader with immediate access to details, if and when clarification of an idea, sequence, or conclusion is required. Timetables, work plans, schedules, activities, methodologies, legal papers, personal vitae, letters of support, and endorsements are examples of appendices.

Evaluation includes a product and process analysis. The evaluation component is twofold: product evaluation, and process evaluation. Product evaluation addresses results that can be attributed to the project, as well as the extent to which the project has satisfied its desired objectives. Process evaluation addresses how the project was conducted, in terms of consistency with the stated plan of action and the effectiveness of the various activities within the plan. Most federal agencies now require some form of program evaluation among grantees. The requirements of the proposed project should be explored carefully. Evaluations may be conducted by either internal staff members, an evaluation firm, or both. The applicant should state the amount of time needed to evaluate, how the feedback will be distributed among the proposed staff, and a schedule for review and comment for this type of communication. Evaluation designs may start at the beginning, middle, or end of a project, but the applicant should specify a start-up time. It is practical to submit an evaluation design at the start of a project for two reasons: (1) convincing evaluations require the collection of appropriate data before and during program operations, and (2) if the evaluation design cannot be prepared at the outset, then a critical review of the program design may be advisable.

Even if the evaluation design has to be revised as the project progresses, it is much easier and cheaper to modify a good design. If the problem is not well defined and carefully analyzed for cause-and-effect relationships, then a good evaluation design may be difficult to achieve. Sometimes a pilot study is needed to begin the identification of facts and relationships. Often a thorough literature search may be sufficient.

Evaluation requires both coordination and agreement among program decision makers (if known). Above all, the federal grantor agency's requirements should be highlighted in the evaluation design. Also, federal grantor agencies may require specific evaluation techniques such as designated data formats (an existing information collection system) or they may offer financial inducements for voluntary participation in a national evaluation study. The applicant should ask specifically about these points. Also, consult the Criteria for Selecting Proposals section of the catalog program description to determine the exact evaluation methods to be required for the program if funded.

Future funding includes long-term project planning. Applicants should describe a plan for continuation beyond the grant period and/or the availability of other resources necessary to implement the grant. Additionally, applicants should discuss maintenance and future program funding if the program is for construction activity. Furthermore, applicants should account for other needed expenditures if the program includes purchase of equipment.

Finally, the proposal should include the planning of a budget. Funding levels in federal assistance programs change yearly. Thus, it is useful to review the appropriations over the past several years to try to project future funding levels. However, it is safer to never anticipate that the income from the grant will be the sole support for the project. This consideration should be given to the overall budget requirements and in particular to budget line items most subject to inflationary pressures. Restraint is important in determining inflationary cost projections (avoid padding budget line items), but attempt to anticipate possible future increases.

Some vulnerable budget areas are utilities, rental of buildings and equipment, salary increases, food, telephones, insurance, and transportation. Budget adjustments are sometimes made after the grant award, but this can be a lengthy process. Be certain that implementation, continuation, and phase-down costs can be met. Consider costs associated with leases, evaluation systems, hard/soft match requirements, audits, development, implementation and maintenance of information and accounting systems, and other long-term financial commitments.

A well-prepared budget justifies all expenses and is consistent with the proposal narrative. Some areas in need of an evaluation for consistency are (1) the salaries in the proposal in relation to those of the applicant organization should be similar; (2) if new staff persons are being hired, additional space and equipment should be considered, as necessary; (3) if the budget calls for an equipment purchase, it should be the type allowed by the grantor agency; (4) if additional space is rented, the increase in insurance should be supported; (5) if an indirect cost rate applies to the proposal, the division between direct and indirect costs should not be in conflict, and the aggregate budget totals should ideally refer directly to the approved formula, and (6) if matching costs are required, the contributions to the matching fund should be taken out of the budget unless otherwise specified in the application instructions.

It is very important for applicants to become familiar with government-wide circular requirements. The applicant should thoroughly review the appropriate circulars since they are essential in determining items such as cost principles and conforming with government guidelines for federal domestic assistance.

Lastly, the review and mailing process concerns the elements of criticism, signature block, neatness, and mailing. At some point in the writing process, perhaps after the completion of a second draft, a neutral third party should review the proposal working draft for continuity, clarity, and reasoning. The idea is to gain constructive criticism rather than wait for the federal grantor agency to volunteer this information during the review cycle. As most proposals are made to institutions rather than individuals, the signatures of chief administrative officials will be required. Thus, these signatures must be included in the proposal where appropriate. The proposal should be typed, collated, copied, and packaged correctly and neatly (according to agency instructions, if any). Each package should be inspected to ensure uniformity from cover to cover. A neat, organized, and attractive proposal package can leave a positive impression with the reader about the proposal contents.

Concluding Remarks

In conclusion, with so many security options available, courthouse administrators must do their homework to determine which choice is most adaptable to their courthouse, visiting population, and staff. Additionally, it must be understood that physical security controls are only one component of a courthouse security protection program. They are not intended to be the sole means of protecting the courthouse; instead, their mission is to complement and enhance other security measures, such as security staffing. All physical security measures are dependent upon trained people to operate or otherwise render them effective. Further, unless the proper security equipment is specified and professionally installed, little positive effect will be realized in relation to reducing crime and saving lives.

Citizens may be taken aback when revelations surface that a courthouse security structure is very weak. In some instances, critical protection postures and capabilities can be easily evaded or defeated. Indeed, some courthouses rely totally upon security officers as a compensatory measure for aging physical security systems or the complete lack of security systems. The decline or lack of safeguards and security program readiness and capability represents a disturbing trend. Especially when one considers the fact that while funding for safeguards and security programs has fallen significantly, program requirements have not. In fact, requirements are growing meaning these systems no longer provide the necessary level of protection required in today's threat environment. There are numerous real-world security threats which many judicial systems continue to ignore or decide to employ "half measures" to thwart.

Many courthouse security forces are managed by subcontractors who hire personnel to staff security manager positions and similar high-priority positions who are not experienced or even trained in security matters. This deficiency becomes apparent when one identifies the plethora of security weaknesses that exist at many of these courthouses. Many security managers have decided to ignore the basic principle of "defense in depth." It is very common for security positions to be laid out in a linear fashion. This means once one security position is breached, the adversaries have penetrated the courthouse. Inexperienced security managers believe that soft alarms and locking mechanisms are valid in-depth security measures. Many courthouse administrators and security subcontractors are more than happy to rely on electronic alarms to somehow thwart physical attack because soft alarms are actually used to replace security officers.

Additionally, many courthouse administrations have dropped exterior fence patrols believing they are a waste of manpower. By ignoring the perimeter, courthouse administrators have expanded opportunities for the adversary to gain access to the courthouse. Adversary(s) may now approach courthouse perimeters without fear of discovery and subsequent officer intervention.

Some courthouse administrators and security subcontractors have also condoned the use of nonsecurity personnel to operate certain pieces of security equipment, to staff security alarm monitoring stations, and/or to conduct other security tasks. Additionally, some courthouse systems manipulate postulated threat identification to suit security force strength (as security forces are cut, the postulated threat is reformed to reflect a lesser threat).

Of course, some readers may be thinking, how can these security concerns be allowed to flourish? The answer is simple: in many ways, courthouse systems regulate, inspect, and evaluate themselves. Since many courthouse systems show little interest in security issues, courthouses security systems are evaluated and always deemed acceptable as a result of any audit. These positive findings are generated for a number of reasons. Perhaps the biggest reason concerns the fact that if courthouse administrators find a courthouse lacking, the courthouse system will have to spend money to fix the shortcomings. Thus, in the interest of cutting security forces and saving money, many courthouse administrations are unlikely to spend any funds on issues such as security. In many cases, the present mission-to-resource imbalance is causing an inability to conduct adequate safeguards and security mission accomplishment. Indeed, as security forces continue to suffer further budget and manpower cuts, the safeguards and security program capabilities continue to fall further behind requirements.

It is the courthouse systems duty to commit to a viable safeguards and security program. Failing to honor security requirements will not only reduce public trust, but more importantly, endanger the citizens and staff it is obliged to maintain. Decisive measures must be taken to stem any reduction of crucial security program resources and capabilities or courthouses will be protected at an unacceptable level.

Of course, security technologies are not the answer to all courthouse security problems. However, many security products can be excellent tools if applied appropriately. They can provide courthouse administrators or security officials with information that would otherwise be unavailable, release manpower for more appropriate work, or be used to perform mundane tasks. Sometimes they can save a courthouse money (compared to the long-term cost of personnel or the cost impact of not preventing a particular incident). However, security technologies are often not applied correctly in courthouses, and are expected to do more than they are capable of, or are not well maintained after initial installation. In these cases, security technologies are certainly not cost effective.

Courthouse administrators cannot simply rely on any existing or projected security/safety system to completely prevent violence from occurring in the courthouse. However, integrated security systems will demonstrate to community organizations and individual citizens that courthouse personnel and law enforcement entities are aware of security concerns and are proactively involved in addressing these issues. A properly designed, updated, practiced, and implemented integrated security system will ultimately increase a courthouse system's success in protecting citizens. The idea is to address physical security and emotional well-being in a concerted effort. Effective integrated security systems using a number of technologies and programs, discussed in this chapter, will serve a proactive role in promoting peace and harmony within the community, and in ensuring the right of citizens and staff members to attend a safe courthouse environment.

Chapter 3

EFFECTIVE RESPONSE MECHANICS

Response Planning Purpose

Court security issues affect many sectors of the community to include differing local needs and serious funding concerns. Indeed, each court operates in its own environment which includes different facilities, different communities and jurisdictions as well as varying resources, including time, personnel, money, and equipment. Consequently each court must determine the level of security that is appropriate for its environment in order to deter, detect, and provide a speedy response to security incidents while remaining accessible to its community.

Thus, an effective response plan should focus on the preparation and compiling of elements of essential information that should be used by police response forces when security efforts have failed and a courthouse violence crisis is in progress. This information is designed to enable police responders to quickly and efficiently develop an entry plan that will streamline response time frames and save lives. The focal point of a rapid effective response is to shift the actions of an active shooter or other type of violent offender from offensive activities to defensive activities.

A response document must be site specific and adjusted accordingly. The end product should contain observed structural and procedural weaknesses and strengths. Applicable recommendations for the enhancement of existing or additional internal defense systems, physical protection devices (hard and soft), and protective forces should be included in applicable attachments. Indeed, a response document can be used as a significant part of a security survey as vulnerabilities or root causes are identified and earmarked for correction. A response document should be developed by compiling elements of essential information concerning a courthouse and the surrounding area into a workable format. An effective response document will neutralize or, at a minimum, decrease security concerns. A condensed oral response briefing should also be prepared and practiced for streamlined presentations.

Further, an effective response plan will enable law enforcement entities to quickly and effectively achieve the following priorities, save the lives of those located in the proximity of the active shooter, protect the lives of citizens located in the area of the event, protect the lives of responding officials, capture and/or neutralize the suspect(s) as soon as possible, obtain area containment, generate communications and multiofficer–multiagency response, and achieve after-event investigation and the return to normalcy of the affected area. Finally, these events are not usually resolved by SWAT teams. Indeed, the first officers on the scene will have to make a rapid assessment of the situation and move to the area where the active shooter is operating, using speed, aggressive tactics, and knowledge gained through the development and use of a response plan.

Response Planning

Response planning is a very tedious process. Courthouse administrators may hear comments from personnel stating that planning is nonessential or useless because no plan ever works as envisioned. These views are voiced by individuals who are inadequately trained in response planning, misunderstand the value of planning, or have never seen or experienced a "wing it" style response go sour. It is guaranteed that even an incomplete weak response plan is better than no plan at all.

Response planning is not just a leadership task, it requires subordinate participation as well. One person should not plan an entire response document alone; if he or she tries, the chances of failure are high due to time constraints, information overload, and limited thinking. One person considering an operation will be limited to his or her personal mind set and experience, but when a whole team of personnel participates, the options are increased. Through team involvement, the plan takes on the identity of a team plan instead of "the plan."

Response Planning Mechanics

To begin planning, the courthouse must be analyzed; therefore, all elements of essential information available must be collected and collated into a workable format. To accomplish this task, a primary question must be answered: **What is the response document's purpose?** The response document's purpose is to serve as a centrally located document containing elements of significant information used in support of an overall mission intended to counter a courthouse violence situation. Finally, a response document is designed to address many complex contingencies by capturing, fusing, and disseminating information to operational entities.

Another question frequently asked concerns the storage of the response document: **Where should the response document be located?** The response document should be removed from the direct area of concern or what would be called during a real-world event, the target site. The response document should be stored in a central location such as the leading law enforcement entity's headquarters. Of course, if desired, copies may be stored in a variety of places such as the courthouse itself, preestablished emergency operations centers (EOC's), rally points, etc. However, these documents should be considered as very sensitive and protected by applying operations security (OPSEC) techniques.

OPSEC Techniques

Operations security (OPSEC) is a countermeasures program designed to disrupt or defeat the ability of people to gain the inadvertent release of courthouse violence crisis response plans outside established control procedures. The central focus of OPSEC is to decrease transmission, sensitivity, and visibility; establish accountability; and increase protection of courthouse violence crisis response plans. OPSEC may be achieved by reducing the accessibility, volume, and dispersion of courthouse violence crisis response plans. OPSEC efforts can be enhanced by requiring access authorization, limiting distribution or restricting further distribution, controlling copies, consolidating activities, and the systematic destruction of data no longer needed.

To implement an OPSEC program, the following principles should be implemented: restrict the distribution of courthouse violence crisis response plans to only those people who have a "need to know"; start the OPSEC program in conjunction with the beginning of the courthouse violence crisis response plan process; keep a low profile when developing, completing, and practicing the actual courthouse violence crisis response plan processes; and finally, identify and utilize designated personnel to handle sensitive aspects of the courthouse violence crisis response plan.

In conclusion, a balance must be struck between the release of nonsensitive and sensitive courthouse violence crisis response plan information. For example, the media (broadcast TV, print media, radio, and electronic media–internet sources), community (community population, families of employees, courthouse employees), special interest groups (labor union), and the general population will be interested in and require some information concerning developing or existing courthouse violence response plans. Other personnel or agencies interested in this information include local governments, state government officials and organizations, and federal government entities. However, only a general overview or concept should be released to these entities in lieu of exactly stating what response actions will be implemented in any situation. Only actual responders and planning entities have the "need to know" projected tactical solutions and response mechanics. If this type of sensitive information is "compromised," offenders may develop plans designed to thwart response efforts, thereby heightening the likelihood of mission failure and endangering the lives of everyone involved in a courthouse violence crisis incident.

The media spokesperson (discussed in detail later in this section) will need to work "hand-in-glove" with the OPSEC officer (usually the chief planning officer—also discussed in detail later in this section) to identify what information may be released and not released. Information not to be released should be a short list. Examples include not releasing information that could jeopardize anyone's safety or information that could jeopardize the management of an incident or investigation; and not revealing key investigative techniques or sources, critical matters of evidence, and/or tactical techniques.

The Response Mission

Our criminal justice system is fundamentally reactive. Indeed, little happens until a crime has occurred; by then, it is too late to design effective response strategies. The courthouse violence response planning system discussed here is designed to be proactive in lieu of reactive, thereby reducing the death, injury, and destruction generated by a courthouse violence crisis event. Furthermore, this system is an effective tool for assisting police officers and other types of first responders to heighten their effectiveness and performance during these types of crises. In short, the courthouse violence response planning mission is to "save lives." Once this goal is reached, the very important role of the criminal justice system can move forward (apprehending and punishing perpetrators).

Response Planning Committee

There is a critical need to form a relationship between courthouse administrations and police personnel before any planning or training can be performed. This relationship needs to result in the development of a courthouse violence crisis response team or a local court security advisory committee. This team not only plans what to do when violence strikes, but it also ensures that staff and employees know how to react during a crisis. This team may also be the personnel chosen to set up and operate an Emergency Operations Center (EOC). This courthouse violence crisis response team should work with police crisis response planners in order to shape and tailor a plan specifically designed to fit the needs of each individual courthouse (each courthouse, police department, and community is unique). Of course, many aspects of a generic planning process will be applicable to all courthouse systems. The idea is not to "reinvent the wheel," but to use applicable planning aspects, "tweak" some aspects, and develop unique aspects when required.

Each team needs to trust and share what its needs are with each other in order to develop an effective response plan. The following planning positions are only suggestions and may or may not be staffed. Additionally, one person may staff a number of positions and/or conduct the activities of one or more other positions as required. Each position should have a job description that includes a job title, reporting line, job function, specific duties and responsibilities, and the qualifications required to staff the position.

A courthouse administrator may have a staff or the administrator may represent the entire courthouse violence response planning committee. The size of the staff needed to carry out courthouse violence response planning will depend upon the size of the courthouse facility; the financial resources available; the courthouse's past history, present threat level, and projected threats of potentially violent situations. How well the courthouse administrator manages the courthouse violence crisis response planning committee depends in part on whether minimum staffing needs are met. Part of the job of a courthouse administrator is to estimate what the staffing needs are or will be, and then plan to obtain that level of staffing. In some instances, especially when courthouses lack financial resources, a volunteer courthouse violence response planning committee may be developed.

Courthouse violence response planning committee positions include the following titles: chief planning officer, administrative support, chief of courthouse security, logistics officer, facility architects and engineers, courthouse medical representative, courthouse legal representative, courthouse media/liaison spokesperson, environmental safety and health officer, and other elements unique to the courthouse, as required.

Chief Planning Officer

The chief planning officer (CPO) has the overall authority and responsibility for the conduct of all activities pursuant to the planning process. The CPO develops and clarifies the concept of the operation to those involved in the planning process, approves the crisis response document, and ensures adequate personnel and resources are available and tasked for completion of the planning process. Additionally, the CPO provides oversight of all aspects of the planning process, keeps higher entities (local, state, and federal agencies, etc.) informed of the status of the planning process as required, and coordinates actions with outside agencies (local law enforcement, fire department, medical support, etc.) as required. Further, the CPO develops a command and control structure (chain of command), develops roles and responsibilities for each position, authorizes policies and procedures, and briefs participating individuals/agencies prior to beginning the planning operation (briefings should continue as needed throughout the operation).

The CPO also authorizes media relations and other policies, for example, OPSEC programs. The CPO is also responsible for training personnel on policies and procedures to include rehearsing the crisis response plan, determining what procedures are needed to meet crisis response plan requirements, coordinating all major activities of the planning process, and establishing and maintaining liaisons/points of contact with all appropriate individuals/agencies. Further, the CPO provides an overall view of the planning document by describing courthouse buildings and the activity conducted in each building, prioritizing each building, establishing the sensitivity of each building, identifying any physical or environmental conditions for each building, and addressing any operational considerations.

Additionally, the CPO must decide what types of threat exist and address them in a priority fashion. These include, drugs, guns, and other types of weapons brought into the courthouse; outsiders gaining courthouse access; vehicle break-ins; graffiti; vandalism; or accidents in the parking lot. Finally, the CPO accounts for all expenses related to the planning operation and is responsible for the development of proactive measures and recording their results, attaching any past security/safety surveys, and compiling concluding comments and instructions.

Administrative Support Staff

This position is responsible for all administrative support pertaining to personnel involved in the courthouse violence crisis response planning process. This person(s) handles routine office work. If at all possible, the CPO should not try to run a courthouse violence response planning committee without some type of administrative assistance. The administrative staff is expected to handle paper work effectively and efficiently. For example, this position provides input to the logistics officer concerning equipment, supplies, and forms needed and reproduces documents as required. Administrative support also publishes and updates phone numbers, contact lists, and locator methods concerning crisis response team personnel; personnel assignment rosters; rosters delineating courthouse personnel responsible for court complex buildings; and courthouse employee information. Finally, administrative support copies all relevant security, safety, and fire regulations for inclusion in the crisis response plan (these regulations may be attached to the master plan through the use of annexes).

Chief of Courthouse Security

This position is responsible for gathering and disseminating intelligence data concerning individuals and groups identified as possible threats; gathers intelligence on expected activities during the planning operation; assesses tactics or actions perpetrators may utilize during a violent incident; and assesses counteractions previously used by law enforcement agencies in response to violent incidents. The SRO also provides the CPO with an assessment of the crisis response planning document; conducts intelligence briefings as directed by the CPO; and is responsible for retrieving visual representation of effected structures (video and still photographs). Finally, the SRO evaluates internal and external security systems; compiles current and potential threat data; and is responsible for establishing a crime scene etiquette program for the courthouse community.

Logistics Officer

The logistics officer determines and acquires all resources required to support the crisis response planning process. The logistics officer also tracks all operational expenses associated with the crisis response planning process and provides the equipment and supplies needed for the project. Finally, the logistics officer provides required resource support concerning all activities focusing on the crisis response planning operation.

Some logistics officers will be assigned the responsibility of financial planning or, at the very least, a person working for the logistics section will be assigned budgeting financial planning duties. Financial planning can be divided into three categories: budgeting, accounting, and reporting. Every courthouse violence response planning committee, no matter how small, must have a budget. A budget is an itemized summary of probable expenditures for a given period of time and is usually prepared on a yearly basis. A courthouse violence response planning committee budget should be developed to maintain an acceptable level of readiness. The size of the budget will depend upon the size of the courthouse; the size of the courthouse violence response planning committee; the past performance of CPO if any existed; the size of the community; the availability of government grants; other appropriations;

and the responsiveness of the local government/community. A look at past budgets will give a general picture of what to expect in the future.

Accounting is another financial term that refers to the keeping of financial records. Accounting is the procedure by which actual expenditures are recorded. Accounting procedures are likely to be well established within any particular courthouse system. The office of financial management will usually be able to assist the logistics officer with proper accounting forms and procedures.

Reporting consists of making a periodic presentation of the budget and accounts to supervisors or other authorities that have oversight responsibilities over the courthouse violence response planning committee. Actual reporting procedures are likely to be standardized and particular to the courthouse system. These reports may be assigned in an annual fashion or more frequently. The logistics officer should try to turn reporting activities into an opportunity to promote the courthouse violence response planning committee.

This position is important due to the fact that without resources (staffing, funds, and equipment) courthouse violence crisis response planning would be impossible. The point is, in order to carry out any courthouse violence crisis response plan, the CPO must know what personnel and assets are available. Resources may be grouped into four areas: those available from the government, those of the courthouse system, those of a neighboring jurisdiction, and those that can be obtained from the private sector. Resource types include emergency services, medical services, assembly areas, transportation, supplies, media sources, individuals, equipment, service agencies, and community groups.

In order to make use of emergency resources, the logistics officer must know what resources are available; where resources are located; and the proper steps in the procurement process, including proper return procedures as required. Thus, a resource inventory should be developed that will enable the best use of resources during a courthouse violence crisis. The resource inventory should contain exactly who controls the resources and how to contact that person. The resource inventory should contain the position, name, phone number (home, office, and cell phone), pager or answering system, complete home and business, and the service or equipment to be provided. The same information should be collected and recorded concerning the primary source's designated alternate in case the primary contact cannot be reached. Additionally, the resource inventory should be listed in a systematic way to ensure efficient use. Also, resources should be sorted into an index by title and page number.

Finally, the resource inventory should be updated as often as necessary, but at a minimum, once a year. A resource inventory is worthless if it is not up-to-date. An out-of-date inventory presents its own hazard. For example, if a courthouse violence crisis occurs and the logistics officer is calling disconnected numbers and promising resources that cannot be delivered, lives may be lost. The fastest way to update a resources inventory is to send a standard form letter to everyone listed in the inventory document. The logistics officer can reproduce previously filed information and send a copy to the contact person, asking him or her to confirm the facts and continued availability of the resource. When the letter is returned, the logistics officer can change information on the inventory record and make note of the last date of confirmation. This process enables anyone using the inventory sheet to identify whether the information is accurate and up-to-date.

Facility Architects and Engineers

Personnel staffing these positions read and interpret blueprints concerning all of the structures located on the courthouse grounds. Facility architects and engineers are responsible for compiling a list depicting the location of supporting utilities, e.g., communication lines, electric lines, water lines, heating and air conditioning, etc. Finally, facility architects and engineers serve as a point of contact for building drawings, blueprints, and other structural information.

Courthouse Medical Personnel

Courthouse medical personnel are responsible for interfacing with local medical support entities; identifying and storing medical supplies designed to meet the needs of mass casualties; assisting in the planning and conducting of mass casualty drills; and answering all questions dealing with medical support operations and programs. Courthouse medical personnel should also establish what levels of injury or trauma hospitals can address and their existing capabilities. Courthouse medical personnel should also become familiar with stress and the resulting trauma (acute stress caused by a sudden, arbitrary, often random event and chronic stress which occurs over and over again such as child abuse). Further, courthouse medical personnel should become familiar with crisis reactions that may appear in the aftermath of a courthouse violence crisis. Crisis reactions include physical responses, cognitive responses, emotional reactions, feelings of loss, regression, behavioral reactions, short-term recovery, long-term crisis reactions, and long-term stress recovery. Finally, courthouse medical personnel should brief all concerned parties on the aspects of crisis reactions, for example:

1. The physical response to trauma is based on animal instincts such as frozen fright, fight-or-flight, or exhaustion. Frozen fright includes physical shock, disorientation, and numbness. Fight-or-flight includes adrenaline being pumped through the body, nausea   or the body relieving itself of excess materials like ingested food, one or more of the physical senses becoming more acute while others shut down, an increase in heart rate, muscle tremors or twitches, chest pain, difficulty breathing or hyperventilation, sweating, elevated blood pressure, thirst, headaches, visual difficulties, grinding of teeth, dizziness, chills, shock symptoms, etc. Weakness, fainting, fatigue and/or exhaustion often occur after prolonged fight-or-flight responses.

2. Cognitive responses to stress reaction include blaming someone; confusion; poor attention; poor decisions; heightened or lowered alertness; poor concentration; memory problems; hypervigilance; difficulty identifying familiar objects or people; increased or decreased awareness of surroundings; poor problem solving; poor abstract thinking; loss of time, place, or person orientation; disturbed thinking; nightmares; intrusive images; etc.

3. Emotional reactions can be broken down into three stages. Stage one includes shock, disbelief, uncertainty, and denial. Stage two includes a cataclysm of emotions such as anger/rage, irritability, agitation, fear/terror, sorrow/grief, confusion and/or frustration, anxiety, apprehension, severe panic, loss of or inappropriate emotional control/ response, depression, feeling overwhelmed, and self-blame/guilt. Stage three includes the reconstruction of a normal/familiar state of equilibrium or balance, putting a stop to the emotional roller coaster.

4. Feelings of loss include loss of control over one's life; loss of faith in one's God or other people; loss of a sense of fairness or justice; loss of personally significant property, self, or loved ones; loss of a sense of immortality and invulnerability, and a loss of future.

5. Feelings of regression include singing nursery rhymes, assuming a fetal position, crawling instead of walking, calling authority figures mommy or daddy, feeling little, wanting mommy or daddy to take care of them, and feeling weak.

6. Behavioral reactions include change in activity. change in speech patterns, withdrawal, emotional outbursts, suspiciousness, change in usual communications, loss or increase of appetite, alcohol consumption, inability to rest, antisocial acts, nonspecific body complaints, hyperalertness to environment, intensified startle reflex, pacing, erratic movements, change in sexual functioning, etc.

7. Short-term recovery includes getting control of an event in the victim's or survivor's mind; working out an understanding of the event; redefin-

ing values; reestablishing a new equilibrium/life; reestablishing trust; reestablishing a future, and re-establishing meaning. While many courthouse employees may live through a trauma and be able to reconstruct their lives without outside help, most people find some type of outside intervention useful in dealing with trauma. Recovery length depends upon the severity of the crisis reaction, the ability to understand what happened, the stability of the victim's and/or survivor's equilibrium after the event, the supportive environment, and the validation of the experience.

8. Long-term recovery includes experiencing crisis reactions for years. Crisis reactions often occur in response to trigger events that remind the victim of the trauma. They can bring back the intense emotion that occurred with the original trauma. Trigger events will vary with different victims/survivors but often include identification of the assailant; sensing (seeing, hearing, touching, smelling, tasting) something similar to something that one was acutely aware of during the trauma event; anniversaries of the event; the proximity of holidays or significant life events; hearings, trials, appeals or other critical phases of the criminal justice process; and news reports about a similar event.

Long-term crisis reactions may be made better or worse by the actions of others. These negative actions are often called the second assault, and the accompanying feelings are known as a second injury. This second injury constitutes the victim's perceived rejection by and lack of expected support from the community. Sources of the second assault may include the criminal justice system, the media, family, friends or acquaintances, hospital and emergency room personnel, health and mental-health professionals, social service workers, victim service workers, employers, victim compensation systems, and the clergy.

Long-term traumatic stress reactions may involve what is called Post-Traumatic Stress Disorder. The following is the description of that disorder referred to in the *Diagnostic and Statistical Manual-Third Edition–Revised,* A309.89 Post-Traumatic Stress Disorder.

1. The individual has experienced an event that is outside the range of usual human experience and that would be markedly distressing to almost anyone; e.g., serious threat to one's life or physical integrity; serious threat or harm to one's children, spouse, or other close relatives and friends; seriously injured or killed as a result of an accident or physical violence.

2. The distressing event is persistently re-experienced in at least one of the following ways: (2a) recurrent and intrusive distressing recollections of the event (which may be associated with guilty thoughts about

behavior before and during the event) (2b) recurrent distressing dreams of the event (2c) sudden acting or feeling as if the event were recurring (includes a sense of reliving the experience, illusions, hallucinations, and dissociative or flashback episodes, even those that occur upon awakening or when intoxicated) (in young children, repetitive play in which themes or aspects of the distressing event are expressed) (2d) intense psychological distress at exposure to events that symbolize or resemble an aspect of the event, including anniversaries of the event.

3. Persistent *avoidance* of stimuli associated with the distressing event or numbing of general responsiveness (not present before the event), as indicated by at least three of the following: (3a) deliberate efforts to avoid thoughts or feelings associated with the event (3b) deliberate efforts to avoid activities or situations that arouse recollections of the event (3c) inability to recall an important aspect of the event (psychogenic amnesia) (3d) markedly diminished interest in significant activities (in young children, loss of recently acquired developmental skills such as toilet training or language skills) (3e) feeling of detachment or estrangement from others (3f) restricted range of affect; e.g., unable to have loving feelings (3g) sense of fore shorted future; e.g., child does not expect to have a career, marriage or children, or long life.

4. Persistent symptoms of increased arousal (not present before the event) as indicated by at least two of the following: (4a) difficulty falling or staying asleep (4b) irritability or outburst of anger (4c) difficulty concentrating (4d) hyper vigilance (4e) physiologic reactivity at exposure to events that symbolize or resemble an aspect of the event (e.g., a woman who was raped in an elevator breaks out in a sweat when entering any elevator).

5. Duration of the disturbance of at least one month. If symptoms continue at least six months after the occurrence of the distressing event.

Note: Not all long-term stress reactions can be described as post-traumatic stress disorder. Furthermore, the intensity of long-term stress reactions usually decreases over time as does the frequency of the reexperienced crisis. However, the effects of a catastrophic trauma cannot be cured. Even survivors of trauma who reconstruct new lives and who have achieved a degree of normality and happiness in their lives will find that new life events will trigger the memories and reactions to the trauma in the future. **Additional note:** Much of the information concerning stress, trauma, and reactions was gathered from (NOVA) National Organization For Victim Assistance–1757 Park Road, N.W., Washington, D.C. 20010.

Some organizations develop Critical Incident Stress Management (CISM) teams to provide peer support (this includes employees, courthouse officials, family members, and emergency response personnel) after a trauma/critical incident to minimize the unwanted effects connected with the critical incident. Some examples of critical incidents include serious injury or death of courthouse personnel; large number of casualties; suicide of an employee; death/serious injury/violence involving a child; expenditure of a large amount of physical/emotional energy without success; incident involving excessive media coverage; bizarre/highly emotional incidents; and an incident involving a friend or relative.

A critical incident often causes some debilitation to the personnel involved. Debilitation makes one unable to function normally. The reactions to the incident are normal under the circumstances for normal people. However, if the reactions are not dealt with, there is a possibility they will appear again at a later date and perhaps cause permanent mental health damage.

An effective way to address debilitating reactions is to employ a debriefing. In these cases, a trained CISM team may create an environment in which an individual can share their feelings and reactions to the incident. Confidentiality is stressed and the session should not be confused with group counseling or any other type of counseling. Rather, debriefing represents an opportunity for the individuals involved in an incident to share their reactions with their peers. The session is conducted by reiterating that the reactions and feelings are normal for normal people under the circumstances.

In conclusion, sometimes one or more of the stress reaction signs described above may predate the incident. These should be considered as signs of critical incident stress only if there is a significant change in their intensity following the incident. Different people react differently to any situation. Indeed, it would be unusual for an individual to experience all of the described reactions. A person may not experience any of the reactions or may experience one or more. The length and intensity of the reactions will also often vary from individual to individual. Symptoms become of concern if they reflect a significant change in functioning from before the incident to after the incident. Symptoms that predate the critical incident are of concern if they significantly increase in frequency of occurrence and/or in intensity after the event.

Courthouse medical personnel should develop a coordinated community response including professionals working within the courthouse district and the greater community. These professionals should be called upon to assist individuals who are displaying severe stress reactions. Effective programs should help the family understand a loved one's reaction to violence, help staff members deal with their reactions to the crisis, and help victims reenter the courthouse environment. Finally, courthouse medical personnel should be fully involved in meeting the needs (validation and healing) of victims of courthouse violence.

Courthouse Legal Representative

The courthouse legal representative is responsible for advising the CPO about any concerns which may be generated as a result of information gathering, compilation, and/or other use. The courthouse legal representative is also responsible for researching the following areas: federal, state and local laws concerning emergency plans; response group interface; and dealing with the press. Finally, the courthouse legal representative should also answer any legal issue or concern as required.

Courthouse Media Spokesman or Public Information Officer (PIO)

The courthouse media spokesperson is responsible for acting as media liaison (broadcast TV, print media, radio, and electronic media–Internet sources), community liaison (community population, victims' families, families of other employees, courthouse system employees), group liaison (labor unions), perpetrator(s) family liaison, and general population liaison. The courthouse media spokesperson is also responsible for governmental liaison; for example, addressing local governments, state government officials and organizations, and federal government entities.

The following information will help the media spokesperson perform his or her duties. The media spokesperson, working in conjunction with the CPO, legal representative, and courthouse administrators, should develop a public information standard operating procedure (SOP). The SOP should outline the framework within which the media spokesperson will work with the media. Essential elements of an effective SOP include a statement of policy, a policy overview, definitions, designated officials, detailed media interface, outline of desired media behavior, what information may be released and not released, information formats, and clarification of access to courthouse facilities.

A statement of policy should acknowledge that the agency is committed to the free flow of information to the media, subject only to the narrow limitations imposed by the law and the legitimate needs of the courthouse system (the federal Freedom Of Information Act (FOIA) as well as state FOIA require the free flow of information). A policy overview simply states the basic principle that will guide the courthouse media spokesperson. For example, the courthouse organization will keep the news media fully, fairly, and accurately informed in a timely manner concerning all matters falling within the administrations area of responsibility, within the limits of law and consistent with the needs of the courthouse community.

Terms used in the public information SOP should be clearly defined. Additionally, top courthouse officials should always make decisions involving formal news conferences and communicate these decisions or needs to the courthouse information officer. Media interface actions should clarify the stance that all courthouse personnel will treat reporters with courtesy and respect at all times. However, the media representative does not have sweeping privileges; he or she also has responsibilities that must be met when involved in a courthouse violence situation. For example, media representatives should be properly accredited and display an appropriate photo ID in plain view. Furthermore, by committing the courthouse organization to keeping the media fully informed, courthouse administrations should expect media accuracy, fairness, and impartiality in their handling of information.

It would be impossible to list every item of information that might be made available to the media; however, the public information SOP should outline, in a general fashion, the information that may be disseminated. Basic information will certainly include "Who, What, Why, When, Where, and How." Once a warrant has been issued for a suspect, additional information can also be released such as name, age, sex, address, nature of charges, further details of the crime, and circumstances of the arrest. For further guidance on what is appropriate to release to the media, refer to the federal FOIA, especially Title 5 U.S.C., subsection b (7), parts A-F; specific state FOIA; the U.S. Code of Federal Regulations (28 CFR 50.2) and the U.S. Department of Justice Rules 7.3, 7.4, and 7.17 governing media policy; and rule 3.6 of the American Bar Association's Model Rules of Professional Conduct.

Information not to be released, in reference to OPSEC principles (discussed in detail at the beginning of this section) should be a short list. Examples include not releasing information that could jeopardize anyone's safety or information that could jeopardize the management of an incident or investigation. Additionally, do not reveal key investigative techniques or sources, critical matters of evidence, and/or names of juveniles. Refer to the resources listed above for additional guidance.

Information formats should outline the different types of contact with the media and who is authorized to make such contact. Information formats include interviews (personal contact or telephone), printed news releases, formal news briefings and news conferences, electronic bulletin boards and e-mail. Access to courthouse facilities should be extended to accredited reporters on legitimate assignment (entertainment type news entities may be handled in a different manner). In conclusion, an SOP will eliminate confusion for the crisis response planning team concerning who can or should say what to whom. It will also have the added benefit of reducing friction and increasing cooperation between the crisis response planning team and the media.

When addressing the media, brief families first; designate one spokesperson; develop a consistent message; schedule news conferences only when news is available; avoid individual interviews; deny requests for exclusive interviews; speak only on issues the media position is responsible for; speak only about known details—do not respond to questions that require more details than are available; don't package human interest stories; be as factual as possible; do not give out any information that has not been confirmed; and make no predictions. Finally, the courthouse media spokesperson should not engage in speculation on what could happen or what is going to happen.

The media spokesperson is very important because courthouse administrators cannot ignore the media. Indeed, courthouse administrators are responsible for presenting information to the public. When a violent event occurs in a courthouse facility, individuals and the community as a whole may experience a heightened sense of fear that additional events will occur or that there may be a larger problem looming in other facilities. Thus, the community has the right to know what the motivation of the crime was, whether the police believe it was an isolated incident or an incident related to others that have occurred in the facility in the past.

Courthouse violence is complicated and not easy to speak about in sound bites. Thus, reporters should be educated on what steps courthouse administrations and police entities have taken to identify, intervene, and react in courthouse violence situations. Most news organizations, especially at local levels, have minimal experience in reporting courthouse violence incidents because it is an area that has received little exposure until relatively recently.

A courthouse media spokesperson must be prepared; a journalist is expected to ask questions and these questions don't stop with who, what, when, where, and how. They also include internal questions about how an issue is covered. Furthermore, not only reporters will be seeking information, loved ones will also be passing along rumors that tend to grow if there is a long delay for an official statement. Some official statement or comment is better than none and can help ensure an accurate depiction is presented. A lack of comment and information unnecessarily fosters suspicion and mistrust.

The key to a better relationship between courthouse administrators, police agencies, community organizations, concerned citizens, and the news media, when a courthouse violence incident occurs, is being aware of the constraints facing each group. Due to public interest, a high-profile courthouse violence incident will be reported regardless of whether a courthouse administrator or law enforcement entity believes it has compiled all the needed facts or is ready to issue a statement. To contain misstatements and avoid inaccuracies by others, courthouse administrators and law enforcement entities should develop a method to distribute information quickly, offering whatever information has been confirmed and explain why more information isn't available. Some information is better than none and any communication, no matter how limited, presents an opportunity to get the courthouse administrator/law enforcement entity's message across to viewers or readers.

Furthermore, a courthouse violence incident will develop into a time-sensitive environment. Thus, it is a good idea to develop media packets before an incident occurs, so it can be followed in the rush of events that will follow an incident. A consistent process should be developed for answering questions quickly. The media packet should contain a protocol on answering media questions. Alternate media contacts should be established if the initial contact person cannot be reached.

Getting a message out in a hectic newsroom setting can also be difficult. Generally, the more contact an administrator has with a news organization, the better. Administrators should fax information or press releases to an assigned desk or assigned editor. Furthermore, if contact has been made with a specific reporter, also fax the information directly to the reporter.

Because many courthouse violence incidents are considered relatively minor offenses (i.e., a fistfight), they rarely make the news. Indeed, the public hears about courthouse violence only when they reach a level the media considers "newsworthy." These incidents are usually presented as isolated incidents and generate a degree of surprise from the community. A courthouse and/or community isn't protected by a lack of information. To address this issue, a media packet may be developed. A media packet should contain the following information: courthouse violence statistics, the responsibilities of the courthouse administration and law enforcement, what steps have been adopted and implemented concerning courthouse violence, a list of courthouse violence definitions and programs, courthouse policy and procedures concerning courthouse violence, a list of local resources concerned with courthouse violence, and sources of further information. This information may be posted on the Web so that both the public and media can freely access desired information.

Courthouse media representatives must also be trained in writing and speaking more sensitively about Asian Americans, Blacks, Hispanics, Native Americans, people with disabilities, women, and other groups. Stereotypes (all Asians are alike), loaded words (Oriental or Negro), loaded images (buck teeth, heavy accents), ethnic slurs (Jap, Chink, or Chinaman), insensitivity (failing to include responses from all groups involved in a crisis), and military metaphors (war or invasion) must be avoided at all costs. The idea is to improve the effectiveness of information while eliminating clichés. Help can be ascertained from groups such as the Asian American Journalists' Association, National Association of Black Journalists, National Lesbian and Gay

Journalists' Association, National Association of Hispanic Journalists, and Native American Journalists' Association.

A courthouse media spokesperson will also have to address electronic media demands. The following information may make addressing e-mail demands easier and more effective. The courthouse media spokesperson should designate a specific person responsible for e-mail replies. To address e-mail inquiries in a timely manner, fact sheets and standard responses should be outlined prior to a violent incident. Further, an area should be set-up for the specific mission of receiving and responding to e-mail messages.

E-mail interaction is not without benefits; for example, e-mail communications may generate tips and information concerning the crisis (naturally, this information should be immediately passed on to investigators). Further, e-mail may be used to refer concerned people to updates posted on the courthouse web site. Finally, e-mail inquiries may be used by the media spokesperson to shape communication objectives.

The courthouse media spokesperson will often be required to present victims' briefings. To effectively conduct these briefings, the spokesperson must show respect, designate a specific person to perform as liaison with victims' families; schedule briefings for victims' families and other affected persons before news conferences; send the same message to everybody; manage expectations; provide credible answers and explain limitations; and manage the outrage. The media spokesperson must not exploit these people. The media should be told that the courthouse media spokesperson has already met with the family. Additionally, the courthouse media spokesperson should involve the clergy and deal with issues before they go public.

The courthouse media spokesperson will often be required to present community briefings. To effectively conduct these briefings, the spokesperson must designate a specific person as community liaison; schedule briefings after news conferences; send the same message to everyone; refer to established e-mail and web site for continuous updates; involve clergy; manage expectations of the community; provide credible answers and explain existing limitations; manage the outrage; avoid the exploitation of personnel or the situation; tell the community that the families have been met with first; determine if there are any limitations placed on the media by a court order; establish a media site/press area and staff as required; ensure that media representatives have media identification; and finally, read media/policy guidelines to all assigned personnel and media representatives.

In conclusion, when a courthouse violence incident occurs, the community as a whole is likely to experience a heightened sense of fear that further incidents may occur, or that the incident may be part of a larger problem in the courthouse community. Any community affected by a courthouse violence crisis has a right to know the motivation for committing the crime, whether the police believe it was an isolated incident or an incident related to other acts that have occurred in the same community. Due to public interest, a courthouse violence crisis will be reported regardless of whether a courthouse administration, police agency, or community organization is ready to issue a statement. To contain misstatements and avoid inaccuracies by others, the courthouse media spokesperson should disseminate information quickly, offer whatever information has been confirmed, and explain why more information isn't available. Some information is better than none because a lack of information will often foster suspicion and mistrust.

Finally, it is in the best interest of courthouse organizations to be as forthcoming with the media and community as possible. Furthermore, courthouse media representatives should work with news personnel throughout the year. A good working relationship may help with useful exchanges of information during a courthouse violence crisis and as familiarity is achieved between entities, the less likely doubts of credibility will occur. Good media relations translates into good public relations.

Environmental, Safety and Health (ES&H) Officer

The ES&H officer identifies the existence of HAZMAT materials. HAZMAT information should include the type, amount, and location of HAZMAT materials and the ease of access to HAZMAT materials. Further, the ES&H officer should recommend the security requirements of HAZMAT materials. Additionally, the ES&H officer should identify the hazard level of HAZMAT materials and, finally, recommend response procedures for HAZMAT material incidents.

Other Elements

Other elements are addressed due to the unique circumstances that may affect any courthouse system. To address unique circumstances, the CPO designates each position by determining necessity, developing and clarifying a scope of duties, directs adequate staffing and responsibilities. **Note:** A variety of community leaders may be asked to support the response planning project by staffing this position; these personnel may include clergy, law enforcement, violence prevention groups, mental health and child welfare professionals, physicians and nurses, business leaders, and other local officials.

In conclusion, courthouse crisis incidents require immediate, planned action, and long-term, postcrisis intervention. Indeed, the crisis response planning team not only plans what to do when violence strikes, but also ensures that staff know how to behave. Courthouse staff will feel secure when there is a well-conceived plan and everyone understands what to do or whom to ask for instructions. Finally, planning will ultimately reduce chaos and trauma generated by any courthouse violence crisis.

Courthouse Violence Response Plan Format and Contents

What should this document include and how should the information be organized? Actually, completing the plan occurs in a variety of steps. While there are no hard and fast rules pertaining to plan development, the basic plan is usually written first. From the basic plan, annexes and appendices may also be developed. The basic plan should be treated as the umbrella document that draws together all other parts of the plan. Its primary audience is the chief executive, planning entities, and police personnel.

A courthouse violence crisis plan should be developed using the following suggested format: introduction to the basic plan; statement of purpose; situations and assumptions; organization and assignment of responsibilities; concept of operations; administration and logistics; plan development and maintenance; authorities and references; and the definition of terms. Annexes to the basic plan, appendices, and standard operating procedures and other procedures should be developed and inserted as needed.

A plan begins with a series of statements that serve as the introduction to the basic plan. These include the promulgation statement, foreword, table of contents, instructions, and change record. The promulgation statement is signed by a chief executive to give the plan authority. Next, a forward is written that describes the planning process, abstracts the contents in an executive summary, and states the goals of the plan. A table of contents should then be developed which lists the total contents to include any annexes or appendices. Another statement concerns instructions explaining the plan's use, the intended audience, and the purposes of its sections and distribution. Finally, a change of record is developed depicting the dates, locations, and specific verbiage of any revisions.

After the introduction to the basic plan has been completed, it is time to develop a statement of purpose. For example, the purpose of the plan is to provide the courthouse community with an effective and efficient courthouse crisis response operation which, when applied, will provide the levels of protection for life and property and recovery assistance which are acceptable to the courthouse system and citizens of the community.

The next section focuses on situations and assumptions. The types of courthouse violence situations that may occur in the courthouse system are described here. The planner must be realistic and develop valid assumptions. The plan of operation for meeting these situations will be based upon the assumptions made in this section. To complete the picture of the situation and assumptions of the plan, a review focusing on the security survey and other proactive measures should be included.

The next step requires planners to establish an organizational structure and assign responsibilities. This is a key section of the plan and will normally be lengthy. It should specifically define the roles of courthouse officials in the planning structure. The organizational structure should also include individuals staffing local government and community positions that may be called upon to provide resources. Certain officials are given specific assignments and lines of authority are identified between the planning positions and emergency responders.

The organizational structure should be as similar as possible to that which is used for day-to-day operations. For example, a courthouse nurse should be assigned as a courthouse medical representative instead of a logistics officer. However, the organizational structure should allow for the expansion and extension of duties as situations dictate. To the greatest extent possible, personnel should continue to work with the supervisor and associates whom they normally work with on a regular basis. This familiarity will often streamline the start-up process by avoiding the need of getting to know new people, establishing territories, dealing with different work ethics, and so forth.

Another important section of the plan is titled administration and logistics. This section should address management of resources, general support requirements, and availability of services and support for all phases of a violence-oriented crisis situation. The plan should establish policy for obtaining and using facilities, materials, services, and any other required resources.

Next, plan development and maintenance should be addressed. This portion is normally addressed after completion of the courthouse violence response plan and includes provisions for review, modification, acceptance, and approval by the head of the effected courthouse system. Of particular importance is the continuous review required to update the plan to reflect improvements needed as a result of experiences in dealing with courthouse violence and changing situations and assumptions.

Any authorities and references that were used in plan development should be stated at the end of the document. Authorities and references may include statutes, executive orders, regulations, formal agreements, general planning guidance, plans of other agencies, plans of other levels of government, and the like. Another section that is valuable concerns the definition of terms. This would include definitions of terms that are not commonly known as well as those used in the plan that could cause confusion if misinterpreted. The terms one chooses to define will depend upon the uniqueness of the courthouse community and the audience addressed.

Annexes may be included in order to describe operations for a particular function. Annexes should define a function and show how activities of various participants in the functional organization are coordinated. Annexes are typically action oriented, and are written for, and preferably by, the person responsible for controlling resources available to accomplish the objectives of the function in a courthouse violence crisis. Annexes may include such functions as direction and control, warning systems, communications, public information, evacuation procedures, law enforcement interaction, fire department interaction, resources management, and the like. Of course, the annexes listed are not meant to be all-inclusive. The selection and definition of functions to be covered in annexes varies from courthouse system to courthouse system depending on such factors as the size, organization, and specific needs of each courthouse. Finally, annexes should be formatted in the same manner as the basic plan. To reiterate, there are nine parts to the basic plan and annexes: (1) introduction, (2) statement of purpose, (3) situations and assumptions, (4) organization and assignment of responsibilities, (5) concept of operations, (6) administration and logistics, (7) development and maintenance, (8) authorities and references, and (9) definition of terms.

Finally, the plan should end with appendices. An appendix contains details, methods, and technical information that are unique to each specific courthouse violence hazard identified as being likely to pose a threat in a particular courthouse. Appendices may also be attached to functional annexes and should have sections corresponding to those in the annex for which supplementary hazard specific information is required.

Crisis action planning staffs may also include standard operating procedures and other attachments that are deemed necessary to support and provide directions to courthouse violence response personnel. These documents may be attached to any part of the plan's elements where they are most readily accessible and most likely to be needed. These attachments may include checklists, charts, maps, standard operating procedures, available resources, call-up lists, and contact lists, etc. Like the basic plan, attachments are living documents. They are changed and revised as required. Indeed, attachments will probably be the most frequently modified part of the plan. Courthouse violence response planners should design the plan in this manner, allowing for the removal and insertion of changes and new pages.

Courthouse Violence Response Plan Information

Of course, as has been previously discussed, courthouse violence response plans are specific and unique to each courthouse system. However, each courthouse violence response plan must gather information valuable in defining a specific courthouse's assets, defining a courthouse's threats, defining a courthouse's weaknesses, defining a courthouse's strengths, and characterizing a courthouse's environment. All courthouse violence response plan information should contain, at a minimum, the following generic information:

Description of the Building(s)

A full description of each building should be compiled to include the exact physical location (street address complete with written directions). This will prevent responding officials from going to the wrong locations or getting lost. Getting lost will waste valuable time and responding to the wrong location can be deadly to everyone involved in the area of responsibility. For example, perpetrators may see response personnel set up at the wrong location and decide to kill people or fire upon unsuspecting personnel. Many courthouses are large and confusing to responders who have never seen the area in question. Further, sometimes buildings look very similar and may generate confusion. Descriptions provide identification by sight and street addresses/ written directions will provide clear physical locations.

Activity Conducted in Each Building

What type of activity is normally conducted in each building? For example: public areas, courtrooms, judge's chambers, jury assembly rooms, restricted areas, prisoner holding areas, evidence storage, and building maintenance areas, etc. Buildings or areas used for mass assemblies are usually attractive areas for offenders to employ courthouse violence actions.

Priority of Each Building

Is one building or facility area more important than another? Is a building considered by the local population as a focal point of importance? Are courthouse buildings protected by security systems operating at different levels?

Sensitivity of Each Building

Sensitivity is an extension of priority. Sensitivity may be assessed as high due to building's contents, importance to the operation of the facility (heat, water, electric power), and the level of protection available.

Physical and Environmental Conditions

When formulating this section, planners should consider the aspects of obstacles, cover and concealment, observation, key terrain, and avenues of approach and/or escape. This is an area that may be beyond many court-house administrator's knowledge, and indeed this verifies the fact that this plan should be developed by the number and type of personnel previously discussed. Police officers should specifically tour each building on the court-house grounds and note the physical and environmental conditions listed above and discussed below. Further, still photographs and videotapes should be produced from all areas of concern. When this is done, there is no ques-tion concerning how effective a perpetrator could be if located in these spe-cific areas.

Obstacles should be noted and described, especially in areas located on routes of travel to and into any structure; for example, do obstacles such as fences, open fields, open parking lots, construction areas, etc. exist that will cause a problem for responding forces. Any area that slows down, stops, or allows a perpetrator to observe responding forces should be considered an obstacle. When these areas are identified, responding forces can formulate plans to either circumvent the area or develop ways to counter the obstacle.

Cover and concealment aspects focus on areas the perpetrator may use as cover and concealment as well as areas that may be used by responding forces. The availability of cover and concealment will directly correspond with the tactical elements of control, security, and speed that responding forces will use to travel to, into, and through an area or building. Strengths and weaknesses should be identified and accompanying methods of counter-action should be recorded.

Observation is also a condition of physical and environmental conditions; for example, does the perpetrator have a good view of an area (through huge windows) or is his or her ability to observe diminished by wooded areas, other buildings, blank walls, etc. Observation is evaluated in two ways: first, responding forces must envision what they believe a perpetrator can see from the tactical area of concern and second, one must consider how well respond-ing forces can see the tactical arena.

Key terrain is also a condition of physical and environmental conditions. For example, can a perpetrator control an area by taking up a position in a specific area? Could a perpetrator take up a position in a bell tower and shoot people at great distances, or can responding forces take up a position in the bell tower and control a large area with effective weapons fire if necessary? If areas are identified as key terrain, responders will have to find ways to cir-cumvent the area, neutralize the area by using various tactics, flush the perpetrator out of the area, or physically occupy the area to prevent the perpetrator(s) from getting in the area.

A final condition of physical and environmental conditions includes high-speed avenues of approach and escape; for example, are there areas conducive to perpetrator approach or escape. If so, these areas must be physically controlled by responders. Further, can these areas be used by responders as approach and/or withdrawal routes? All nontraditional ingress and egress routes should be identified, for example, air conditioning ducts, elevators shafts, air vents, maintenance tunnels, and adjoining structures.

Of course, the above explanation is only a sampling of physical and environmental conditions that are important to responders. These principles should also be used when evaluating the inside of any structure; for example, obstacles, cover and concealment, observation, key terrain, and avenues of approach and escape will also exist inside all structures to some extent. This is another example of why courthouse violence response plans are site specific and unique to each courthouse.

Courthouse Personnel Responsible for Each Building

Who is actually in charge of each building? These people are sometimes know as building managers. A primary and secondary building manager should be identified to include primary and secondary contact methods. These personnel should know more about their assigned building than anyone else on the courthouse grounds.

Operational Considerations

Will the loss of a particular building affect other parts of the courthouse? Could operations conducted in a building prove valuable to a perpetrator?

Supporting Utilities

A list depicting the location of supporting utilities, e.g., communication lines, electric lines, water lines, heating and air conditioning, etc. should be compiled for each building. A survey of power supply systems should be conducted to include the type of power supply, for example, on-site power, off-site power generation, power supply capacity, capacity for expansion, and condition of power facilities. Distribution systems and emergency back-up systems may be identified by number, location, capacity, and condition. The fuel supply for power systems should also be evaluated for type, quantity, security, and location.

Visual Representation of Courthouse Structures

Visual representation should include the following types and areas of concern: photographs depicting the interior and exterior of each building to include rooftops. These photographs should include aerial still photographs, ground level still photographs, and still photographs taken from a variety of angles. Videotapes are also required to include aerial video, ground-level video, and video taken from various angles. Photographs and videos should also include contents of rooms, location of all emergency lighting systems, location and type of all security alarms and monitoring stations, location and type of fire suppression systems, location and type of telephones to include numbers, and the location of all intercoms.

Blueprints and drawings are important and should include building floor plans depicting hallways' length and width, direction of travel and destination, and any branching areas. All rooms should include dimensions, door structures, door swing directions, type of door locks, location of light switches, type of lighting to include emergency lighting, location of closets and other hiding places, room use, and window locations and type (can they be opened and closed, thickness, coating materials, curtains, and blinds or other covering). What can a person see from this position and are there alternate points of ingress and egress?

Further points of interest include adjoining rooms, structures or hallways, air conditioning and heating ducts, sewer access, basement access, rooftop access, and access to elevators and/or elevator shafts. Wall material and thickness are also important. Stairwells should be described by type (straight or winding), dimensions, direction of travel, number, and location of ingress and egress points. Finally, planned structural modifications should be addressed, including proposed blueprints or drawings.

A new technology that combines all of the above visual representation methods into a very effective response planning tool is called "Interactive Virtual Floor Plans For Emergency Response Planning & Tactical Operations." This virtual floor plan developed by Interactive Tactical Group (ITG) uses advanced 360-degree digital imaging to produce photo-realistic visual maps that are accessible on CD. ITG integrates maps, databases, and high-definition visual images into a package that can be quickly deployed and allows responders to "walk through" a building (unknown physical environment), moving from room to room, without physically entering the facility.

Internal and External Security Systems

These security systems include intrusion detection systems (IDS), structure locking mechanisms, building access control, campus access restrictions, etc.

Generally, security systems are designed to discourage unauthorized access, provide a warning that an intrusion is occurring, notify staff members that a security problem exists, and delay or scare away a perpetrator. However, security systems can work against responding forces and tip off offenders that a response mission is in progress. Thus, the type, number, location, and capabilities of all security systems must be recorded.

Evaluation of Lighting Systems

The evaluation of lighting should focus on types and effectiveness; for example, lights can be identified as timed, manually operated, motion activated, sound activated, or photo-electric. The type of lights used by a courthouse may be of great importance to police officers. Lights can compromise a mission so officers need to know the type of lighting used in order to formulate effective plans to defeat their operation.

Lights should be evaluated for effectiveness by observing their functioning at night, noting times of operation, brightness, area covered, and ease of access to wires and bulbs. Light beams may be designed to overlap one-another in a continuous arc or designed to highlight specific areas. All dark areas should be noted and evaluated for attractiveness as an ingress/egress points. Any malfunctioning lights should be noted and replaced as soon as possible (perpetrators hate lights and may telegraph intentions by breaking or removing light bulbs a few days prior to an attack). Finally, lights should be evaluated for any interference caused by foliage such as weeds, shrubs, bushes, and trees. Foliage must be trimmed or removed if it is causing shadows or completely blocking light beams.

There are also some nontraditional lighting systems that may be encountered; they include infrared (IR) or near infrared lighting. These lights may be conducive to responding units who plan to use active and/or passive night vision devices.

Evaluation of Fence Lines

Fence lines should be evaluated for the following points of information:
1. Age and condition
2. Fabric tension
3. Fence material
4. Existing holes to include their size and location
5. Interface of the fence fabric to the ground, anchors, and bottom railing
6. Wire design
7. Properties of the ground

8. Washouts or other erosion
9. Concrete support
10. Gravel base
11. Asphalt base
12. Strength and physical appearance
13. Fence attachment to support poles
14. Condition and location of gates
15. Top guard type and condition
16. Overall fence stability
17. Lighting type and effectiveness
18. Existing intrusion defense systems
19. Foliage type and density

All of this information will assist responders in deciding if, how, and/or where a fence can best be breached.

Evaluation of Parking Facilities

All parking facilities should be noted and the following information should be included: exact physical location, distance from courthouse, observation points located in the courthouse, amount and types of vehicles parked (during hours of operation and off-shift hours), access requirements, ingress and egress points, lighting requirements, existing defense systems, and the ability to support response force vehicles and associated operations (field command post, tactical operations center, medical aid station, etc.).

Evaluation of Site Security Forces

Security forces should be examined and the following information should be gathered: size of the available force, training level, intended mission, duty locations and functions, equipment available, and security vehicles number and type.

Evaluation of Communication Systems

Communication systems should be noted and the information gathered should include types (telephones, cell phones, cordless phones, intercom systems, two-way radios, etc.), capacity, installation (above or below ground), potential for exploitation, current assignments–exact locations, condition, and identified dead spots (areas where radios will not transmit or receive).

Figure 31. Advanced vegetation growth obscuring a fence line.

Figure 32. Washed-out fence bottom guard.

Figure 33. Improperly maintained gate. The gate may easily be climbed over, crawled under or a person may easily pass between the gate and securing post. A gate in this condition completely circumvents the fence.

Figure 34. Gravel fence base.   Figure 35. Cement fence base.

Evaluation of Existing Vulnerability Countermeasures

Vulnerability countermeasures may include the following topics: Barriers–natural or manmade, active or passive, command-activated or intruder-activated, safe havens–indoors and outdoors, evacuation procedures and routes, and existing explosive mitigation devices.

Evaluation of Perimeter Terrain

During an incident where a suspect(s) is either at large or at a standoff with law enforcement, setting up a perimeter is vital to a successful conclusion, and the sooner the perimeter is established the better the chance for success. Not only are perimeters necessary for the apprehension of the suspect(s), but for the protection of citizens as well. Therefore, the following aspects of perimeter terrain should be noted: grade–flat and level, rolling and hilly, or mountainous; proximity of the perimeter to bodies of water; high volume vehicle traffic; pedestrian traffic; aircraft landing strips; railways; ground cover–defoliated, rock/gravel, paved/asphalt surfaces, grassy/weedy, heavily foliated, or forested areas; soil composition–type, compaction, stability, drainage, surface coloration, and surface reflection. All of these terrain aspects of terrain can either work in the favor of law enforcement officials or the perpetrator(s). If certain terrain features are identified as working against law enforcement officials, steps should be taken to neutralize the situation.

Employee Information

The following employee information should be captured: turnover rate; overtime worked; absenteeism; morale; biographic information; current full-face photograph; physical characteristics–height, weight, build, hair color, eye color, race, scars, marks, tattoos, preferred clothing, preferred jewelry, spectacles; medical concerns; marital status; point of contact and method; military experience; and any special skills.

Prisoner Information

The following prisoner information should be captured: discipline record–arrest history; absenteeism; biographic information; current full-face photograph; physical characteristics–height, weight, build, hair color, eye color, race, scars, marks, tattoos, preferred clothing, preferred jewelry, spectacles; medical concerns; marital status.

Current and Potential Threat Data

Current and potential threat data should focus on the following: past threat activities, past actions and outcomes, firearms used or otherwise available, explosives used or otherwise available, other violent methods, effected areas, and any past demands and deadlines.

Security, Safety, and Fire Regulations

These regulations should include natural emergency plans and standard operating procedures, evacuation routes—primary and alternate; rally points; accountability procedures; security procedures; and containment positions to include police; fire equipment; and ambulance set-up.

Environmental, Safety, and Health Considerations

Environmental, safety, and health considerations will normally be categorized as hazardous materials (HAZMAT). Hazardous materials include substances or materials that because of their chemical, physical, or biological nature pose a potential risk to life, health, or property if they are released. A release may occur by spilling, leaking, emitting toxic vapors, or any other process that enables the material to escape its container, enter the environment, and create a potential hazard. Hazardous materials may be categorized into explosives, flammable and/or combustible substances, poisons, or radioactive materials.

Explosives are substances that release pressure, gas, and heat suddenly when they are subjected to shock, heat, or high pressure. Flammable and/or combustible substances are easy to ignite. Related hazards are posed by oxidizers that will lend oxygen readily to support a fire, and reactive materials which are unstable and may react violently if mishandled.

Poisons (or toxic materials) can cause injury or death when they enter the bodies of living things. Such substances can be classified by chemical nature, for example, heavy metals and cyanides; or by toxic action, such as irritants, which inflame living tissue; and by corrosives, which destroy or irreversibly change tissue. One special group of poisons includes etiological (biological) agents. These are live microorganisms, or toxins produced by the microorganisms, that are capable of producing a disease. Finally, radioactive materials are a category of hazardous materials that release harmful radiation. In conclusion, it must be understood that the above listed HAZMAT categories are not mutually exclusive; for example, acids and bases are listed as corrosive materials but can also act as poisons.

The risk associated with any particular hazardous material depends on the source, the availability of pathways for the HAZMAT to reach the receptor, and the characteristics of the receptors. No single piece of information alone is sufficient, and incomplete information can be highly misleading. To assess a HAZMAT risk, the following questions must be answered:

1. What are the hazard properties of the substance and what kind of effects can it have on living things or on the environment?
2. How much of the substance exists at the source, and in what concentration?
3. In what form is the substance?
4. What are the chemical and physical characteristics of the substance?
5. How is the substance contained?
6. What pathways of exposure exist?
7. Where is the population located in relation to the source?
8. What are the characteristics of people who are at risk? The susceptibility of any individual to a toxic substance varies depending on age, weight, sex, and individual characteristics; for example, juveniles are more susceptible to the effects of HAZMAT than adults.
9. How long does the exposure to the chemical last?

Many of these questions can be answered by referring to a substances Material Safety Data Sheet (MSDS). Any HAZMAT material located on a courthouse complex should include this information. The MSDS is usually prepared by the manufacturer or distributor of hazardous substances. An MSDS form will include the following information: the identity of the substance, physical and chemical characteristics, physical hazards, health hazards, routes of entry, permissible exposure limits, existence of carcinogens, safe handling methods, control measures, first aid procedures, date of preparation, and manufacturer information.

Another information source includes the National Fire Protection Association (NFPA) 704M system. The NFPA 704M label is diamond shaped, and is divided into four parts, or quadrants. The left quadrant is blue, and contains a numerical rating of the substance's health hazard. Ratings are made on a scale of 0 to 4, with a rating of 4 indicating a danger level so severe that a very short exposure could cause serious injury or death. A zero, or no code at all in any quarter, means that no unusual hazard would result from the exposure.

The top quadrant of the NFPA symbol is red, and contains a numerical rating for a fire hazard. Again, the numerical codes range from 0 to 4, with a 4 representing the most serious hazard. The right quadrant of the NFPA symbol is yellow, and contains a numerical rating for explosive or other reaction. Once again, the numerical codes range from 0 to 4, with a 4 representing the most serious hazard.

The bottom quadrant of the NFPA symbol is white, and contains a numerical rating for any special hazards that may apply. There are three possible codes for the bottom quarter: OXY, meaning the material is an oxidizer; W/, indicating the material reacts with water to release a gas that is either flammable or hazardous to health; and the tri-blade symbol, designating a radioactive material that will emit radioactivity. It is important to note that this system is chemical-specific. No chemical identification system can accurately assess the synergistic effects of one chemical combining with another, or the possible effects of combining unknown amounts of several chemicals.

Evaluation of Courthouse Interface with Local Governments and Population, Communication Methods, and Points of Contact

To begin this evaluation, key personnel and resources must have been identified beforehand. This includes the identification of key agencies, businesses, social institutions, etc. Leadership must also be identified early to include formal and informal leaders (individuals in the community who are important and have clout as perceived by the community). Potential leaders are also identified as those who have status, power, and/or wealth. Of course, all of these key personnel should be listed by address and communication methods (telephone—home and office, pagers, cell phones, radios, etc.). Some of the important key contact agencies, resources, and personnel may be broken down into the following headings: emergency services, medical services, assembly areas, transportation, supplies, media, individuals, equipment, service agencies, and community groups.

Emergency agencies typically include fire, police, public works, and public utilities. Medical agencies typically include hospitals, clinics, doctors, dentists, nursing homes, and medical associations. Assembly areas may include parks, shopping centers, schools, churches, government buildings, warehouses, and community centers. Transportation resources may include buses, trucks, vans, four-wheel drive vehicles, tractor trailers, taxicabs, power boats, air assets, snowmobiles, and swamp buggies. Supplies typically include food and medical items. Media resources include newspapers, radio stations, television stations, and news services. Individuals include local government officials, military entities (military assistance to back up response forces or provide equipment), clergy, doctors, dentists, nurses, pilots, amateur radio operators, and building contractors. Equipment may include farm tractors, construction equipment, excavation equipment, chain saws, portable power plants, etc. Service agencies may include the Red Cross and/or Salvation Army. Finally, community groups may include the chamber of commerce,

Kiwanis, Lions Club, Moose, churches, American Legion, VFW, women's clubs, and even senior citizens groups.

Once key organizations and individuals have been identified, memorandums of understandings (MOU's) should be signed by each agency delineating who will provide what resources and services. MOU's, at a minimum, will require an on-going liaison between the police, courthouse, and community officials. At the least, MOU's should address the chain of command—who is in charge, crime scene processing, interviewing procedures and processes, media interface, victim services, and other agency support.

Counseling Services

Intervention counseling for personnel and their families should be established in advance of any violent event. Information concerning program development and implementation can be gathered from the National Organization for Victim Assistance's Crisis Response Team. Employee assistance programs and other counseling services can be developed and implemented by contacting local services or by researching existing programs. Of course, the entire community must be informed as to where victim services are located. Finally, this service should be isolated from the media.

Crime Stopper Programs

The heart of any crime stopper program must include the identification of anti-social behaviors which carry established consequences which will be enforced to the letter. Crime stopper programs may consist of a number of options; they include telephone tip lines, anonymous tip line box(s), zero tolerance programs, reward programs, training administrators and employees to recognize people at risk of engaging in violent behavior; and finally, background checks should be performed on all personnel working in any courthouse facility. Of course, for any of these programs to work most staff members will need to perceive their actions as constructive to establishing a safer and more secure working environment.

Telephone Tip Lines

This program may consist of a telephone tip line staffed by trained personnel 24 hours a day. All personnel should be trained in information gathering processes and effective recording formats. Of course, a clear line of contact personnel must be established in order to pass on time critical information in a coordinated and timely manner. Employees should be briefed on the purpose of the telephone tip line and how to contact the service. The idea is to provide employees with a safe process for reporting threats, intimidation, and other security concerns. This briefing should include the consequences and seriousness of making hoax threats.

Anonymous Tips Line Box(es)

This proactive measure is a viable option for courthouse systems that cannot afford a fully staffed telephone tip line. This box should be readily accessible from both inside and outside of a facility's structure. Of course, the box should be constructed so that unauthorized personnel cannot readily access the contents. Anonymous tip line box(es) must be emptied and the contents evaluated before each workday begins. Like the telephone tip line, a clear line of contact personnel must be established in order to pass on time critical information in a coordinated and timely manner. Of course, it is imperative that information be passed on to the police in a timely manner. Naturally, employees should be briefed on the location and purpose of anonymous tip line box(es). Like the tip line, the idea is to provide employees with a safe process for reporting threats, intimidation, and other security concerns. This briefing should also include the consequences of tampering with the tip line box and the seriousness of making hoax threats.

Zero Tolerance Programs

It is important to establish a zero tolerance program targeting weapons, alcohol, drugs, and/or threats made by anyone entering the courthouse. For example, when a person makes threats to kill or assault others, immediate action should be exercised. Furthermore, if appropriate, psychological evaluation and intervention should be provided in a timely manner. Each institution must set clear limits on antisocial behavior and determine consequences for offenders. A zero tolerance program must identify exactly which behaviors will not be tolerated, be fairly and consistently applied and, above all else, be unbiased.

Reward Programs

These programs may be designed to monetarily reward a person who comes forward with information concerning a pending or actual courthouse violence incident. Of course, the reporting person's identity will have to be protected as much as possible. The reward offered will also have to be considered attractive by the general population. Cost associated with this program will often be offset by intervention, the speed of investigation process, and a heightened level of perpetrator identification. The reader must understand that many courthouse systems cannot afford real-time detection and real-time response to security incidents. Information concerning a pending incident or after-the-fact investigation is extremely important to these facilities. Reward programs may enable investigators to quickly identify, catch, and deal with perpetrators. As a result, perpetrators may have second thoughts about engaging in antisocial behaviors in the courthouse.

Courthouse Police Officer Assignment

Courthouse personnel and law enforcement officials must work together in order to secure a courthouse. This process is obtained by establishing and integrating liaison, trust, training, and intelligence into an effective mixture designed to prevent a violent act. Officers should also develop intelligence systems targeting potential or planned acts of violence; however, intelligence must drive investigations—investigations should not drive intelligence.

The importance of this position should preclude any temptation a police department may harbor in the assignment of substandard officers to staff this position. It will do little good and may generate a negative response if officers have been chosen to staff these positions due to poor performance, negative attitude, or a lengthy disciplinary history. This is not the place to "hide" a problem performer. This position should be chosen through a selection process designed to balance sound police skills with strong interpersonal communication skills. Extra training focusing on the American juvenile justice system may also be required.

Further, courthouse administrations may choose to hire full-time security personnel in lieu of police officers. If this is the preferred action, courthouse administrators must check the security contractor's business practices focusing on background checks and training issues. Many states do not require background checks or formal training. Little effective proactive results will be realized by organizations that insist on cutting cost when hiring personnel. When a budget concern is weighed against the cost of providing a safe courthouse environment, the choice should be clear.

Of course, courthouse officers should not make up the only police presence in courthouses. Patrol officers should include courthouses into their daily patrol responsibilities. Periodic visits by patrol officers become extremely important in courthouses located in areas where courthouse administrators cannot afford to assign a dedicated courthouse officer(s).

Background Checks on All Courthouse Personnel

Background checks to include a simple criminal record check should be listed as a condition of employment. Criminal record checks are inexpensive (approximately $20.00 per individual criminal record search) and are often valuable in revealing a person's criminal history and/or some psychiatric problems. Indeed, routine background checks should be performed on all personnel seeking work at any courthouse facility and the results of these checks should be obtained prior to the hiring of any individual.

Preemployment background checks may also include resume and employment application verification as well as data research from other sources. In some states, falsification of a job application is a criminal offense. Most information comes from public records, except for credit reports, which require a signed release. Some other good sources of information include driving record, education verification, civil litigation, and social security number verification. Employers are normally on firm legal ground as long as the inquiries comply with applicable laws; for example, the Fair Credit Reporting Act, Americans With Disabilities Act, Equal Employment Opportunity Act, Title 7 of the Civil Rights Act of 1964, and the Age Discrimination in Employment Act.

Background checks may be assimilated into a personal assurance program made up of four components: supervisory review, medical assessment, management evaluation, and security determination. Supervision review may include properly executed documents, drug testing, and a preemployment check. Medical assessment may include physical, mental, emotional, behavioral, substance and alcohol abuse. Management evaluation may include review of the supervisory review and medical assessment, evaluation based on unannounced drug testing, and rehabilitation or reformation results. Security determination may include initial access authorization, annual or other periodic security access authorization, and termination of access authorization. Of course, a courthouse administration does not have to implement the full complement of the above listed components. The administration may pick and choose applicable components that fit their courthouse system's particular needs.

Finally, employees designated to participate in personnel assurance program should be required to report arrests, other legal issues, mental conditions requiring medication or treatment, observed unusual actions or mannerisms conducted by other employees, criminal matters, and fraud, waste, and abuse. Of course, some of these issues may be protected by state or federal law; thus care must be taken to avoid gathering information deemed as legally protected. Legal council should be contacted during the development and implementation of any personnel assurance program.

Supporting Policies

This section is titled in a rather generic manner due to the number of proactive measures to be discussed, for example, searches of courthouse property. Searches of courthouse property are valuable in bolstering the effects of courthouse security especially if they are random and conducted without warning. Lockers and desks are courthouse property, and employees have little Fourth Amendment protection from search and seizure of items stored there. However, the results of many searches will be challenged and may lead to evidence suppression and/or possible civil suits. Thus, it is imperative that legal council be sought while developing and before implementing policies concerning the searching of employees' personal belongings, lockers, desks, and vehicles parked on courthouse grounds.

Officers and courthouse officials must have a clear understanding of search and seizure law as it pertains to searches on courthouse property. Finally, it must be understood that state law may be more restrictive than federal law; if so, officials must adhere to the more limiting state law requirements. Of course, the same concept applies to federal law; if federal law is more limiting than state law, federal law will supersede state law.

Without going into too much depth, there are some exceptions concerning the search warrant rule. Exceptions include plain view, search incident to a lawful arrest, stop and frisk, vehicle inventory, consent to search, automobile searches, and miscellaneous circumstances. Plain view includes but may not be limited to the following: the officer must be at a location where he or she has a legal right to be; the discovery of the seized items must have been inadvertent; and the items seized must appear to be incriminating.

Search incident to a lawful arrest includes but may not be limited to the following: the arrest must be lawful and the search must concentrate on the suspect's person or be within the suspect's area of immediate control—also known as the lunge area. Stop and frisk includes but may not be limited to the following: when a police officer has reasonable suspicion that the person has been, is, or is about to become engaged in criminal activity, the peace officer must have a reasonable belief that the person is armed and dangerous, and the stop and frisk is focused on outer garments only in order to discover weapons which may injure the officer.

Vehicle inventory includes but may not be limited to the following: a matter of standard practice by a peace officer's department performed each and every time to maintain consistency; performed as a care-taking policy indicating that the search is performed for the protection of the owner's personal property; as protection against false claims of theft lodged against officers; protection for the officer from unrecognized danger; and the procedure must not be used by the officer solely to discover evidence.

Consent to search includes but may not be limited to the following: must be freely and voluntarily given; must be based on the totality of the circumstances. The most critical analyzation process will occur after the arrest has been made, and third party consent focusing on whether the third party has control over the premises or items to be searched. Automobile searches include but may not be limited to the following: exigent circumstances such as probable cause to believe that the vehicle or containers located within the vehicle contain sizeable items. Proactive search of the vehicle includes but may not be limited to the following: lawfully stopping the vehicle; with reasonable suspicion that the vehicle contains weapons, the search may extend to the passenger compartment.

Miscellaneous searches include but may not be limited to the following: fire scene searches with certain specifications; crime scene searches with exigent circumstances; inventory searches at jail which are custodial in nature; abandonment of property that has been voluntarily relinquished and has no expectation of privacy; canine search establishing probable cause. In conclusion, these rules are subject to constant interpretation and may vary from state to state so annual updates should be given to officers by qualified instructors.

Interviews and Interrogation

There is a difference between interviewing and interrogation. An interview concerns the process by which an official seeks, obtains, and evaluates information given to him by persons who have personal knowledge of an event or circumstances of a crime, accident, or other matters of official interest. An interrogation involves a process by which an official endeavors to obtain information about an event, crime, or accident from an individual who is suspect in that event, crime, or accident and is unwilling to provide that information. Miranda warning is required if an interrogation is custodial in nature. Thus, special care must be observed in order to keep the interrogation noncustodial. Every state has its own laws governing interrogation especially if juveniles are involved.

The purpose of an interview is to obtain facts, information, and background in order to determine the truthfulness of a matter under investigation. Facts are items known and without question, for example, names, dates, and locations. Information includes all other information gained from victims, witnesses, and others possibly interested in the matter; and background concerns finding out all pertinent information about an individual prior to the presentation of facts and related information.

There are four elements of consideration for conducting an interview: timing, setting, physical barriers, and preparation. Timing includes conducting the interview, as soon as possible, after any incident. However, an official may delay questioning if the person is cold, sleepy, hungry, or otherwise physically uncomfortable. Emotional states may make a person an unsatisfactory subject to interview until a later date. The setting should include a private interview area. Familiarity of an area may be conducive in gaining cooperation and calm an emotional person.

Physical barriers include minimizing physical distance between the official and person interviewed; however, personal space should not be violated. Officials should be aware of the arrangement of chairs if the interview is being conducted sitting down. Chairs may be inadvertently positioned in such a manner that open conversation will be uncomfortable. For example, when an official is positioned at one end of a table or on the other side of a desk and the interviewee is at the other end of the table or on the other side of a desk, the perception is one of domination which may negatively impact the free flow of information.

There are six qualities necessary in a good interviewer. First, the interviewer should have a good personality, one that reflects confidence, sincerity, and alertness. Second, the interviewer should possess a breadth of interests, in other words, be able to discuss many different topics with a variety of people. Third, the interviewer should be an actor or be able to act a part. Fourth, the interviewer must be a salesman having the ability to sell himself or herself to another person to gain their trust and confidence. Fifth, the interviewer must have the ability to remain in control of the interview and keep the discussion focused on the topic at hand. Finally, the interviewer must be pleasant.

Upon completion of an interview, the official should close the conversation in a courteous and friendly manner. The official may also wish to summarize the conversation. Finally, the official should let the person know their cooperation is appreciated. Of course, the information gathered must be evaluated. Evaluation may be conducted according to five criteria. First, is the information relevant to the issue at hand? Second, is the information related to all other known facts? Third, is the information source trustworthy and competent? Fourth, is the information accurate and verifiable? Finally, is the information potentially powerful enough to establish proof?

Defense-in-Depth

Of course, each measure described above should be designed and implemented in an effort to make the introduction of weapons and/or dangerous contraband onto courthouse grounds as difficult as possible. These measures are called supporting policies because, if they are initiated as a stand-alone policy, their effectiveness will be limited if not totally insignificant.

Referring to the defense-in-depth security concept addressed in the physical security portion of this book, an effective measure should be developed in the following manner. Courthouse officials may stagger reporting times to lessen foot traffic and accompanying mass interaction, activity should be physically monitored by courthouse officials as people enter the courthouse facility, closed circuit television (CCTV) systems would monitor and record activity, personnel should monitor the CCTV, courthouse officers should be prepared to immediately respond to any incidents, everyone should be processed through metal detectors, all hand-carried items should be inspected, and random searches of courthouse property should be conducted. The idea of a defense-in-depth process requires perpetrators to defeat a number of security measures in order to introduce a weapon into the courthouse. Thus, the ultimate idea is to make the introduction of weapons and/or dangerous contraband into any courthouse facility so difficult that people will not even consider, much less attempt it.

Past Security/Safety Surveys

Please refer to Chapter 2 of this book for a full explanation of the information contained in a security survey. If a courthouse facility has not performed a security survey, the author recommends that one be completed, by a security professional, as soon as possible.

Crisis Procedure Checklists

These checklists may include subjects such as lock-down procedures, evacuation procedures, emergency notification lists, emergency operations center (EOC) or incident command system (ICS) involvement, and crisis aftermath procedures, etc. A courthouse administrator may attach natural or technological emergency procedures to this portion of the response plan; however, these types plans are inadequate for courthouse violence response situations. Granted, parts of these plans are valuable and should be used, but there are portions of a courthouse violence response plan that will require different response actions.

For example, a courthouse experiencing a violent attack such as an active shooter will require a police response that will require tactical actions such as cordon operations, scouting operations, a tactical operations center (TOC) (this is totally different from an incident command center or emergency operations center), over-watch evacuation routes and accompanying rally points in order for innocent civilians to be screened for perpetrators, search and clear operations, neutralization of perpetrator(s), and subsequent criminal investigation.

Lock-Downs

Lock-down, safe haven, or evacuation procedures are not as clear-cut as they seem. Indeed, these procedures are frequently emotional and dangerous events. Courthouse administrators are unlikely to understand that the situation they face during any courthouse violence crisis is tactical. This is an important point because, once a situation has turned tactical, solutions also become tactical. Tactical situations are often very fluid and tactical principles are also subject to change. Tactics must be flexible in nature and are always subject to change in a moment's notice. Tactics are chosen to fit the situation; the situation does not fit the tactics.

For example, if a violent action is occurring outside a courthouse facility, it is probably wise to employ lock-down procedures in order to provide a barrier between the courthouse occupants, situation, and perpetrator. However, if a situation is occurring inside the courthouse itself, it may not be a good idea to lock-down the occupants. A lock-down will fix personnel in place and provide numerous defenseless targets of opportunity for the perpetrator; plus there will be many more personnel for responding officers to assess while performing dangerous search and clear operations. Would it not be a better choice to evacuate personnel from the crisis area? The answer is dependent upon the tactical situation.

A freely moving perpetrator will endanger everyone in the courthouse while a fixed-in-place perpetrator will only endanger people in the immediate area. In the former situation, evacuation would probably be a good choice, while the latter situation would probably require a lock-down. Of course, any tactical situation can be argued in many different ways that only verifies the concept that tactics and tactical responses must remain flexible in relation to rapidly changing tactical developments. Therefore, neither a lock-down nor evacuation procedure should represent the sole decision of the responsible administrator. Furthermore, one procedure may come into play or both procedures may be applicable; for example, only part of the courthouse may be locked-down while the remainder of the courthouse is evacuated.

Furthermore, evacuation and/or lock-down procedures must be carefully chosen in order to fully protect visitors and staff from harm. Indeed, it is critical that courthouse administrators identify safe areas "safe havens"—a form of lock-down where courthouse staff and visitors can go in a crisis situation. A safe haven is actually part lock-down and part evacuation. When implementing a safe haven procedure, personnel actually leave the immediate area and proceed to an identified safe area. Many of these areas may actually be located inside the courthouse in lieu of evacuating to outdoor areas. Several areas must be chosen as safe havens because a courthouse violence situation may take place anywhere on the courthouse grounds. For example, according to the situation, an area normally considered safe may be subject to perpetrator access or weapons fire and therefore becomes unsafe.

Safe Havens

The best safe havens are solely dedicated to this purpose and are clearly identified and discussed with courthouse staff members. Safe havens should not be externally locked due to problems associated with key control. Safe havens can be protected from tampering through the use of plastic or paper seals (tamper indicating devices) and frequent status checks. If a seal is broken, a complete inventory of the safe haven should be performed. Of course, safe havens can be monitored through the use of security systems or frequently patrolled by courthouse security. Some safe havens may be dual use and serve other purposes than just security needs.

At a minimum, any area designated a safe haven should have a telephone, emergency telephone numbers, a flashlight, and a lockable door. Safe havens should have a means of escape (ground floor doors, outdoor stairs, secondary ingress/egress doors, etc.). Safe havens should be located in areas that have natural choke points (stairs, hallways, channeled entrances, etc.). Choke points restrict free movement so these areas may be avoided by perpetrators. The idea is to choose a safe haven that provides courthouse staff with the ability to move while outside choke points restrict the perpetrators ability to maneuver.

If possible, safe havens should be stocked with emergency supplies and a disaster supply kit. These supplies should sustain the courthouse staff for at least one day. If emergency supplies cannot be stored in a safe haven(s), these supplies should be stored in a sturdy, easy-to-carry container such as a backpack, duffel bag, or covered trash container. Disaster supply kits should include seven basic kinds of supplies, for example, water, food, first aid items, sanitation items, tools and accompanying supplies, bedding, and special items. Disaster supply kits can be protected from scavengers and/or pilferers through the use of plastic or paper seals (tamper indicating devices) and frequent status checks in the same manner as safe havens.

Water should be stored in plastic containers. Containers that will decompose or break should be avoided. Most people need to drink two quarts of water a day; of course, hot environments and/or intense physical activity can double that amount. As a general rule, store one gallon of water per-person-per-day. At least a one-day supply of nonperishable food should be stored. These foods should require no refrigeration, cooking, or other preparation, and little or no water. Food items should also be compact and lightweight.

A first aid kit should also be developed and stored in the safe haven. This kit should contain the following items:

Sterile assorted bandages in assorted sizes
Two-inch sterile gauze pads (8 or 12)
Three-inch sterile roller bandages (3 rolls)
Hypoallergenic adhesive tape
Scissors
Moistened towellettes (8–10 individual packages)
Tube of petroleum jelly or other lubricant
Bar of soap
Tongue blades and wooden applicator sticks
Latex gloves
Aspirin or nonaspirin pain reliever

Antiseptic or hydrogen peroxide
Three-inch sterile gauze pads (8 or 12)
Triangular bandages (3)
Two-inch sterile roller bandages (3 rolls)
Tweezers
Needle
Thermometer
Cleansing agent/soap
Antiseptic spray
Assorted sizes of safety pins
Basic first aid book
Eye wash
Rubbing alcohol

Sanitation items should include the following:

Toilet paper, towellettes
Plastic garbage bags and ties
Soap, liquid detergent

Feminine supplies
Plastic bucket with a tight lid
Household chlorine bleach

Tools and supplies should include the following:

Mess kits or paper cups, plates, and plastic utensils
Flashlight and extra batteries
Fire extinguisher, small canister, ABC type

Plastic sheeting
Battery-operated radio and extra batteries
Non-electric can opener, utility knife
Pliers

Tape	Compass
Matches in a waterproof container	Aluminum foil
Plastic storage container	Signal flare
Paper, pencil	Needles, thread
Medicine dropper	Whistle

Bedding should consist of one blanket or sleeping bag per person

Note: The first aid kit should be sealed and periodically checked in the manner discussed in the disaster supply kit section of this book.

Courthouse staff members must know where safe havens are located and what routes are safe to follow in order to reach them. At least one staff member should travel the route to the safe haven and quickly check the safe haven to ensure the area is clear of perpetrators and explosive devices. Other staff members should then travel to the safe haven. Next, staff supervisors should immediately account for their staff members upon reaching the safe haven. Supervisors should also check staff members for injuries and render treatment as required. This procedure will help responding personnel avoid needless and dangerous searches for missing persons. Trying to find out where staff members are located can be the most stressful part of a courthouse violence crisis.

Supervisors should control staff members while occupying the safe haven. The door to the safe haven should be locked once all staff members are accounted for and heavy objects should be used to reinforce the door. Personnel should not be allowed to wander around the room; they should be instructed to remain on the floor, near a wall, in a far corner away from the door. The door should remain under observation at all times. Personnel should call 911 as soon as possible and give a complete location of the emergency (address, floor and room number, city or town, nearest cross street, and any helpful landmarks), provide your name and telephone number, describe what happened, pass on how many people need help and what is being done to assist them, and finally, let the person on the other end of the line hang up first.

A supervisor should also call the police and tell them what is happening and where, if anyone is injured, where the safe haven is located, and give a complete description of the perpetrator(s), (height, weight, build, age, race, hair color, eye color, clothing worn, weapon(s) number and type, equipment carried, and a name if known). A checklist should be developed listing these and other topics and this checklist should be posted near the telephone. A procedure should also be planned for getting courthouse facility keys into the hands of the police if required (a complete set of keys should be stored with the emergency crisis response plan). However, if police officers request keys, they may be thrown from a window to responding units. To plan for this option, keys should be placed on an oversize device to avoid the possibility of losing them in the dark or in high foliage. Courthouse employees should not leave the safe haven to assist police with search and clear operations. **Courthouse personnel should never pick up a weapon and approach the police!**

Courthouse personnel should remain in the safe haven until physically contacted by police officers. Additionally, personnel must remain calm, alert, aware of their surroundings, and avoid the mental state of denying that a courthouse crisis event is occurring. The mental mind-set must be one of survival and winning a confrontation, not panic and defeat. Finally, all instructions issued by the police should be followed to the letter. Complying with these instructions will heighten the chances of a safe and successful conclusion to a very dangerous situation.

Indeed, personnel released from a safe haven by police officers who have entered the crisis site may be in shock or become hysterical. This is understandable and should be expected, especially if responding police officers are dressed in tactical gear including protective masks. Shock and hysteria may be more pronounced if officers have been shooting weapons and/or using distraction devices. Thus, released personnel may panic and react by running for exits, trying to hide, or even physically attacking police officers themselves.

Officers will likely be prepared for such actions and maintain visual and physical control of all suspects and personnel discovered in the crisis site and keep personnel in place, with hands in sight, and call for support personnel backup (usually designated as snatch teams). These team members, as soon as possible, begin instituting a nonhostile authority by using calming techniques; being firm, avoiding anger or disrespect; showing understanding, but not being overly sympathetic; modeling calm behavior; reassuring personnel that everything is under control; repeating instructions as needed; ignoring nondisruptive emotional behavior; and using distractions such as focusing group attention on something or someone else.

When giving members of this group directions, police officers will likely order only one action at a time; use the shortest sentences possible; repeat directions frequently; give acknowledgment and encouragement when needed; and only a team leader will give directions while team members observe personnel to make sure all instructions are understood and followed. If personnel are to be moved under exigent circumstances (a chance of additional firing or the crisis site is not fully cleared), officers will likely take the following actions: keep in place all handheld items until inspected by bomb squad and/or investigating officials; require each person to place his or her hand on the shoulder of the person to the front, for control purposes, and move in a single file until absolutely clear of any danger; maintain a calm but firm in-charge manner; ensure personnel take proper actions; give clear and concise instructions; use physical guidance, if necessary, especially for hysterical individuals or if subsequent gunfire erupts; and keep personnel reassured until the crisis site is cleared.

There will be a tendency for rescued personnel to rush to families or friends; however, people moved from the crisis site will often be directed to a prepared, secured, holding area. Support personnel (including female officers) should be preselected and standing by to perform the following actions: conduct professional body searches for hidden weapons, masquerading active shooters, and body bombs; use prearranged code words or hand signals to alert other officers of any active shooters discovered among rescued personnel; maintain close observation; be alert for suspicious behavior; reassure personnel that normal procedures are being followed; and be constantly prepared to deal with fear reactions or emotional hysterical behavior.

To prepare courthouse personnel for the possibility that a courthouse violence situation could occur and that the above actions may be taken, information should be passed in a manner that will not frighten personnel. Steps that will enhance lock-down, safe haven, or evacuation procedures should be thoroughly discussed. The idea is to instill in each staff member that the possibility of a courthouse violence crisis is real while raising confidence in the chances of survival. Confidence in survival will be heightened as each staff member learns the appropriate actions to take before, during, and after any courthouse violence crisis.

All staff members should learn how to render basic first aid to include cardiopulmonary resuscitation (CPR). Emergency telephone numbers should be posted near all telephones and all staff members should be taught how to effectively summon help in an emergency. For example, call 911, give a complete location of the emergency (address, floor and room number, city or town, nearest cross street, and any helpful landmarks), give your name and telephones number, describe what happened, pass on how many people need help and what is being done to assist them, and finally, let the person on the other end of the line hang up first.

Evacuation

The next task is to discuss with courthouse staff members what steps to take in the event of an evacuation. Evacuation can be a frightening experience; knowing what to do can make the process safer and more efficient as well as reduce the fears and uncertainty of leaving. It is a good idea to develop an evacuation checklist in order to remember what to do during an evacuation. This checklist should include the steps to be taken and who is in charge of performing each step. The following items should be included, but this list should by no means be considered all-inclusive.

1. Answer how personnel will be evacuated from the courthouse in a safe and orderly manner.

2. Plan for transportation in case a full courthouse evacuation requires completely leaving the courthouse grounds. When transportation is assembled to transport personnel away from courthouse grounds it should be inspected for immediate security concerns and law enforcement personnel should be assigned as security escorts. Transportation should be positioned in a manner designed to expedite a safe and rapid traffic flow. Drivers should have in their possession copies of evacuation routes and be familiar with them to include the destination. Personnel may be held inside the transportation conveyance unless other plans to safely secure them have been made. No vehicle should leave the courthouse grounds unless a roll call is performed and everyone is accounted for.

3. Each supervisor should have a "grab and run" emergency kit that is designed to be as light as possible. The kit should include a work section roster, emergency contact information, emergency medical information, small first aid kit, flashlight, and other items deemed necessary by the individual courthouse administrator.

4. A buddy system should be used by staff members; if for any reason staff members become separated from the main group, they will have someone looking out for them. The buddy system will often lessen or even prevent panic.

5. It is a good idea to designate at least two ways out of each room and/or building.

6. An area should be designated for assigned personnel to meet family members and explain the situation and if practical, set up a procedure allowing personnel to check out.

7. All staff members should listen to and follow all instructions issued by emergency officials.

8. Police officers will normally treat all evacuated personnel as suspects. This precaution is taken because active shooters may try to escape or even attack people after they have mixed into the evacuating population. Thus, everyone who exits the scene will be directed to a safe area, frisked, separated, and perhaps handcuffed until a debriefing is performed (normally in a secure area).

In conclusion, the best way to develop evacuation or lock-down procedures is for courthouse administrators to work with staff members, police administrators, and other emergency responders by participating in a number of mock courthouse violence scenarios. Mock scenarios will often reveal the best options to choose in a number of circumstances. The more mock scenarios that can be practiced, the higher the likelihood that an effective deci-sion can be made in a real-world crisis. Furthermore, practice will help staff members to evacuate an area in safe and orderly manner. Staff members with knowledge and who are assigned responsibilities often feel less vulnerable or panicky during emergency situations. The central focus should be on the sharing of responsibilities and working together as a team.

Emergency Notification List

An emergency notification list is more stable and clear-cut than lock-down or evacuation decisions. Indeed, this is one area that can be directly pulled from a well-planned Incident Command System (ICS) procedure. Emergency notification lists should be in place so that in the event of an emergency, the assigned person(s) can go down a list notifying the needed agencies and per-sonnel as designated. The emergency notification list should be structured in a hierarchical fashion. Of course, emergency responders should be listed and contacted first. Finally, the time of notification should be recorded next to the contacts name or agency instead of using a check mark or other symbol.

Incident Command System (ICS)

An Incident Command System (ICS) is the model for command, control, and coordination of a response and provides a means to coordinate the efforts of individual agencies as they work toward the common goal of stabilizing an incident and protecting life, property, and the environment. ICS is a sound program and federal law requires the use of ICS for response to HAZMAT incidents. Indeed, many states have adopted ICS principles for responding to all types of incidents. However, many courthouse administrator's are overly dependent on incident command systems. This is a dangerous mistake in relation to a "real-time" courthouse violence crisis. Consider the fact that inci-dent command systems are time and information dependent, meaning, by the time a full-blown ICS is operational, the perpetrators inside the courthouse facility will be or have been free to commit any acts they originally planned.

Granted, ICS is valuable in the long term, if situations continue over a period of time and when performing aftermath operations. However, an ICS will do nothing to stop perpetrators from continuing to kill courthouse per-sonnel. A well-planned courthouse violence response plan implemented immediately upon notification that a courthouse violence crisis is occurring will enable police officers to stop the violence.

Of course, parts of any existing ICS should be used when developing rapid response operating procedures for courthouse systems. The reader will find many of the elements of the ICS to be valuable. Some of the more important areas include the emergency operations center, incident command post, and staging areas.

Aftermath Checklist

Aftermath checklists should include such things as media releases, notification of family members, injury assessments, damage assessments, assisting with criminal investigations, debriefing courthouse personnel, and getting the courthouse back into operation.

Acquiring Response Planning Information

Where do courthouse administrators acquire response planning information? Information gathering methods are diverse and unique to each location, but generally, the methods consist of the following:

1. Reconnaissance and surveillance—administrators should observe the area of concern from as many angles and heights as possible. One view may reveal what another cannot. Air assets are valuable, if available. Administrators should make maximum use of photography, video, and sketches. Furthermore, the area should be observed at different periods of the day and night in order to record any significant changes such as vehicle traffic, pedestrian traffic, lighting conditions, etc.

2. Conversation—enter into general conversation with staff members; these personnel may see, hear, or know elements of essential information. Hot lines may also be established to gather this type of information. Also, converse with building managers, workers, custodians, etc. to verify and identify any courthouse building weaknesses or unusual circumstances. It is interesting to note that in many workplace tragedies, the shooters actually talked about their intentions to other people or associates.

3. Records—Personnel, medical, and work performance information should be developed into an information bank complete with updated photographs.

4. Documents—Analyze all notes and messages obtained during day-to-day courthouse operations.

5. Maps, photographs, terrain models, and touring similar buildings. Procure maps of the immediate and surrounding area. Procure photographs, videos, and all other means of visual representation including photographs of the immediate and surrounding area. Procure floor plans of courthouse building(s) and adjacent buildings. Question build-

ing managers, workers, custodians, etc. to verify floor plan accuracy. If possible, develop a three-dimensional model of the courthouse site.

6. A professionally developed courthouse site security survey will contain a great deal of essential information that can be easily assimilated into a courthouse violence response plan.

Response Procedure Completion

The elements of essential information gathered by the different team members should be evaluated, compared, and ultimately compiled into one master response document. When complete, the leading courthouse administrator should review the response document in order to ascertain effectiveness. An effective response document should be evaluated for workable format, completeness, and feasibility. The response document should then be filed in a known central location complete with facility keys. **Note:** The response document may be useless when only one person knows the location or has sole access to the document.

The leading courthouse administrator is also responsible for critiquing the end product, rendering assistance during information gathering efforts, and answering questions concerning the end product. The goal is to keep the information flow focused, efficient, and effective. Ultimately, the courthouse crisis response planning procedure should serve as a process for securing immediate external support from law enforcement officials and other relevant community agencies. All provisions and procedures will also require monitoring and review by the core developers and the lead administrator.

Characteristics of a Good Plan

A plan must be based on facts or, at the least, valid assumptions. If assumptions must be made, they should be checked out to make sure they are as close as possible to the actual situation. The plan must also provide an organizational structure and should clearly define the relationship between the various functions and fix the responsibility of who is to do what. To strengthen organizational structure, personnel should be assigned functions which are close to their day-to-day operations and existing work groups should be kept intact as much as possible.

Cumbersome words and long sentences should be avoided so the plan will not be misunderstood. Additionally, the various elements of the plan must be coordinated and fit together. Finally, a completed plan must be reviewed and revised as necessary. Indeed, there may not be agreement from everyone on every point. Thus, the CPO may have to serve as a negotiator between departments. If no agreement can be reached, the CPO will have to recommend a final course of action and present the plan to managing entities as required. The final page of any plan should contain signature blocks for all effected administrators and heads of entities to sign signifying they are all in agreement.

In conclusion, a plan is considered good if it provides for an organizational structure and offers a definite course of action to meet a courthouse violence crisis. Finally, for any courthouse violence crisis response plan to be effective it must be evaluated for validity. Validity may be measured by testing methods designed to see if the plan will actually work. The most effective way to test a plan is by simulating a real courthouse violence crisis in order to exercise responsible personnel and applicable procedures.

Response Plan Exercises

The most effective way to evaluate a plan and accompanying programs is to perform a dry run or exercise. An exercise will often identify strengths and weaknesses in any plan that can then be addressed, revamped, and/or corrected. Further, procedures can be modified or deleted as necessary. Finally, exercises provide personnel with specific emergency response assignments to understand and practice the exact duties they are expected to accomplish. The goal is to eliminate any confusion in the accomplishment of an assignment.

There are five different types of exercises that may be used to test a courthouse violence crisis response plan. Each exercise is progressively more realistic, more stressful, more complex, and more difficult to conduct. Therefore, courthouse systems should plan on exercising in successive steps—each building on the experience of the past exercise. These five exercises are designed to provide both individual training and improve the response system as a whole.

The five types of exercises include orientation, drill, tabletop, functional, and full-scale exercises. The orientation exercise is a preparatory training exercise that uses simulation materials to set the stage. This exercise is very low-key and is used as a building block to other, more difficult exercises. The second type of exercise, called a drill, is typically a single emergency response function targeting single agency involvement. This exercise is often used to evaluate a field component during a full-scale exercise. **Note:** For more information concerning a drill, see the description of a drill and full-scale exercise listed below.

The third type of exercise is called the tabletop exercise. The characteristics of this exercise include low stress, little attention to time, lower level of preparation effort, and only rough attempts to simulate reality. The focus in these exercises is on training and familiarization with roles, procedures, responsibilities, and personalities working in the courthouse violence crisis response system. The tabletop exercise introduces participants to messages that simulate a realistic courthouse violence event. It is to these messages that individuals respond with decisions. Thus, the tabletop exercise serves the purpose of emphasizing the many problems associated with coordination among responding agencies.

The more advanced exercises include functional exercises and full-scale exercises. The functional exercise normally takes place inside a classroom or actual emergency operations center (EOC). This exercise involves complex simulation supported by various forms of message traffic (written, telephone, radio), and exhaustive attempts to recreate a realistic environment through simulation. Training is realized through the practice and testing of personnel and procedures under complex conditions which generate high stress levels that in turn evoke responses approximating a real courthouse violence crisis, even though actual equipment and personnel are not physically operating. The functional exercise typically brings key personnel into the EOC to run through their decisions and responsibilities.

This exercise tests the organization of the plan, its task assignments, and the liaison necessary among responding agencies. Conflicts in authority or responsibility often emerge in a functional exercise, as do gaps in task assignments in the plan. These authority and responsibility conflicts plus gaps in task assignments can be identified and neutralized during the training exercise in lieu of an actual situation (authority and responsibility conflicts plus gaps in task assignments can easily result in additional death and destruction in a "real-world" courthouse violence crisis). In conclusion, the conducting of regular and periodic functional exercises should be a major goal for every courthouse violence crisis response program.

A full-scale exercise typically combines a functional exercise with a drill in which field personnel, representing one or more responding emergency services, actually operate. The actual movement of equipment and personnel is important for emergency service organizations, but a drill alone does not suffice to test the courthouse violence crisis response plan. Too often, agencies feel confident that they have tested their plan after running a drill. However, unless the EOC is activated and full interagency coordination has been exercised, there is no complete system test. Therefore, the goal of exercising should be to conduct a full-scale exercise to include EOC activation. Drills alone cannot substitute for simulation of emergency coordination—the most important task of the courthouse violence crisis response manager.

Drills do serve a valuable purpose in support of a full-scale exercise. For example, before conducting a major exercise, the courthouse violence crisis

Figure 36. Example of a full-scale exercise.

response manager or designated person should make certain that the plan calls for the alert of all required personnel by conducting a notification drill. This drill consists of pretending that a courthouse violence crisis has occurred and observing whether the correct people and agencies were notified at the proper time. This drill achieves the purpose of making certain the plan contains the proper information concerning roles and responsibilities. Of course, any of the annexes can also be tested in this manner by observing annex initiation, response, and effectiveness. Drills also enable the testing of specialized activities such as the EOC and communications equipment to verify that it is in working order.

Conducting Drills and Full-Scale Exercises

In order to conduct a drill and a full-scale exercise, a great deal of preparation activity will have to be made. Safety is paramount in conducting exercises involving firearms, explosives, chemical agents, pyrotechnics, vehicles, unarmed self-defense techniques, tactical individual movements, and tactical team movements. Collectively this material provides the essential ingredients for effectively planning and carrying out exercises designed to support training and evaluation efforts in a safe manner. Of course, the magnitude and scope of a particular scenario will determine the applicability of the following observations.

These observations will be broken down into the following headings: general safety, participant responsibilities, weapon safety, blank ammunition, pyrotechnics, vehicle safety, rules of engagement, explosives, preexercise briefing, command and control functions, controller/evaluator training, and concluding remarks.

GENERAL SAFETY. Safety rules must be followed to minimize the potential for accidents/incidents during exercises. Maximum effort should be made by management, controllers, and participants to anticipate and react to unsafe situations. As a matter of exercise policy, realism must be achieved and safety must be considered in the actions of all participating personnel. By integrating realistic safety requirements into exercise scenarios, safety application by participants is enhanced under both operational and exercise conditions.

All exercises must be governed by plans that specifically address safety issues while remaining consistent with realistic training. Safety plans should include procedures for any materials, equipment, and/or operations that are identified as potential hazards during the conduct of a specific scenario. Preparations should also be made to react with appropriate levels of medical assistance to situations that could occur.

Exercises and related activities should be regulated by controllers who have the final authority regarding safety matters. During an exercise, controllers are responsible for ensuring that operations are conducted safely. Controllers may stop exercise activity for safety or administrative reasons. Any individual may stop exercise activity for safety reasons.

PARTICIPANT RESPONSIBILITIES. Personnel acting as aggressors and response force operators must be briefed on their individual responsibilities; they include the following:

A. Avoid identified hazardous areas.
B. Monitor personal physical condition for signs of overexertion.
C. Render first aid and notify a controller if injuries or assistance is required.
D. Report injuries, no matter how slight, to the nearest controller or safety officer.
E. Handle and use all weapons in a safe manner.
F. Inspect weapons, equipment, and personnel to ensure that no live ammunition is   present in the exercise area.
G. Limit physical contact during an arrest or physical control maneuver to searching and handcuffing, refraining from violent physical contact.

H. Refrain from attempts to disarm any individual by grabbing their weapon or person.

 I. Ascending or descending from elevated positions by a ladder, stairway, or other safe method, jumping from elevated positions should be avoided.

 J. Avoid hot propellant gasses vented from weapons.

K. No person acting in the role of a hostage may be physically abused.

 L. All personnel occupying a target facility must be provided with appropriate safety equipment during assault phases.

M. Any damage to vehicles, equipment, or facilities must be reported to a controller by the end of the day's exercise.

N. Eliminated participants must immediately cease fire, movement, communication, and other actions, and remain in place until the exercise is terminated or upon release by a controller.

WEAPONS SAFETY

A. All weapons should be equipped with approved blank fire adapters or blast deflectors.

B. Exercise firearms should be inventoried by serial number and stored separately from live ammunition.

C. All exercise weapons, if possible, should be fitted with live round inhibiting devices to prevent the accidental introduction of live rounds.

D. All exercise weapons must be inspected at the beginning of each scenario, clearly marked as an exercise weapon, closely controlled, and kept separate from any weapon not associated with the exercise.

E. Exercise weapons should not be loaded until authorized by an exercise controller.

F. Blank firing weapons are to be fired only at participants who are at least 10 feet away from the weapons muzzle.

BLANK AMMUNITION AND BLANK FIRE ADAPTERS

A. Only blank ammunition magazines, clips, and belts that have been distinctively color-coded and modified to inhibit live rounds may be used.

B. Blank ammunition must be stored separately from live ammunition and inspected prior to issue by an exercise controller.

C. Prior to each exercise and each scenario participants must inspect their weapons and person to ensure that only blank ammunition and marked exercise weapons are in use.

D. Prior to each exercise and each scenario designated controllers must inspect exercise weapons and all ammunition to ensure that only blank ammunition and marked exercise weapons are in use.

Hand-Thrown Pyrotechnics, Distraction Devices, and Chemical Agents

A. Participants should never pick up thrown pyrotechnics, distraction devices, or chemical agents. Duds should be reported as soon as possible to the controller.

B. Duds must be handled by following the manufacturer's disposal recommendations or site-approved procedures implemented by properly trained personnel.

C. Pyrotechnic devices may be used only in areas identified as safe in the exercise plan.

D. When pyrotechnic devices are authorized for use in an exercise, appropriate fire fighting equipment must be readily available.

E. Participants who will be using pyrotechnics, distraction devices, chemical agents, or other hazardous materials must have appropriate training.

F. A chemical agent decontamination area and method (natural, passive, or active) should be set up and organized to facilitate the decontamination of personnel suffering from chemical agent exposure.

Vehicle Safety

A. Only specifically designated vehicles may be used by the participants during an exercise.

B. Vehicles may only be mounted or dismounted after they have come to a complete stop.

C. All personnel in moving vehicles equipped with seat belts must wear seat belts at all times. Personnel in the open back of moving vehicles must remain seated within the body of the vehicle.

D. Vehicles may only be driven within posted speed limits and in accordance with safe driving rules.

E. Vehicles may not be used to crash, block, or endanger another vehicle in any way.

F. Vehicles may not be used to chase down personnel.

G. A vehicle must be turned off, placed in park, and the emergency brake set, prior to the driver departing the vehicle.

H. All nonexercise vehicles will be conspicuously identified, and the identification methods will be included in participant briefings.

Rules of Engagement. Specific rules of engagement should be developed and documented for each exercise. Typical rules of engagement focus on halting the exercise. An exercise may be halted at any time for safety, emergency, or administrative reasons.

A. Exercise Freeze: An **"Exercise Freeze"** is a command that is used to halt an exercise when it is necessary to correct safety-related problems or respond to a "real-world" emergency. Any person observing a life-threatening safety problem should announce "Exercise Freeze." Controllers should relay the "Exercise Freeze" announcement throughout the exercise area and on the radio net. Every participant must immediately freeze in place (i.e., stop at his or her location and cease fire, movement, communication, and other related actions) until the command "Resume Exercise" is given by the controller. A code word may be designated to serve as the order to freeze the exercise.

B. Administrative Hold: An **"Administrative Hold"** is a command used to halt an exercise when it is necessary to correct exercise problems of an administrative or procedural nature. The effect of an "Administrative Hold" will normally be limited to specific locations rather than the entire exercise. The command "Administrative Hold" will not be used to correct safety problems or respond to emergencies. Only a controller can administratively halt exercise activities. The controller will announce the hold in the affected area and all participant activity in that area will immediately halt until the controller gives the command "Resume Exercise."

EXPLOSIVES

A. Organizations handling explosives must provide safe operating procedures to the Safety Staff. These procedures will identify the hazards, assess the risks, and establish the necessary safeguards for the particular operation.

B. Explosives will only be authorized for use by tactical units that are thoroughly trained in the use of such devices, and in applicable safety requirements.

C. The quantities of explosives used will require review and preapproval by the Senior Controller and Senior Safety Officer.

PREEXERCISE BRIEFING. The following example is not meant to be all-inclusive for every scenario. Briefings should be tailored to specific exercises and to the participants. Specialized briefings may be necessary to ensure that selected participants are aware of detailed information and/or requirements pertaining to a specific event or role. Responsible personnel must ensure that participants are provided these briefings.

A. Scenario
B. Assignments and Responsibilities
C. Communications Requirements, Procedures, and Methods
D. Safety

1. Controllers
2. Safety officers
3. Participants
4. Equipment, weapons, ammunition, etc.
5. Vehicles
6. Risk assessment reports, hazards, and mitigating controls
7. Actions to be taken in the event of emergency
   E. Questions and answers
   F. Identify the number of scenarios to be conducted
   G. Establish pass/fail criteria
   H. Exercise control measures
      1. Exercise control chain of command
      2. Describe controller responsibilities specific to the scenario
      3. Describe nonparticipant control
      4. Describe exercise and emergency communications systems
      5. Describe accountability and control of weapons and ammunition
   I. Identify required supplies
   J. Safety/health issues
   K. Training Requirements
   L. Exercise coordination requirements
      1. Emergency medical personnel
      2. Fire department
   M. Compensatory measures
      1. Safe exercise halt procedures
      2. Emergency response into an exercise area
      3. Weather
      4. End of exercise accountability (personnel, weapons, ammunition, and equipment)
   N. Coordination and approval
      1. Site specific control authority
      2. Facility authority
      3. Environment, safety and health

COMMAND AND CONTROL. A system of command and control is necessary to maintain an environment free of the recognized hazards associated with major drills/full-scale exercises and performance tests. The command and control system helps to ensure that rules of engagement are followed, specific hazards and safety concerns are appropriately addressed, and exercise continuity is maintained. The chain of command is as follows.

A. *Exercise Director:* Responsible for assuring that all appropriate safety measures are in place prior to the start of the exercise and during scenarios, plus has the final authority for exercise halts due to potential safety problems.

B. *Senior Controller:* Reports directly to the Exercise Director and is responsible for coordinating, establishing, and supervising the exercise controller staff; identifying the number of personnel required to control the exercise; ensuring that appropriate controller training is conducted and developing and implementing the concept of operation for the Exercise Director.

C. *Controller:* The controller staff must be organized in a manner that facilitates the control of all affected locations and the control and coordination of all events to be initiated during the exercise. Individual controllers may have several duties assigned depending on where they are and what activities are occurring in their areas of responsibility. Their first and foremost responsibility is ensuring safety during exercise activity. This includes that ensuring all participants adhere to the safety procedures and rules of engagement. In most cases, the event controllers at a particular exercise location will be the only personnel watching for potentially hazardous situations during the exercise and they must be prepared to take prompt action to prevent accidents or unsafe conditions. In   the event these situations develop, controllers take action in accordance with established safety procedures. Personnel assigned as controllers are responsible for enforcing and/or implementing the following general requirements during exercise:

1. Conducting safety checks and inspection of all personnel under their control for live rounds, prohibited articles, and general safety, and reporting the results to the Senior Controller prior to the beginning of the exercise.

2. Ensuring no live firearms or ammunition of any type are allowed within the exercise area.

3. Ensuring exercise participants wear appropriate safety equipment.

4. Ensuring that personnel under their control comply with the exercise plan to include the rules of engagement and the safety regulations.

5. Stopping a specific activity or the entire exercise if unsafe conditions or acts are observed.

6. Ensuring the accountability of personnel and equipment at the termination of the exercise, and reporting the results to the Senior Controller.

D. *Safety Controller:* The safety controller is responsible for assessing the exercise plan, conducting walk-downs of the exercise area, and conducting safety briefings which specify the rules of engagement, medical response, munitions and weapons safety, and vehicle and personnel safety. The Safety Controller reports to the Senior Controller and should   remain in contact with the Senior Controller at all times during the exercise. In addition, the Safety Controller:

1. Assists the Senior Controller in the development and conduct of pre-exercise controller training.
2. Ensures that adequate safety walk-downs are conducted to determine site suitability prior to the exercise.
3. Conducts a safety walk-down with the Exercise Director, Senior Director, Event Controllers, and other selected controllers prior to the exercise.
4. Ensures emergency medical and fire protection services will be present or on call for the duration of the exercise.
5. Establishes high-speed avenues of ingress and egress to facilitate the movement of medical personnel.

E. *Event Controllers:* Event Controllers report to the Senior Controller and are responsible for executing control over specific categories of exercise activity including one or more exercise events. Event Controllers are responsible for ensuring that non-participating facility personnel in the exercise area are aware that an exercise is to be conducted and that they are not to interfere with the flow of the exercise. Event Controllers must ensure that all exercise participants under their control:

1. Are aware of procedures for halting an exercise for safety reasons or actual emergency.
2. Are not in possession of any live weapons or ammunition.
3. Are fully trained and qualified if programmed to deploy hand-thrown pyrotechnics, distraction devices, explosives, and/or chemical agents.
4. Are instructed that if distraction devices are used, they are not to be thrown within 50 feet of personnel in open areas or into occupied areas or rooms.

F. *Special Controllers:* In those exercises involving special weapons, explosives, pyrotechnics, rappelling, etc., the exercise plan should specifically designate controllers for the special activity. Special Controllers are responsible for ensuring that the following safety requirements are implemented, as applicable to their assigned area of involvement:

1. All exercise participants are fully trained and provided with specific instructions on the hazards of special weapons, explosives, and other similar devices prior to the exercise.
2. Distraction devices are not to be thrown within 50 feet of personnel in open areas or into occupied areas or rooms.
3. All explosive simulators are returned to their point of issue at the conclusion of the exercise activity.

CONTROLLER/EVALUATOR TRAINING. The command and control system is dependent on a contingent of personnel selected and specifically trained to control drills and full-scale exercises. In addition to being trained to oversee exercises, controllers must receive training commensurate with the scope, complexity, and special nature of the activity. Based on the nature and complexity of the exercise, specific controllers may be required for special or high-risk activities. Training should focus on formal and scenario-specific aspects. Formal training should include the following topics:

1. Controllers/Evaluator
   a. Purpose
   b. Responsibilities
   c. Duties
2. General knowledge
   a. Equipment/pyrotechnics
   b. Safety
      1. Firearms
      2. Vehicle use
      3. Participants
      4. Environment, safety and health
      5. Medical
3. Exercise plans
   a. Schedule
   b. Scenarios and variables
   c. Participant actions
   d. Controller/evaluator actions
   e. Role player actions
   f. Suspension/resumption/termination
   g. Rules of engagement
   h. Communications
   i. Administration

Scenario Specific Training should include the following:

1. Briefing on tasks and responsibilities. Brief on the specific tasks and responsibilities prior to exercise initiation.
2. Rules of engagement. Brief each controller on the procedure for the following: exercise freeze, administrative hold, rules of engagement for participants, vehicle safety, explosives, weapons and ammunition, distraction devices, pyrotechnics, general safety, and actual emergencies.
3. Documentation. Describe and demonstrate the desired method for recording information concerning the events that transpire during the exercise. Describe required reports.

 4. Simulation/artificialities. Describe planned simulations/artificialities; how they will effect the exercise; when they will be injected; and the procedures for formulating and introducing other simulations/artificialities, as needed, after exercise initiation.

 5. Transportation arrangements. Describe how controllers, exercise participants, data collectors, and visitors are transported to the exercise location.

 6. After-action meeting. Describe the purpose of the after-action meeting, the information that should be brought to the meeting, and the location of the meeting.

 7. Equipment. Describe the location of the issue and turn-in of equipment, accountability measures, and detailed instructions on the equipment required for each controller during the exercise.

 8. Radio usage and call signs. Provide a detailed description and demonstration of the radios the controllers operate during the exercise. Explain the importance of operating only on the channel and frequency specified in the communications plan.

 9. Route familiarization and exercise site. Provide each controller with a map depicting the route of the exercise site and walk-down the exercise site with all controllers as necessary.

 10. Emergency procedures. Review and provide all controllers with a copy of exercise emergency procedures.

 11. Information protection. Review the guidelines for information control and established policies and procedures for the protection of exercise-related information.

 12. Controller identification. Describe how controllers will be identified and demonstrate the proper method of donning and wearing any apparel to be used for identification purposes.

 13. Nonplayer/observer identification. Describe how nonplayers or observers will be identified and demonstrate the proper method of donning and wearing any apparel to be used for identification purposes.

 14. Controller meetings. Provide directions to and scheduled time for any controller meetings.

 15. Scenarios scripts. Participants must stay faithful to scenario scripts or be ejected from the exercise by the controller.

In conclusion, full-scale exercises must be conducted with the highest regard for the safety and health of personnel, protection of the environment, and the protection of property. Safety issues must be considered from the inception of any exercise to the completion of a scenario. Furthermore, planners should conduct a test of all or part of the courthouse violence crisis response plan. Planners should take notes as the test is in progress and pay

Figure 37. Officers practicing courthouse violence drills.

Figure 38. Officers practicing courthouse violence drills.

Figure 39. Officers practicing courthouse violence drills.

Figure 40. Officers practicing courthouse violence drills.

Figure 41. Officers practicing courthouse violence drills.

Figure 42. Officers practicing courthouse violence drills.

Figure 43. Officer practicing courthouse violence drills.

particular attention to what went as expected and what went wrong. A review should be held after the test to discuss the outcome, and the plan should be modified as necessary. Additionally, exercises should not be "one-shot" efforts; rather, exercises should be an integral part of improving each courthouse violence crisis response plan. Finally, advanced exercises, especially full-scale exercises, should not be attempted until all participants and agencies have participated in the more basic exercises and drills. The surest way to fail the test of any plan is to attempt to launch a full-scale exercise with insufficient practice of basic exercises and drills.

Concluding Remarks

In conclusion, once the courthouse violence crisis response plan has been completed and tested, this is an excellent time to begin a full information push concerning courthouse violence and accompanying programs. It is also an excellent time to do a little promotion within the courthouse system. Courthouse administrators should use the completion of the plan as an opportunity to renew contacts with other agency officials, volunteer groups, and the public. The information shared with different groups will depend upon the type of group, its role in the plan, and stated interest in the plan.

Chapter 4

TACTICAL CONSIDERATIONS

The purpose of this chapter is to focus on some information and tactics that have been used or will likely be used when responding to courthouse violence crisis situations. Reading this information will help courthouse officials to understand some of the reasons why law enforcement entities perform certain actions. This information will also assist law enforcement officials to develop new skills or perhaps refine dated skills.

Training Issues

All agencies should develop and provide basic (recruit) and in-service training programs for all sworn employees who work in the court security or transportation of prisoners function. Furthermore, all newly assigned officers to the transportation and/or court security functions should receive a minimum of 80 hours of formal classroom instruction in the following subject areas:

1. Report writing
2. Legal issues
3. Fire emergency and evacuation processes
4. First aid certification
5. C.P.R. certification
6. Communication skills
7. Dealing with the public
8. Rights and responsibilities of courthouse staff
9. Use of lethal and nonlethal force
10. Searches of cells, facilities, courtrooms, visitors, guests, and defendants
11. Negligent release and negligent supervision avoidance
12. Operation of security equipment and technology
13. Litigation procedures
14. Patrol of courthouse and facilities

1.5. Understanding problems of prisoners
   a. Suicide prevention
   b. Alcohol and drug emergencies
   c. Diabetes, epilepsy, and infectious diseases
16. Supervising prisoners (male, female, and juvenile)
   a. Principles and skills
   b. Security
   c. Transportation
17. Media relations guidelines
18. The nature of court violence and security threats
19. The court system and how it functions
20. Methods of intelligence gathering and threat assessment
21. How to handle court disruptions
22. Parking lot, parking garage, sally port, and perimeter security
23. Explosives, weapons, and contraband search/identification
24. Defensive tactics
25. Firearms training and qualifications
26. Identifying disguised and concealed weapons
27. Protecting persons at risk
28. Crowd control
29. Hostage situations
30. Handling sequestered juries
31. Roles and duties of bailiffs

Additionally, all sworn employees who work in the court security or transportation of prisoners function should be provided with 40 hours of annual in-service training in compliance with the certification requirements of specific state peace officer standards and any existing training commission. For legal protection of both the agency and its officers, all officers should be thoroughly tested to make certain that they have learned the necessary knowledge and skills to perform each task correctly. Finally, the agency should keep complete written records on all officers, specifying what they were taught, when the training was conducted, how officers were tested, and whether the officer was required to keep retesting until the relevant skills were learned.

Concealed or Disguised Weapons

Illegal prohibited articles may be difficult to identify. Indeed, since the 1950s, the marketing of concealed and/or disguised weapons has blossomed, and designs have been copied at an enormous rate. These weapons are turning up on many American street corners and will increasingly find their way into courthouse areas. Concealed weapons are manufactured in all sizes and shapes, thus the following list of descriptions is not intended to be all-inclusive. Some of these deadly devices are fabricated (there are numerous publications available to the public which provide detailed descriptions of how to construct concealed/disguised weapons) for sale on the black market, fabricated in home workshops for personal use, and/or sold through specialty magazines and at flea markets. Many of these devices are advertised as self-defense tools and are shipped directly to the buyer's residence with few or no restrictions on the purchase. Numerous novelty shops are also currently selling these items. Finally, some of these devices are of high quality and expensive; others are of poor quality and inexpensive.

The following list is compiled to serve as a guide to familiarize security officers, and courthouse officials with the types of concealed/disguised weapons typically encountered on the street. The first device, the executive ink pen, looks and works like an ordinary pen. However, this pen pulls apart to reveal a blade approximately three inches long. These pens are normally painted black or silver. Another device disguised as an ink pen is called the "Executive Protection"; this device is a 360 degree pivot, one handle Balisong-type knife. The Executive Protection is .50 inches in diameter, has a 2.85 inch long blade, is 5.5 inches long when closed, and 8.5 inches long when opened. This knife comes in the following colors: black, blue, burgundy, silver, or gold. Finally, some pens do not conceal edged implements, but are actually disguised tear gas dispensers, for example, the tear gas pen. This device is a five-inch long pen and contains a 10 percent formula of Oleoresin Capsicum (OC). The effective range is approximately 12 feet.

There are a number of knives disguised as harmless devices. For example, the bracelet knife pulls apart to reveal a thin one-inch blade. Another device, the sword umbrella, is made from a telescoping umbrella that has been modified to conceal a 10-inch blade complete with a sturdy fiberglass handle. The blade is housed in an undetachable sheath located inside the base of the umbrella. The belt buckle knife is a clever device that houses a three-inch, double-edged knife in what appears to be an ordinary belt buckle. The blade can be quickly detached without loosening the belt. Some models contain a knife hidden in a built-in sheath. Another device, the comb knife, is an 8 1/4-inch fully functional comb that snaps apart to reveal a three-inch blade. These combs are available in a number of colors. The walking cane sword is a clever device, used to house are a number of different-sized blades. Approximately 36 inches overall, they typically offer either one sword blade or a combination of a long blade and a shorter dagger-type blade fitted in the handle. These devices are available in black lacquer or a mahogany finish.

Another edged weapon, a common necklace type knife, is called the cross knife. The cross knife contains a one-inch long by two-inch wide blade. Furthermore, some knives are disguised as the common key. The key knife is approximately 1.2 inches in length and two inches wide. These devices are commonly attached to key chains and may be easily overlooked. There are also credit card knives, which are approximately twice the thickness of a normal credit card. These devices house a retractable two-inch long by two-inch wide blade and are easily concealed in a wallet or purse.

An additional device, the lipstick knife, is a cleverly disguised 1.2-inch knife, housed inside an aluminum lipstick tube. This device is available in a number of different colors and the blade is extracted by twisting the tube's base. A final device used to conceal edged implements is the hollow wristwatch. This device is not a weapon in itself, but can be used to conceal weapons. These units consist of a leather or nylon wristband, and a molded plastic watch face that opens to reveal a hollow compartment large enough to conceal two standard razor blades.

There are also a number of plastic weapons readily available on the open market. These devices are actually made from fiberglass-filled nylon or other space-age plastics. These devices include plastic knives, the devils dart, etc. Plastic weapons typically do not have great slashing and cutting power; however, they do have incredible penetrating capabilities. Thus, users adopt plunging-type attacks. These devices usually weigh less than one ounce, are very tough, and won't register during metal detection efforts.

Beepers and pagers are sometimes used as a disguised weapon or to hide weapons. One device looks like a personal beeper/pager but is actually a pepper spray (oleoresin capsicum) device. This pepper spray pager is the same size as a personal beeper/pager and may be attached anywhere a conventional pager would be placed. The pepper spray pager contains a 10 percent formula of oleoresin capsicum and has a range of approximately 10 feet. An additional device that uses a pager as a disguise is not a weapon itself; however, this hollow pager shell is capable of concealing a small firearm inside the cavity. When in use, the case pops open and hinges downward at the press of a button allowing instant draw of the weapon. Another variation of this device includes a hollow pager case that houses a small handgun that is fired while contained in the pager case by pressing an externally positioned firing button.

Many devices are disguised firearms; for example, the cigarette lighter gun is made from a traditional Zippo-type lighter. This weapon is capable of firing a .22 caliber round by opening the lighters cover and applying pressure to a firing mechanism located in the base of the lighter. Another disguised firearm, the tire gauge gun, appears to be an ordinary tire gauge. This spring-loaded weapon is capable of firing a .22 or .25 caliber round when a striker is pulled to the rear and released.

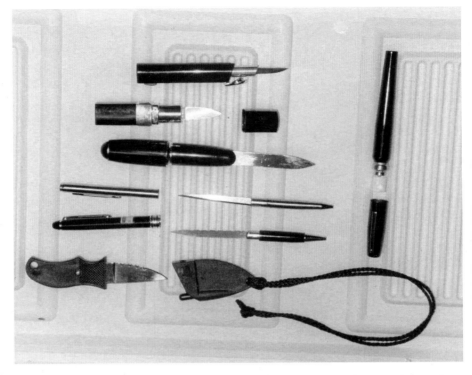

Figure 44. Various disguised knives. The device on the far right is a chemical agent designed to look like an ink pen.

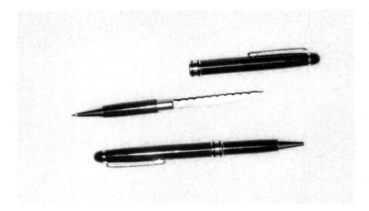

Figure 45. A knife disguised as a black ink pen. The top portion shows the device open and the bottom portion shows the device closed.

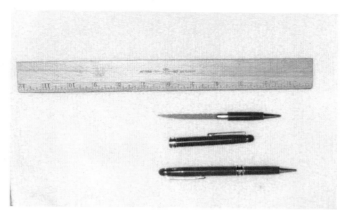

Figure 46. A knife disguised as a burgundy ink pen. The top portion shows the device open and the bottom portion shows the device closed.

Figure 47. Hollow containers used to conceal weapons and contraband.

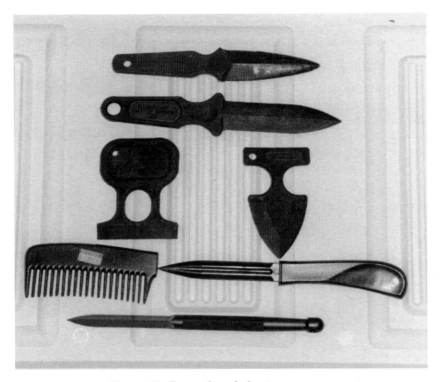

Figure 48. Examples of plastic weapons.

Some disguised firearms such as the bolt gun resemble a normal piece of hardware but are capable of firing a .25 caliber round. The bolt gun is fired by pointing the threaded end of the bolt toward the intended target, pulling rearward on the spring-loaded bolt head, and releasing the bolt head which moves forward firing the round. Another disguised firearm, the pen gun, is available in numerous calibers–the two most common being the .22 or .25 caliber. These devices are available in a variety of designs and many display quality machine work. Pen guns are spring-loaded, thus the operator points the device at the intended target, pulls back on a cocking knob which is in turn releases, driving the firing mechanism forward, firing the round.

Stun guns may also be discovered at courthouse entry control points. These devices are usually easily recognized; however, one device, the stun gun umbrella is not so obvious. The stun gun umbrella resembles an ordinary collapsible umbrella measuring approximately 18.2 inches overall. This device is capable of delivering approximately 80,000 volts.

The Knife Wielder

Probably more people are carrying knives or other edged weapons today than at any time in history. Attacks by knife-wielding subjects are becoming more common. Even though firearms and explosives receive the most publicity, the primary weapon in many violent incidents is the edged weapon. Officers should not judge knives in relation to their small size. A dedicated wielder using the element of surprise can cause serious injury or death by attacking a victims eyes, face, and throat area. Indeed, it is amazing what damage even a small two-inch blade can do to human flesh. A small knife can be hidden easily and can be used to penetrate an artery before the victim realizes what has happened. A small knife can be manipulated in the hand with ease and can be used in a wide variety of ways by an attacker. Make no mistake; any edged weapon can be used to kill.

However, many officers do not respect or realize knife wielders' capabilities, know their tactics, or understand their intent. This section will cover these points so the reader will know to beware of the knife wielder. The knife is one of the most vicious weapons available and is used in a staggering number of homicides and assaults. Once a knife attack begins, it is almost impossible to stop without sustaining injury. Most people attacked by a knife wielder won't even know a knife was involved until after the fact.

The knife wielder may possess no training or skill and still inflict serious injury or kill. Normally, all that is required is a series of rapid slashes or thrusting motions. Officers should never evaluate the knife wielder's capabilities due to stance, appearance or grip on the knife. A trained knife wielder will use surprise, stealth, aggressiveness, and ruthlessness to devastating effect. He will usually slash repeatedly with the intent to rupture arteries, sever nerves, and destroy tendons. His goal is to injure or destroy life-sustaining organs and to incapacitate his victim quickly.

Many knife wielder's learn knife fighting techniques from street fighting experiences, martial arts schools, and other formal or informal schools. There is an abundant amount of schools that teach knife fighting—some good, some bad. Furthermore, anyone may acquire knives with little or no restriction and learn to use these knives by purchasing and watching videotapes extending distance learning instruction on the deadly use of knives and other edged weapons. There are also a variety of ways knife wielders grip knives; the two most common are the straight grip and the back hand. The straight grip involves grasping the knife by the handle with the blade tip pointing away from the attacker. Slashing may be accomplished from this grip, but plunging is more likely. The back hand grip involves grasping the knife by the handle with the blade pointing toward the attacker and is usually hidden behind the inside of the forearm. Slashing is very comfortable from this position and it lends itself well to speed and power. Stabbing can still be accomplished from this position as well. Whichever grip is used the knife wielder will often conceal the knife behind his body or an object until it's time to strike. This is why in any type of possible physical confrontation the adversary's hands must always be watched.

Stabbing or plunging targets include the solar plexus, abdomen, bladder, kidneys, and clavicle artery, all targeted in an effort to destroy vital organs. Stabbing in these areas avoids the body's protective chest and rib bones. Slashing targets include the neck, forehead, inside the arms, inside the thighs, stomach, pelvic area, and chest. The goal is to sever arteries causing the victim to bleed out, to cut tendons and muscles to disable the victim, or in the case of the forehead strike to blind the victim through profuse bleeding. A quick cut not delivered with full slash momentum is often called a flick. The flick is designed to cut the hands, knuckles, fingers, forearms, etc. of an officer fending off a knife attacker by using his or her hands and arms for protection. The goal is to cause the defending person to drop his or her arms and uncover vital organs.

A trained knife wielder may also be adept at throwing his knife accurately up to 16 feet or more. The trained knife thrower will usually carry anywhere from three to six knifes. This assailant will not normally throw his one and only knife. Also, officers shouldn't expect the knife thrower to remain stationary, they practice throwing while moving forward, backward, laterally, and diagonally. The knife may be thrown handle first, blade first, overhand, underhand, weak hand, backhand, or sidearm.

A knife thrown with only moderate force can be buried up to the handle in a person's breast bone. Even if the knife only penetrates an inch or two, massive injury and blood loss are likely. The knife doesn't even have to penetrate to cause severe injury. Upon impact, the knife will start to penetrate, causing an initial incision and puncture wound. As the knife ricochets off a bone, the knife will often continue to cut in a twisting, turning, or sliding motion. Each knife has its own wound signature due to balance, mass, weight, and blade design. Once the assailant has thrown a knife, he will disengage, throw another, or close the distance to continue the attack.

Regardless of the type and size of the knife, all are deadly, if used properly. Many people have the misconception that the attacker's knife will be a fixed blade hunting, chopping, carving, fighting, military, switchblade, or exotic type. Far more prevalent are the folding types due to their ease of carry and conceal ability. Indeed, extremely large folding knives are easily carried and concealed. Further, folding knives are so common place that they normally never attract attention when seen by the public.

When an officer encounters a knife wielder, he or she should maintain distance: remember, a person can cover seven feet in approximately two paces or in about one second! A 40-yard dash can be completed by a great many people within six seconds. Do not crowd a knife wielder! The tactic for the officer involved in a knife attack is to disengage and gain distance, if possible.

If a safe distance or disengagement is impossible, the officer must be mentally prepared to sustain a cut(s). This mind set will help the officer deal with the enormous psychological effect that profuse bleeding causes. Officers must try to protect their torso with their hands and outer arms, if no other defensive or offensive device or technique exists. They must also convince themselves that they will survive. Defending oneself from a knife wielder requires specific training in controlling the knife, stunning the attacker, grounding the attacker, and disarming him if possible. An officer may seek knife defense training taught by police academies, martial artists, or some personal defense companies.

Concealed Carry Methods

Concealed weapons can be hidden virtually anywhere; for example, behind/inside the sweatband of hats or the underside of the brim; front and back surface of the neckline. Weapons may be held in place by a holster, cord, or decorative chain to dangle down the back or the center of the chest; obese subjects may conceal weapons in folds of the skin and overhanging masses.

Additional concealment locations include the belt line–inside the waistband, attached to a belt, on the underside of belts or belt loops, and inside, on or behind belt buckles; wrists–all surfaces can be used with rubber bands, elastic bands, velcro strips, or tape; ankles–again, all surfaces can be used, inside socks, inside shoes, boots, or other types of footwear; jackets–inside internal or external pockets, inside front panels, inside sleeves or down the back; pants–pockets, groin/anal area, along the inside of the leg, sewn inside belt loops in the middle of the back, and packages–internal and external compartments, between hidden dividers and inside hidden compartments.

Finally, males most commonly attach items to the waistline, especially in the small-of-the-back for a number of reasons. One reason concerns the fact that law enforcement professionals handcuff perpetrators with their hands placed behind the back before a search is conducted. The perpetrator's hands and cuffs now obscure this search area; a concealed weapon may be accessible, and many officers do not like to put their hands in this area because a perpetrator can use a twist of the hands and trap the officers searching fingers inside chain link handcuffs. Males also tend to hide items in pockets, the groin or ankle area, and/or in briefcases or fanny packs. Females commonly hide items in pockets, bras, purses, and other types of handbags. Females may also

Figure 49. Waistband carry.

attach items to the waistline and like males may favor especially the small-of-the-back. Experienced female suspects know many officers will avoid this area because it is sufficiently close to the buttocks that officers fear false allegations that they sexually fondled a female in custody.

Thus, when officers employ security scanning devices, physical search techniques, or approach suspicious individuals, great care must be taken to watch for any movements involving the person's hands. Officers must be aware of the inventiveness and deceptiveness of the modern criminal. Thus, caution must be practiced with every item found on a suspicious person. Close examination of seemingly harmless items may appear unorthodox, but may save the lives of courthouse personnel. For the most part, a visual search will not be enough.

Free Carry

To use this technique, the person either sticks the weapon in his or her waistband or in a pocket. While sticking in the waistband, the weapon is not secure and may fall down into the pants or out onto the ground during the wearer's normal range of movement. To avoid these problems, the wearer may not move naturally. A weapon carried in this manner may also be prone to printing (the outline of a weapon imprinted on clothing). People may try to avoid printing by placing a handkerchief between the weapon and the outer material, causing the area to be very bulky. Further, a weapon carried free style may cause pockets and/or a waistband to sag or the weapon's weight may pull the supporting garment to one side, telegraphing the possibility that a weapon is being carried. Finally, a person using the free carry method will often telegraph the fact that he or she is carrying a concealed weapon by frequently adjusting the position of the weapon as it moves around on the body.

Elastic Medical Aids

These devices are elastic bands made in a variety of sizes to fit a variety of extremities. Small weapons may be inserted under these bands. The ability to conceal the weapon is good, due to the bands ability to tuck the weapon into the body. Even if the band is seen, it will be considered a medical aid and not a concealed carry device.

Officers may see parts of the weapon, especially the grip of a handgun, supported under the band. The handgun's muzzle may also extend past the band. An especially popular carry position is inside the weak side forearm with the grip of the weapon pointed toward the hand. In this position, the weapon is accessible from almost any position. Offenders may use the ploy of crossing their arms at the first sign of danger. This action will normally be perceived as non-threatening, but the weapon will be instantly available. However, vigorously moving the weak arm may cause the weapon to flip out on the ground and additional ammunition (reloads) will often be carried elsewhere on the body.

Naturally, these elastic bands may be worn under an outer garment and tight shirts will often be avoided. Shirts having loose cuffs or stretchable cuffs such as those found on sweatshirts are often favored. The shirt may be shoved back in order to draw the weapon, or the hand will be slipped under the cuff. People with larger forearms may be able to carry larger firearms.

Paper Bag Carry

A variety of weapons can be carried in a paper bag–the limitation is the size of the bag. Naturally, the bag can't be translucent. Further, the weapon may be housed in a holster or free carried inside the bag. The advantage of this technique is the ability to fire the weapon without opening the bag. The

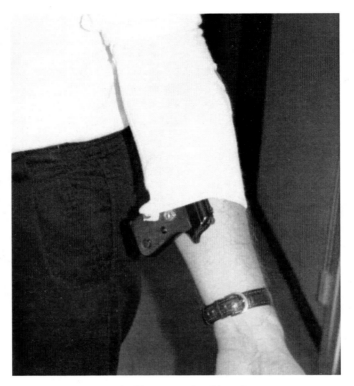

Figure 50. Elastic medical band carry.

offender just stabilizes the handgun, pushes the trigger finger through the bag, and fires. A bag can even be prepared ahead of time, by taping the weapon down and tearing a small hole for finger insertion. Like the other carry methods described, reloads will have to be carried on the body. Normally, the bag will not look threatening and accuracy won't be precise; this is a close-range proposition. Another option is to approach areas with the weapon already in the hand, but still enclosed in the bag.

Cardboard Box Carry

The cardboard box carry is the same as the paper bag carry except that it is not quite as flexible. Offenders may or may not open the box to access the weapon. If firing from the box is chosen, the offender will often prepare the box ahead of time—a hole may be cut for hand access. Further, the weapon is stabilized so that, when the hand is inserted, the weapon is readily available.

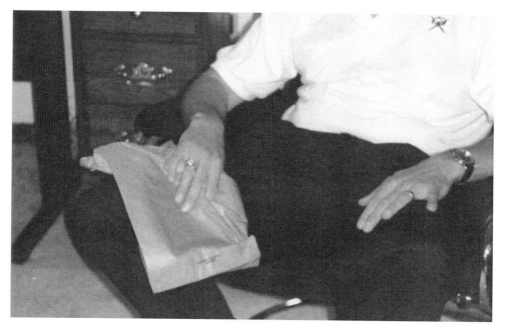

Figure 51. Paper bag carry.

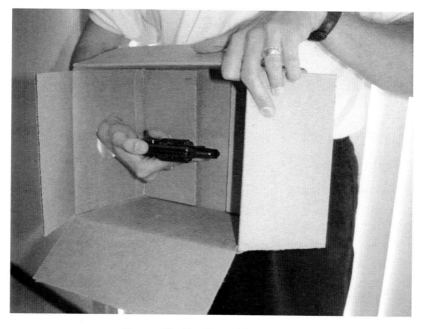

Figure 52. Cardboard box carry.

Figure 53. Garment over-the-hand carry.

Garment Over-the-Hand Carry

This type of carry uses a weapon already held in a firing grip. Usually, the weapon will be cradled in front of the users body by one hand, and a garment is draped over the weapon hand for concealment purposes. The weapon may be fired through the garment or the garment may be flung to the ground just prior to firing.

Briefcase Carry

The briefcase carry is a variety of a purse, day-timer, portfolio, camera bag, and/or camcorder bag carry methods. Any of these devices are commonly observed on courthouse grounds and often attract little, if any, attention. All of these devices offer good concealment, since they house the handgun inside an outer covering that prevents casual observation and printing. These devices also offer the user the option of carrying larger weapons, and more reloads than are usually carried on the body. Further, these devices are not prone to flagging others that a handgun is concealed due to their prevalence in our society.

Figure 54. Briefcase carry.

Figure 55. Portfolio carry.

Vehicle Methods

Vehicles provide a person with a vast number of places to conceal weapons. The following examples represent only a few places where weapons can be concealed. Furthermore, the vehicle itself may be used as a weapon. These examples illustrate why vehicles should be parked in a controlled area.

A weapon may be holstered or free of any covering and simply placed under a vehicle seat. Many people will think this is not carrying, but it is. Many states consider any weapon within "lunging distance" or "arm span," inside a vehicle, as carrying.

A vehicle's glove box is slightly more common and secure than placing a weapon under the seat. This is due to the user's ability to control the weapon by locking the glove box. The size of glove box will dictate the size and number of weapons carried. Further, the weapon may be holstered or free carried in the glove box. A variation of this concealment method is the console carry.

Another possible carry technique consists of placing the weapon in a map pocket. Map pockets are elastic topped pouches or molded indentations found on the lower part of a vehicle's front and back doors. The only security these devices provide is the housing of the weapon in a small area. The size of map pocket will dictate the size of handgun carried.

A rather unique carry method is accomplished by using a Doskocil Hang 'n' Hide. The Hang 'n' Hide is a plastic box fitted with a lock and a strap that is designed to be slipped over a garment pole or hook. The box is large enough to house two or more handguns plus spare ammunition. A garment is hung over the device concealing the system.

A final technique involves a vehicle's trunk. Even though this is not a true concealed carry method, it is an option for transporting a firearm in the general vicinity of the vehicle operator. Indeed, most states do not recognize this method as carrying. When using this method, a great number of weapons, ammunition, and explosives can be transported.

Body Cavity Carry

Some people carry weapons in their body cavities such as in the mouth, between the breast, between the anus cheeks, and/or inside the anal cavity and vagina cavity. Typically, this type of concealed carry is only effective with very small weapons; however, larger weapons may be carried in the vagina by extending part of the weapon into the canal, with the rest supported by the underwear. The weapon may be covered with plastic wrap for hygiene purposes. The mouth carry offers the best accessibility of the body cavity meth-

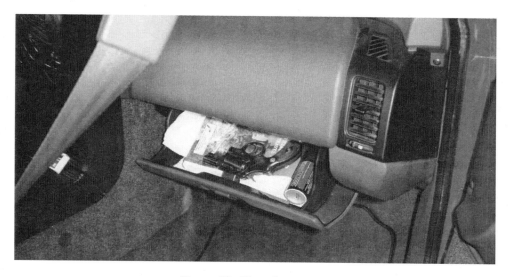

Figure 56. Glove box carry.

Figure 57. Map pocket carry.

ods. Of course, small firearms may be taped under the arm, in the cleavage area of heavily breasted women and/or between the buttocks.

Lanyard Carry

This system is unique to small weapons attached to a key ring-type device that is attached to a lanyard. The lanyard will typically be worn around a person's neck and under an outer garment. When used with athletic apparel, the lanyard may be mistaken for a whistle. For extra control, the weapon may be taped to the chest using medical tape. The weapon may be accessed, by simply pulling the lanyard out of the shirt.

Belt Buckle Carry

This system is also unique to small weapons attached to an ornamental belt buckle or a skeleton type belt buckle. The weapon is held in place by metal clamps. This system may be covered by a pullover type outer garment or left in the open, in hopes the general population will mistake the weapon for an ornament only.

Self-Contained Firearm/Holster Combination Carry

A system unique to the North American Arms revolver is the attachment of the firearm to a plastic device that serves as a carrying device and handgun grip. This plastic device may be clipped to a pocket or carried as a pocket holster. It is effective in avoiding printing, and the device enhances the handling of such small grips found on this small revolver. There are also some leather devices designed to both contain the weapon and enable the user to fire the weapon without withdrawing the weapon.

Hollow Book Carry

Many of these "secret compartment" books are made of actual pages that have been glued together, and hollowed out in the center. A plastic insert is often placed in this hollow space intended to store valuables or small handguns. These books are covered with a variety of titles so no one title is indicative to the carry system. This book is a very effective way to conceal handguns in a car, in briefcases, or when hand carried, etc.

Medical Sling Carry

A weapon can be easily carried in a standard medical sling. The weapon can be inserted between the "injured" forearm and sling material. The

Figure 58. Belt buckle carry. The top view shows a .22 revolver attached to a belt buckle and the bottom portion shows a mounting plate attached to the weapon for a belt buckle.

Figure 59. Self-contained firearm holster with a weapon inside.

weapon's grip will often be facing toward the open end of the sling. The weapon is quick and easy to reach by inserting the opposite hand into the open end of the sling. The "injured" arm may also be pulled free of the sling to provide a two-hand firing grip. A medical sling is very disarming and may give the offender the edge in a violent encounter.

In conclusion, the above carry methods are by no means all inclusive. However, they do represent the majority of concealed carry methods likely to be encountered on a courthouse grounds. Officers and courthouse officials should all be briefed on these concealed carry methods. Any suspicious

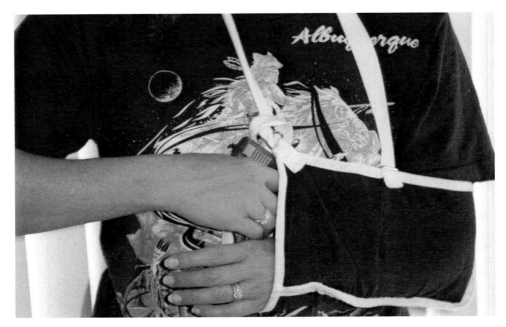

Figure 60. Medical sling carry.

actions or items should be inspected in accordance with courthouse policy and procedures.

Emergency Operations Center (EOC) Operations

In the law enforcement arena, tactical operations will often require the manning of an EOC, tactical operations center (TOC), and a field command post (FCP). For the purposes of this book only, the EOC will be discussed due to the fact that during a courthouse violence crisis response, this is the only location where both the courthouse administrators or courthouse violence crisis response planners/committee members and law enforcement operators will intertwine in order to resolve the crisis.

The EOC should be developed to coordinate all available resources required to deal with courthouse emergencies effectively–to include courthouse violence crisis events, thereby saving lives, avoiding injury, and minimizing economic loss. The EOC should be staffed by personnel responsible for guiding the direction of emergency operations. Staffing is a departmental/courthouse system management function. Their mission is to manage and support the response to emergency situations, keeping required personnel informed about the status and plans for crisis resolution.

The EOC approves the responder's operations order unless compromise procedures are initiated and the EOC also coordinates the responder's request for support or logistics, for example, explosive ordinance personnel, canine handlers, lightly armored vehicles, etc. Finally, the EOC maintains contact with other officials, the media, and public as required. Note: *The EOC is not a command and control element for responders operating in a tactical arena.* To clarify: The EOC approves and orders the mission but does not command and control responder processes or tactics. Support is the key concept.

The EOC may be established anywhere except in the crisis area or mixed in with the TOC. If the EOC is too near the crisis area, its ability to function will be curtailed. Also, if the EOC is set up in conjunction with the Tactical Operations Center (TOC), meddling, confusion and disruption of operations will result. The ideal place for an EOC is in a local government building that may be already equipped with the necessary communications equipment and other support features. How the EOC is made operational and how the response phase is controlled will often determine the success of plan implementation and subsequent effective results. Staffing the EOC may mean as little as moving people out of their offices and down the hall, or it may be as difficult as moving people all over town.

A sequence of steps is required in order to make the EOC fully operational; of course, these steps may vary depending on the scope of the courthouse violence crisis. The following operational steps are common: alert EOC personnel; activate communications equipment and support facilities; initiate the message flow system; ready appropriate logs, maps, and status charts for the operations board; prepare a shift schedule; announce briefing schedules; and provide for necessities.

The alerting process should be clearly stated in the courthouse violence crisis response plan as a standard operating procedure (SOP). A common alerting process requires a chain of calls where one person calls another on an alert roster. If one person cannot be reached, alternate names should be provided to ensure that the EOC is fully staffed. Activating the communications equipment and support facilities normally requires the activation and testing of communications equipment. Activating the support facilities may include anything from starting an emergency power generator to plugging in the coffee pot.

Initiating the message flow system is simply a method of recording messages as they arrive so that they are documented and appropriate/timely action can be taken. Usually all incoming messages are routed through one person who records the messages and forwards them to an operations officer. The operations officer then assigns the responsibility to act on the message to someone within the EOC. The operations officer should then be advised of the action taken. Actions taken should always be recorded and posted. To simplify matters, some type of preprinted form should be developed to document and handle incoming and outgoing messages. The form should be an easily recognizable document and contain space for the members of the staff to take notes. A good format contains the following: title of document; status—incoming or outgoing to include time and date, method of information delivery; name, position, and title of person receiving the information; name, position, and title of person acting on the information; name, position, title, and location of person requesting information; message space; action taken space; and notes space.

This information processing is one of the keys to the success of any courthouse violence crisis response effort. How well personnel perform will often depend upon how well they respond to the information received. Thus, information processing includes how information goes into the EOC, how the information is passed along inside the EOC, and how the information flows out of the EOC. Furthermore, written information is important because it documents the actions taken during the response phase. This information may be referred to in the event verification of actions is required.

It is vital that personnel maintain a log of events within the EOC. Of course, other support documents will also be required such as maps, photographs, videos, drawings, blueprints, and the location of utilities, etc. EOC personnel must be prepared and many of these items should be prepared well in advance of any courthouse violence crisis. It is a good idea to create a set of credentials that will allow only certain personnel access to the EOC.

If the EOC is to be in operation for any length of time, a duty roster should be developed and posted within the EOC so that personnel are not on continuous duty. This schedule should include on and off duty times as well as relief breaks. This is done due to the fact that operations can get very intense and accompanying fatigue is likely. Fatigue of key personnel should be avoided if at all possible.

Briefing schedules should be established and announced as soon as possible. The EOC staff should be briefed when shifts change, and at any other times when situation changes or major events and accompanying decisions are required. It may be a good idea to develop and position an update chart or status board just inside the entrance of the EOC. This action informs newly arriving staff of the situation as well as provides a central place for the staff to update themselves. The media will also need a briefing schedule so that they know when to expect a report from the EOC. Finally, providing for the necessities of operating an EOC includes appropriate food, water, clothing, and housekeeping supplies.

It is essential to control access to the EOC. The EOC is no place for nonessential personnel. The idea is to be able to run the EOC with minimum interference from those who are not part of the emergency management effort. The best way to do this is to have controlled access to the EOC. As soon as the EOC goes into operation, some type of check-in procedure should be established. A guard may be placed at the EOC door to check for EOC credentials and/or an access list. Anyone who does not have credentials and/or is not on the access list should be cleared through the EOC operations officer prior to admittance. Two lists may be required: one list would contain those individuals who have EOC access at any time, while another list may identify individuals who have only limited access to the EOC. It is also a good idea to have some type of sign-in procedure, so that at any time one can tell who is in the EOC. A separate room should be established outside the EOC for media personnel and other visitors. If logistics do not enable the establishment of a separate area, a restricted area may be established inside the EOC to accommodate these personnel. However, they should not be allowed to loiter; once their task is complete, they should be escorted out of the EOC.

In conclusion, once the staff arrives at the EOC, there should be no question as to what they should do. Each staff member should have a personal copy of the EOC standard operating procedures. EOC personnel should be briefed on the situation as soon as possible. This can be done through the use of a quickly prepared handout that is given to them as they sign in or through a general briefing. The initial briefing will normally be brief while follow-up briefings will be more detailed as additional information arrives over the course of the crisis event. The EOC should be placed into operation as soon as physically possible.

Tactical Containment Operations

Courthouse officers, being police officers, quite frequently participate in containment operations in response to natural disasters, accident scenes, crowd control functions, and in support of tactical operations, etc. All of these containment operations have many elements in common; however, tactical containment operations require a variety of unique requirements that must be considered. Poor containment operations can endanger the courthouse population, contiguous civilian population, law enforcement officers, support personnel (firemen, emergency medical technicians, tactical consultants, command, control, communications and intelligence personnel, etc.), and permit adversary attack, reinforcement, and/or escape. Proper containment operations will diminish or avoid many unnecessary situations thus heightening mission success and officer survival.

Once an incident has developed into a containment situation (a subject has taken a defensive posture), e.g., hostage situation, barricaded subject, hostile takeover of an area or valuable asset, etc., immediate steps must be taken to gain control of the situation through the implementation of a tactical containment operation. Containment procedures should be initiated to achieve the following goals: contain the problem in the smallest area possible; confine the perpetrator to his current location; isolate the perpetrator from all outside contact; provide 360-degree observation and fields of fire; and slow down the adversaries action so tactical units can plan and prepare to resolve the crisis through applicable negotiations or tactical actions.

The first officer arriving at or otherwise encountering a crisis scene should perform steps designed to contain and, if possible, confine a perpetrator in the smallest area possible by establishing and maintaining an inner perimeter. This concept is of vital importance to response teams that may have to eventually enter a stronghold (the smaller the area these officers have to search and clear or assault, the safer the operation will be). Smaller areas often enhance logistics, manpower, tactical solutions, team techniques, and time factors, etc., which all directly reflect upon officer survival and may even heighten the chance that hostages may be rescued. Granted, a lone officer will probably be unable to contain a perpetrator completely; however, he can help ensure that the adversary will be contained quickly when additional officers arrive by first, taking cover; second, establishing and maintaining communications with the dispatch section; and third, maintaining surveillance of the perpetrator. The most important goal, at this point, is for the officer to stay alive and to act as an intelligence collector until additional officers arrive.

The inner perimeter should isolate the perpetrator from all outside contact. Outside contact must be controlled or the perpetrator may call for reinforcements from family, friends, or criminal associates, coordinate with the media causing detrimental peripheral problems to develop, or gain sympathy from the general public, etc. The inner perimeter should also provide 360-degree observation and fields of fire (blind spots, dead space, or otherwise unobserved areas may allow the perpetrator to escape, enable the adversary to plan a method of attack, or generate feelings that the perpetrator still possesses some control of the situation). As officers arrive, the initial officer should provide safe approach directions and verbally guide officers into containment positions located on diagonally opposing corners or other configurations in order to gain 360-degree observation and containment.

Finally, the inner perimeter should slow down the adversary's actions and gain tactical units time by (preventing perpetrator escape, generating feelings of surrender vs. deadly confrontation, fostering a willingness to negotiate a solution, etc.). A strong inner perimeter will often enable tactical units the opportunity to thoroughly plan and prepare the resolution of a crisis through applicable negotiations or tactical actions.

Naturally, the size and shape of the inner perimeter will be determined by the location of the suspect, the perpetrators' weaponry, manpower constraints, physical constraints of the target area, and by the physical characteristics of the surrounding area. A perpetrator located on a first floor may have access to multiple escape routes, but may not be able to view very much of the tactical arena. A perpetrator located on a second floor may be able to see more of the tactical arena but may not have many escape routes. A perpetrator located on a rooftop may be able to observe a huge portion of the tactical arena; however, to do this, the perpetrator will often have to silhouette his or her body against the horizon offering a clear target for precision riflemen or containment forces. Plus, there may be no escape routes on a rooftop.

The perpetrators' weaponry will impact the size and shape of the inner perimeter. For example, officers may be able to choose containment positions located closer to the target area, if the perpetrator has a two-inch barreled revolver in lieu of a scoped hunting rifle. Manpower constraints also impact the size and shape of the inner perimeter. For example, multiple adversaries will require more officers to be deployed in order to cover additional threat areas. Furthermore, if fewer officers are available, different containment configurations will have to be chosen in order to provide effective target area coverage.

Physical constraints of the target area will also impact the size and shape of the inner perimeter; for example, a multifloor courthouse will be much more difficult to contain than a single floor court facility. Finally, the physical characteristics of the surrounding area will impact the size and shape of the outer perimeter. For example, heavily wooded areas may allow officers to choose containment positions that are very close to a target area while large open areas (huge mowed lawns, parking lots, etc.), may cause officers to choose containment positions located a great distance from the target area. Of course, armored vehicles or other heavy-duty vehicles may be used in these situations to provide closer containment positions while also providing cover and concealment.

Containment positions may be located in a diagonal shape (on two opposing corners), or square shape for 360 degree coverage, U-shape to cover three sides of an area, or an L-shape to cover two sides of an area. Of course, all of these configurations may afford partial views of other areas. To further develop an inner perimeter, officers should take up positions that afford cover and concealment, permit observation of the largest area possible while avoiding cross-fire situations, cover all possible routes of escape or high-speed avenues of approach, and deploy weapons which can effectively cover required distances; e.g., a two-inch barreled revolver will be of little use deployed 100 yards distant from the contained area. **Note:** Inner perimeter officers should not be tasked to perform any duties that would detract from their primary containment duties.

An ingress/egress (control) point should be established in order to control all personnel moving into or out of the containment area. **Note:** Uncontrolled ingress/egress will weaken containment efforts and may be dangerous (unidentified police personnel may be mistaken for escaping perpetrators). Established control points may also be used as safe routes to evacuate citizens or released hostages, coordinate negotiated deliveries, and facilitate the movement of support personnel. Of course, tactical units may use other avenues of approach other than through an established control point; however, all perimeter personnel must be advised that tactical units are moving inside the area, especially when an assault is underway.

After the inner perimeter is in place, officers should develop an outer perimeter. Outer perimeters are designed to isolate the area of operations, further contain the perpetrator (if a break-out is attempted and the inner perimeter is breached, the outer perimeter acts as a safety net), and prevent unauthorized personnel from entering the area. Of course, more than one outer perimeter may be developed depending on the tactical situation. An inner perimeter coupled with an outer perimeter provides defense in depth both inside and outside the crisis area (layers of officers will have to be penetrated during any escape attempt or penetration from outside assets).

Inner and outer perimeters are actually made up of a series of blocking positions. Blocking positions can be established in two ways: observation and fire, or physical blocking. Observation and fire techniques allow officers to block more than one escape route. A containment position conducive to this technique must allow observation of any movement within an established sector, provide proper cover and concealment, provide clear fields of fire, and be within range of the officers weapon. There is no need to fire a weapon from a location that is beyond the weapon's effective range or the officer's ability to accurately engage a perpetrator. Indeed, doing so may endanger officers located in the general area due to resulting inaccuracy! There is a "golden rule" officers must adhere to in this situation (containment officers should not fire into a stronghold once a tactical team has entered; likewise, tactical teams should not fire outside of the stronghold once they have entered). Violations of this golden rule heighten the chances of friendly fire casualties! Officers must exercise discipline and honor designated areas of responsibility.

Physically blocking a perpetrator involves developing positions that will require the perpetrator to overrun during any escape attempt. Blocking positions should be manned by more than one officer (one officer cannot remain alert at all times especially during operations that become protracted). Indeed, the field commander may have to institute relief systems in order to feed, water, or otherwise take care of officers manning perimeter positions. Physical blocking techniques may require the massing of available materials; utilization of vehicles—especially large trucks, spike sleds, or other tire puncturing devices; utilization of existing terrain features; utilization of existing obstacles, e.g., dumpsters, adjacent buildings, fences, etc. The idea is to completely block the route of travel. Furthermore, physical blocking positions must be under observation and fire techniques at all times. Finally, containment positions are not necessarily static—officers may reposition themselves at night, in order to operate more effectively during the hours of darkness, then move back to the original position for daylight operations.

In conclusion, proper containment operations protect the courthouse population, civilian population, law enforcement officers, support personnel (firemen, emergency medical technicians, tactical consultants, command, control, communications and intelligence personnel, etc.); thwart adversary attack, reinforcement, or escape attempts. Furthermore, proper containment operations will diminish or avoid many unnecessary situations, e.g., crossfires. Finally, proper containment operations will heighten mission success, and the chances of officer survival.

Responding to Explosive Devices

The intent of this section is not to train officers on how to construct or use explosives, but instead, to increase their awareness and ability to search for certain explosive devices. This new knowledge concerning an explosive device threat will enable officers to be prepared through preconceived response procedures and safety guidelines to prevent inadvertent initiation. This skill may well mean the difference between life, death, suffering, or serious injury when an explosive device is encountered.

Many courthouse violence crisis response incidents have included the threat or actual use of explosive devices. In the last completed statistics published by the ATF during the five-year period of 1993–1997, there were a total of 13,510 actual and attempted incendiary or explosive bombings nationwide. A notable majority of these actions (10,318) involved the use of explosives. During this period, 314 people lost their lives; 2,915 were injured; and property damage ran into the millions.

The most common types of containers were pipe bombs and bottles. Dynamite sticks, cans, boxes, pressurized cartridges, and grenade hulls were also used. An FBI 1995 Summary focusing on explosive devices stated that pipe bombs accounted for 31 percent of all improvised explosive devices. The most common explosive filler used in bombs include flammable liquid, chemicals, photoflash and fireworks powders, black powder, commercial high explosives, smokeless powders, match heads, blasting agents, C4 and TNT. Dynamite and black powder ranked at the top of the list as being the most stolen high explosives.

Explosive devices are attractive to some offenders because they do not necessarily require sophisticated explosives, controlled or hard-to-obtain components, or materials. The deadliness of an explosive device is limited only by the builder's imagination. Further, explosive devices generate considerable media attention when discovered or detonated, and provide an easy impersonal means of causing damage, injury, death, or terror without the perpetrator's presence. A single explosive device can receive more publicity than many murders and it may take considerable time, assets, and effort for authorities to catch the perpetrator. Explosive devices are particularly vicious because they do not discriminate between intended or unintended targets—they are solely designed to neutralize targets of opportunity. Finally, officers involved in a courthouse violence response operation must be aware of the possibility that explosive devices may be deployed in the target area. An officer should always look before acting.

Prerequisites for Explosive Device Deployment

Before a person deploys an explosive device, he or she must first develop a motive. After a motive has been established, three basic conditions must be satisfied in order to field a device. First, the perpetrator must have the know-how to construct and deploy the device. Second, he or she must have access to explosives or the raw material from which the explosive device can be made, and third, he or she must have the opportunity to place the device at the desired target area. The threat of explosive device use is great today because each of these prerequisites can usually be satisfied.

Explosive Device Information Sources

Information concerning how-to-build many types of explosive devices is easily accessed and readily available to the public. A number of specialty publishers produce books devoted to the subject showing how-to-build booby-traps using improvised materials, commercial products or surplus military components. Another source of information are military manuals; for example U.S. Army Manual, FM5-36. Military manuals can be purchased over the counter at any number of Army surplus stores, found in yard sales, or obtained from the personal libraries of armed forces veterans.

Not only are books or pamphlets available, the INTERNET is also becoming a major source for this type of information; for example, in 1992, booby-trap plans were posted on a computer bulletin board. This booby-trap information was first gathered by college students, then high school students. As a result, this specific booby-trap was popularized, experimented with, and/or actually deployed a number of times. This device, known as a Drano bomb, pool acid bomb, or soda bottle bomb consisted of a one or two liter plastic or 16 ounce glass soft drink bottle, locally available acid, and metal filler. As the acid and metal interact, they rapidly produce hydrogen gas within the capped bottle. Usually, within 15 to 90 seconds, the bottle will shatter, showering the immediate area with acid and fragments from the container. In addition, if an ignition source (open flame) is close to the detonation area, the escaping hydrogen gas will explode into a large fireball. Furthermore, acid residue may burn the skin, destroy clothing, or damage equipment and property. This device became so popular that it was adopted for use by some crack house operator's. The device was designed to function when entry teams kicked in a door. Once initiated, this device cannot be stopped, or if it misfires, cannot be safely approached by officers due to the danger it may still explode (bomb technicians can render this device safe).

Explosive Device Use

Explosive devices may be used to provide a number of functions; for example, to warn the perpetrator that someone is approaching. This warning enables the offender to choose between the options of fighting, fleeing, or a combination of the two. If the perpetrator has ample advanced warning and the desire, he or she may choose to fight, if for only a brief period of time before fleeing. The idea may be to cause additional injury or death through the use of small arms fire prior to making an escape or committing suicide. If a number of perpetrators are present, they may decide to spring a hasty ambush on the approaching officers. After all, once an explosive device has been tripped the adversaries will know that response personnel are in the area and their direction of approach.

Explosive devices may also be used to impede access. The first device triggered may cause the response team leader to choose an alternate route costing the police time and gaining the offender time. Also, the first device triggered will certainly cause officers to initially stop, then proceed slowly, while looking for additional devices. Explosive devices may also be used to slow or stop the police pursuit of a suspect, the perpetrator may plan an escape route which goes directly through an area seeded with explosive devices. The perpetrator will know where the devices are, but pursuing officers will not. When pursuing officers trip the first explosive device, all officers will, at a minimum, slow down or even discontinue further pursuit.

Explosive Device Construction

An explosive device may consist of a stolen military device, a clever well-constructed device, or may be a crude device, as dangerous to the maker as the intended victim. Explosive devices may be constructed from stolen military components, purchased commercial components, or from improvised components; for example, common household commodities and common chemicals can be used for making improvised components. Improvised components include cheap commonly available components such as gunpowder, household chemicals, farming chemicals, lumber, batteries, pipes, and common electrical wire.

Firebombs

Various types of chemical firebombs can also serve as supplements or substitutions for explosive devices. These devices often consist of bottles containing flammable liquids designed to break or otherwise mix, when dropped. One such device consists of a container filled with a chemical and wrapped in paper or cloth soaked with another chemical that will ignite upon contact. This is known as a binary device—both chemicals may be stable by themselves, but once mixed become unstable. The attractiveness of this device is found in the ease and safety of transport to the target area (the reacting chemicals are kept separate until the device is deployed). Another device consists of a light bulb, modified to contain gasoline or explosive compound, once an electric charge is introduced into the improvised filler an explosion or fire will result.

Explosive Device Initiation

Initiation of some kind is necessary to "set-off" all explosive devices, and runs the gambit from simple to complex. Explosive devices may be initiated by mechanical, electrical, chemical, or a combination of these triggering devices. No attempt has been made to cover all existing triggering devices since, like explosive devices, the amount and combinations of triggering devices available is limited only by the builder's imagination. **Note:** mechanical and electrical triggers are by far the most common initiators.

Mechanical Triggers

Mechanical triggers set the explosive device into motion through the physical relation of force and matter. Examples of mechanical triggers include pull types—a fine wire attached to the triggering device, pressure types—spring loaded device designed to fire when pressed, and pressure release types—a spring loaded striker armed when pressure is applied and fired when pressure is released.

Electrical Triggers

Electrical triggers set an explosive device into motion through the use of a power source, usually batteries. Electrical triggers are popular due to their capability of firing several devices in a chain reaction—almost simultaneous fashion. The number of devices fired is limited only by the power of the electrical current and the capability of the wire to carry the current.

Chemical Triggers

Chemical triggers set an explosive device into motion through the use of a chemical reaction. Corrosives such as acid are often used in chemical triggers. An example consists of a binary device: as the acid eats through a barrier material, two flame-producing chemicals interact causing fire. Chemical triggers may be used when a consistent time delay isn't necessary. A great deal of expertise is required to obtain consistent short duration time delays.

Combination Triggers

Combination triggers consist of different types of triggers working in conjunction with one another, for example, a pull-type electric trigger, pressure-electric device, or magnetic-electric device. A pull type-electric trigger is initially activated by the mechanics of pulling to allow an electric source to initiate the actual device. A pressure-electric trigger is initially set off by the mechanics of pressure to allow an electric source to initiate the actual device, and a magnetic-electric device is initially set off by the mechanics of pulling the magnet from its position allowing an electric source to initiate the actual device. Combination triggers are sometimes used by perpetrators as built in safety devices.

Multiple Triggers

Multiple triggers are stand-alone triggers attached to an explosive device acting as a back-up to another trigger or to booby-trap an explosive device. When used as a back-up, if one trigger fails, the other trigger may initiate the device. Multiple triggers serve as a very good reason for letting only "Bomb Technicians" disarm booby-traps.

Discovering and Reacting to Explosive Devices

Explosive devices may or may not look like dangerous devices and may or may not be concealed. The thoroughness of any search and likelihood of success depends on the skill of the searchers and the ingenuity of the perpetrator. To avoid explosive devices, the officer needs to know where they are likely to be deployed.

Explosive devices may be used as point defense devices, most useful for blocking an approach or defending a specific place. Perpetrators may place a few explosive devices at the side of a hallway where officers may seek cover during an operation. Hallways and other approach routes such as stairways and roof hatches are logical places to place explosive devices. Any gate or doorway is also a logical place to put an explosive device, because the suspect knows exactly where the officer will be upon passing through.

Explosive Device Recognition

Even though perpetrators who utilize explosive devices have devious minds, and they disguise their work cleverly, there are some telltale signs. First is location; the officer must be very suspicious and alert around any access point leading into a suspected area. Second is physical evidence—naturally if a trip wire is visible, the officer must be cautious. Remember, just because a trip wire has been discovered doesn't mean the explosive device has been located—the trip wire only represents the triggering device. The explosive device may be very close to the discovering officer or a fair distance away; indeed, other officers may actually be closer to the explosive device than the officer discovering the trip wire. Some bombers use secondary or even a third device designed to injure, kill, and hamper as many law enforcement officers and first responders and civilians as possible.

A light piece of cloth may be used by an officer to detect a trip wire; for example, the cloth is held at arm's length and moved slowly from the ground to waist high, then waist high to over the head in an attempt to brush against and reveal any hidden trip wires. Many times an officer can squat or lay on the floor looking upward in order to silhouette a trip wire against dark-colored objects. Flashlights may be valuable for spotting booby traps in darkened areas. Mirrors are also valuable for looking into small or other hard to observe areas. Mirrors may also be used to reflect light into dark areas.

Officers should also look for abnormal depressions in the floor; these may suggest tampering with the structure. Officers should be wary of any rearranged objects; a pile of papers observed in a particular spot where there are no other papers may hide an explosive device. Further, imprints on the floor from recently moved objects such as filing cabinets, a desk, office equipment, etc., may represent a warning sign that objects have been moved to other locations. Officers must be wary of any object or area which channels foot traffic into a specific area; for example, a filing cabinet may be placed in a hallway to either conceal an explosive device designed to initiate if the filing cabinet is moved or the filing cabinet obstacle may be designed to force officers to circumvent the object and thus walk into an explosive device.

Officers should also look for shiny objects, colors, shapes, and other suspicious items. Finally, officers must be suspicious of inconsistent odors and lack of movement and follow "gut feelings." An explosive device may contain a component that is highly reflective which the criminal may not realize during the set-up process. The reflection may also only occur during certain parts of the day according to the sun's position or the use of a structure's lights. An officer should look for colors that are inconsistent with the area. Electrical wires are often brightly colored and other parts of an explosive device may be brightly colored as well. If a color is inconsistent with the immediate area, beware!

The officer should be wary of items not normally found in certain areas. Officers should take note of discarded empty packages and be especially observant to what they originally contained. These empty packages could mean explosive devices are in the area. Officers must be wary of any item apparently left behind; it may be an explosive device. Often, attractive boxes, pornographic magazines, bogus documents, possible evidence, etc. will be left behind to either conceal an explosive device or be an explosive device.

Officers should use their sense of smell; petroleum based products used in incendiary devices may be detected by their odor. Officers should look for unnatural movement or lack of movement; for example, a fan may move objects supporting an explosive device in a different direction than surrounding items or the weight of an explosive device may hold an item still while the air moves other items. Again, officers should follow their "gut feeling"; if something doesn't look or feel right, it probably isn't right. Any object or condition perceived to be out of place should be viewed with suspicion.

Officers should suspect packages that are lopsided, have protruding wires or string, have oily stains on the wrapper, emit strange odors, lack a return address, appear to be excessively heavy, are addressed to titles only, display no names, are directed to incorrect titles, have visual distractions, have foreign postmarks, have air mail markings, are marked special delivery, possess restrictive markings such as addressed to confidential personnel, have postage that has not been canceled, are secured by excessive packing tape, and/or have addresses that are poorly typed or handwritten.

Officers may receive a bomb threat over the phone so they must be ready to gather as much information as possible. As many phones as possible should be capable of caller identification. When a bomb threat is received, an officer should at a minimum log the number at which the call was received, the length of the call, time of the call, and date of the call. The exact words of the threat should be reported. The officer receiving the bomb threat should also ask the following questions: When is the bomb going to explode? Where is the bomb? What does the bomb look like? What kind of bomb is it? What will cause the bomb to explode? Did you place the bomb? Why did you place the bomb? Where are you? What is your name? Frequently, the more information the caller leaves, the more the threat should be taken seriously.

Officers receiving a bomb threat should also listen and try to determine the caller's sex, age, and note any accent. The caller's speech should be evaluated for the following mannerisms: calm, angry, excited, slow, rapid, soft, loud, laughing, crying, normal, distinct, slurred, nasal, stutter, lisp, raspy, deep, ragged, throat clearing, deep breathing, cracking voice, disguised, foreign, and/or familiar. If the voice sounds familiar, whose voice did it sound like?

Officers should also listen for background sounds, for example, street noise (buses, cars, etc.); airplanes; voices; PA systems; music; household (dishes, TV, etc.); motors (fans, air conditioners, etc.); office or factory machinery; animal noises; clear, static connection; local or long distance call, phone booth, or any other noise that is distinct. The officer should also listen to the language and note if it is well spoken (educated), foul, irrational, incoherent, taped, or if the message is being read. Finally, all phones should have a Bomb Threat Aid card located next to the phones in order for a person to fill in boxes and areas depicting the above information. If possible, the officer should fill out the card while on the phone; if not, the card should be filled out as soon as possible after the caller hangs up. All of the above information should be reported to first responders. This information may very well cause an administrator to request a bomb search.

Searching for Explosive Devices

Officers should not succumb to the movie or television tactics of having the perpetrator search for an explosive device. Remember, the perpetrator may be suicidal and deliberately trip the device or the perpetrator may make a mistake and injure or kill him or herself and the accompanying officer. The act of letting a perpetrator actively search for an explosive device, voluntary or not, will likely be viewed by the public the same as soldiers using prisoners of war to walk through mine fields—a definite war crime. Of course, there is nothing wrong with interviewing the perpetrator to ascertain the presence, type, description, working mechanism, and location of an explosive device.

Note: except for the most unusual circumstances, bomb technicians do not perform searches. In fact, in some large metropolitan areas, local bomb teams do not even respond to a bomb threat until a suspicious object is discovered. Indeed, even Army explosive ordnance teams (EOD) are prohibited by Army regulations from searching any building or area.

Bombs are usually found in places where the public has general access. Bombers choose to set explosives in public areas because there is a low probability that the act will be discovered by courthouse security personnel. These general access areas include restrooms, public corridors, conference rooms, probation areas, and courtrooms. While court personnel are not qualified to conduct searches for bombs, their familiarity with their work areas should enable them to detect items which do not belong or are suspicious. If such items are detected, they should not be touched or moved; security personnel should be notified.

It is the duty and responsibility of the judge, police supervisors, or other designated authority to decide whether an explosive device search will be conducted; if so, the search must be planned, organized, and implemented through the use of trained personnel. A variety of conventional bomb searching methods can be used; a common technique follows:

First, the building should be broken down into segments (room by room) and established search patterns should be developed. Search patterns enable searchers to conduct methodical thorough searches designed to avoid the likelihood of missing devices that unorganized random searches often generate. Second, and perhaps the main ingredient for an indoor booby-trap search is "trained search teams." These search teams should contain officers who are trained in search techniques and explosive device recognition. Once the search team is formed, officers will need to make sure the effected area and adjacent areas have been evacuated.

Standard operating procedures should direct the practice of conducting the search from an established exterior perimeter to the buildings interior and from bottom levels to top levels. One team may be formed and assigned the task of searching the outside of the target area and another team assigned the indoor search. Outdoor searches should begin at ground level and focus on ledges, ornamental facings, porches, overhangs, trashcans, shrubbery, and parked vehicles. The outdoor search team must be very cautious since the adversary will know that many of the areas listed above will be searched by police officers during the collection of evidence. The outdoor search should be conducted before the indoor team approaches the building. This procedure will clear the way for the indoor search team to approach the building.

The indoor search team should approach the building when the outdoor search team has given the "all clear." Before entering the building, the indoor search team should peer into windows and any other points of observation and scan the interior for obvious devices or suspicious areas and items. When entering a building, it may be best for the search team to enter through a non-traditional point such as a window. Officers must be conscious of the difference between nontraditional points of entry and seldom-used points of entry. Nontraditional points of entry, such as upper story windows, usually won't have explosive devices attached to them, but seldom used entry points such as alternate doors to the same area are logical areas for explosive device placement. Multiple doors to the same area enable the perpetrator to choose which door(s) to booby-trap and which one(s) to use as a primary ingress and egress point. Note: if a suspect is observed leaving an area through a window instead of a door, it is a safe bet that the building contains one or more explosive devices.

Once the building has been successfully entered, rooms will have to be searched. The best technique for room searches is the utilization of two man teams—one member will be in charge of the area searched. Once again, the search team should look into the room prior to entry. If the room's lights will be used, the officer must first examine the switch for signs of tampering—paint chipped off retaining screws, uneven or crooked cover plate alignment, visible wires, etc. Be advised that the light switch may be used as a triggering device for an explosive device. Next, the officer should examine the light fixtures for visible wires or devices affixed to light sockets. The light bulb itself should be examined for solid or liquid fillers. One popular light socket booby-trap involves filling a light bulb with explosives or gasoline; when the light switch is turned on the electric current will fire the device. Finally, the light switch should be operated from outside the room, if possible, by reaching into the room in lieu of complete entry. The officers may decide to search the room with the extensive use of flashlights—a difficult procedure.

Upon entry, the room should be divided into two equal parts or as near equal as possible. This equal division should be based on the number and type of objects in the room to be searched and not on the size of the room. An imaginary line is then drawn between two objects in the room, e.g., the edge of the window on the south wall to the desktop on the north wall. Next, the average height of the majority of items resting on the floor should be noted. This procedure establishes the first searching height, usually from the floor to waist high, or to the working level of the room such as desktops.

Both searchers should begin at one end of the room—the starting point, and start from a "back-to back" position. Searchers must walk softly checking for trip wires, bulges in carpeting or area rugs, or unevenness in other floor coverings. Next, searchers should check all items on the floor around the wall

Figure 61. Officers beginning an indoor bomb search.

area, scanning in a horizontal sweep. **Warning:** nothing should be inadvertently moved, tilted, jarred, or lifted! "Hands off scanning" is the order of the day. When the searchers meet at the opposite end of the room, the middle of the room is checked upward to the preselected height.

Searchers then return to the original starting point and select a second search height, usually from waist height to the top of the head. The second search is conducted in the same manner as the first and usually covers pictures on the walls, tall table lamps, cabinets, etc. When cabinets, doors, or drawers are manipulated, one should slightly open the area of concern and peer inside with the aid of a flashlight, then inch-by-inch check for signs of an explosive device until the area is cleared. Fiber optic scopes are excellent tools for looking into areas without disturbing contents or surfaces.

Again returning to the starting point, searchers begin a third search height, normally from the top of the searchers' heads to the ceiling. Areas to be searched include air conditioning/heating ducts, hanging light fixtures, intercom ports, etc. The final search pattern includes returning to the starting point and searching the area above false or suspended ceilings, attics, lofts, etc. When the final search pattern is completed, the room should be marked to ensure that no rooms or areas were overlooked. Indeed, some departments require search teams to trade areas and perform a redundant or back-up search.

If while conducting any of the above search patterns, the searching officer discovers an explosive device or suspected explosive device, he should freeze, sound the alarm–avoid using the radio, clear the area, mark the area (with tape, paint, felt markers, signs, etc.), isolate the area, and notify police supervision who, in turn, will notify the bomb technicians or explosive ordnance personnel. If absolutely necessary, place sandbags, bomb blankets, mattresses, etc. around the suspicious object, but do not attempt to cover the object. ***Do not attempt deactivation–this is a job for specially trained and experienced personnel!*** Upon arrival, bomb technicians will take appropriate action with any object determined to be of a suspicious nature.

The above search method represents only one of many methods and may be used to search any enclosed area. If another search method is chosen, it must possess the same methodical and careful steps. As the reader can imagine, indoor searches are dangerous, time and manpower consuming, and best left to specially trained personnel.

Searching for Explosive Devices in Vehicles

The number of triggers, types of explosive devices, deployment locations, and complexity of remote entry procedures make vehicle searches more dangerous than searching outdoor locations or the interior of buildings. The only advantage a vehicle search has over the aforementioned locations is the condensed search area. ***Note: only personnel specifically trained in bomb disposal and vehicle search procedures should physically search a suspect vehicle.*** Officers should conduct only a "hands off" visual scan of the suspect vehicle and surrounding area. According to ATF statistics gathered from 1993 to 1997, the prime locations for attaching a bomb to a vehicle are in or under car seats, under the vehicle frame, in or around the gas tank, and in wheel wells.

Visually searching a vehicle should follow the same procedural pattern as searching a building. The officer should start the search at an established perimeter: 50–75 yards is often used as a reference distance. Perimeter searches should start and finish at the same point; begin at ground level and focus on dumpsters, trashcans, shrubbery, and other parked vehicles. The vehicle should never be touched or otherwise moved, and officers should avoid using radios near the vehicle.

Next, the exterior of the vehicle should be scanned. The officer should look for mud, dirt, or snow knocked loose from the underside of the vehicle. An excess of vehicle fluids located underneath the vehicle should be noted; this may signal vehicle tampering. Ground impressions should be evaluated for the possibility that someone knelt or laid next to or under the vehicle. Handprints, fingerprints, and other smudges on a dusty or muddy exterior may signal tampering. The exterior of the vehicle should also be scanned for fresh signs of forced entry or tampering around the doors, window seals, hood, trunk, hatch latches, gas tank cap, hub caps, or wheel covers. Finally, all loose wires or strands of wires located around the vehicle's lighting systems should be treated as suspicious.

Next, the officer should scan the interior of the vehicle through all of the windows and windshield. A flashlight should be used to illuminate the floorboards and other dark areas. Particular attention should be paid to vehicle operating pedals, switches, door panels, and storage areas. Unusual packages or items located inside the vehicle should be noted.

Finally, the officer may check the underside of the vehicle by using a small hand-held mirror or larger inspection mirror. If the mirror image is dark, the officer may shine a flashlight onto the mirror's face and reflect the light into the area of concern. The mirror inspection should be conducted slowly and thoroughly, beginning at the front of the vehicle, moving from one side to the other, then rearward. Particular attention should be paid to the engine compartment, exhaust system, fender wells, both sides of tires, under bumpers, top of the drive train, under the gasoline tank, and other crevices. If a suspicious item is observed in the mirror, another officer should look into the mirror and state consensus—some officers are aware of what car parts look like, others do not. If while conducting any of the above search patterns, the searching officer discovers an explosive device or suspected explosive device, the same process should be employed as described in the section above.

Bomb Dogs

Bomb dogs may be a valuable asset when searching for explosive devices; however, they may also be a hindrance. For example, dogs can trip booby-traps the same as their human counterpart. If explosive booby-traps are

Figure 62. Officers training on how to perform a bomb search of a vehicle.

expected in an area, dogs may be useful in detecting them by odor. However, remember that a booby-trap may not incorporate an explosive compound for the dog to detect.

Perhaps the most effective bomb dog breeds are Labrador retrievers, spaniels, and German shepherds. Through training, these dogs learn to shut out all odors except the odor they are trained to detect, even when other overpowering odors are in the area. Perpetrators may try to confuse or otherwise disguise an odor by lacing the area with pepper or other irritants. Normally, these actions will only cause the dog's nose to run and actually, once the dog has finished sneezing and the mucus has cleared, the dog's sense of smell may be enhanced. Note that a dog working alone is useless, but when teamed with a competent dog handler, a dog is often an effective resource.

Reacting to Explosive Devices

The first action the officer must perform upon seeing something that appears to be an explosive device is FREEZE. Next, announce in a loud voice, "device or booby-trap." This is accomplished as a warning to alert other officers that an explosive device has been found and that more devices may be in the area. Other officers in the area should also freeze and resist the temptation of rushing over to the discovering officer's position in order to see the device. Not only may the officers' rushing over to the discovered explosive device's location set off another device, but the discovered device may be command detonated. The perpetrator may be watching and waiting for officers to "bunch up," then detonate the device.

Officers must look carefully around the area before taking another step in any direction. Never assume that the trip-wire, trigger, or device discovered is the only one in the area. The best thing to do is to leave the device alone, mark it, work around it, and send for a bomb technician to disarm it. One way to mark an explosive device is with a spray can of paint to ensure that the discovering officers and others will see it upon return for disarming procedures. Plastic ribbon, string, or crepe paper make good marking tools. If retreat from the area is the chosen option, the officers must make every attempt to exactly retrace their steps.

If an explosive device has been discovered the hard way, "tripped," all officers should FREEZE. Rushing to cover or throwing oneself to the floor may set-off other devices. Next, announce in a loud voice where the device was and if there are any casualties. Other officers in the area should also freeze and resist the temptation of rushing over to assist injured officers. Officers rushing over to the wounded officers' location may set off additional devices, resulting in more casualties. Assisting officers should be quickly designated (usually the closest officers to the scene) and look carefully around the area before taking another step in any direction. Never assume that the tripped explosive device is the only device in the area! Assisting officers should plan a route to the injured officer and work slowly and methodically while negotiating the area. When retreating from the area, the officers must make every attempt to exactly retrace their steps. Naturally, civilian medical personnel should be alerted and stationed at a safe location. Requiring civilian personnel to enter the booby-trapped area is not a good option.

If the urgency of a situation requires that the officer immediately do something with the device, they must work carefully, placing personal safety first. Officers should remove any hats, unnecessary equipment, loose equipment, loose clothing, etc. before working around an explosive device. Unnecessary equipment and loose items may snag or hit the device setting it off.

Next officers must conduct a "hands-off" scan of the triggering device and explosive device before touching anything. Never try to deactivate an explosive device alone; always work, at a minimum, in a two-man team configuration. A team concept generates both a psychological and physical advantages. Two men will conduct a more thorough search and personal security is heightened. An officer can never be sure that, while all of their attention is on the device, a suspect won't attack. The officer needs someone to watch his or her back and perimeter while operating in the tactical arena. Always leave disarming an explosive device to the experts!

An explosive device may be moved in lieu of disablement because trying to disable or dismantle a device is tricky and the officer might set it off during the attempt. Another problem is that the officer may not find all of the triggers leading to the device. If the officer must move the device, the simplest way is to attach a light rope or wire to it and pull the device from a safe distance, while remaining behind cover. Do not succumb to curiosity and watch the device, if the officer can see the device, he certainly isn't behind cover. Remember, even a device that appears to be nonexplosive may be a ruse.

Before any device is moved, all officers in the area should be warned, accounted for, and assume a covered position. Next, the officer must check the entire area for additional trip-wires, and examine each end of any trip wire found because a chain of devices may be wired together. Other officers may be in the vicinity of these connected devices. Never cut any electric wire found until the officer knows what is at the end of it. If the wire is part of a firing circuit, cutting it will deactivate the device; however, if it is part of an arming circuit, cutting it will activate the device. The officer should never pull a slack wire or cut a taught wire. Leave the tripping or disarming of an explosive device to the experts!

Explosive Device Training Courses

The author strongly recommends all officers involved in courthouse crisis response operations attend an explosive device familiarization class. Good explosive device courses are few and far between. When considering a class, look at the following areas: class focus, length of class, class displays, instructor's background, practice exercise "jungle walk," and an emphasis on teamwork.

In conclusion, the odds are against encountering an explosive device, but if an officer becomes the unlucky one, knowledge is the first line of defense. Knowledge of personal limitations will also keep an officer safe by accepting the concept that dismantling an explosive device is a job for a specialist. Keep these points in mind, and the chances of officer survival are greatly enhanced.

Specialty Impact Munitions

Specialty Impact Munitions (SIM) are becoming sterling examples of less-lethal systems that may be ideal for use in a courthouse. One definition widely preferred by law enforcement personnel concerning less-lethal systems is stated as follows: "A weapon system or device that, when properly applied, can stop the undesirable action of an individual and induce compliance by means that have a low probability of producing lethal effects." The concept of a SIM is the reduction of the number of fatalities produced in encounters where lethal force was previously acceptable and within the rules of engagement. When a less-lethal munition is used as the first round, knowledgeable courts and investigative boards frequently recognize this action as a legitimate attempt to avoid lethal injury. Indeed, the desired effect should be incapacitation of the intended subject to a point which allows officers to take control of the situation, and make a decision on what follow-up actions are required.

SIM are not new; as early as the 1960s American law enforcement organizations were experimenting with and using SIM with varying degrees of success. For example, wooden baton rounds were used to quell riots and the first "beanbag" rounds appeared. Recent years have seen a great deal of interest placed on SIM, resulting in increased research and subsequent new developments. For example, a great interest in SIM has resulted from the rising occurrence rate of "Victim Precipitated Suicide" or "Suicide By Police" and other frequent encounters with mentally disturbed individuals. Victim precipitated suicide is a clinical term for the action of an individual who chooses to be killed by law enforcement personnel as an alternative to a conventional suicide. Keep in mind that these individuals are very dangerous because they may kill a law enforcement officer in the process of achieving their goal.

SIM addresses the dangerous gap that exists in the range of use of force tools generally available to police officers. Historically, the most common use of force tools, the baton and firearm, were found to be too weak or too strong in many response situations. Thus, officers may have to choose an unnecessarily strong response for lack of an effective alternate weapon. Additionally, SIM are extremely valuable use of force tools designed to provide effective law enforcement while at the same time minimizing the risk to life. Finally, SIM can be viewed as an alternative to deadly force and as an effective tool designed to subdue subjects with little or no harm.

SIM offer a viable choice in controlling target specific situations and civil disturbance situations. Target specific situations include barricaded subjects and the arrest of some violent subjects. Statistics reveal that the majority of incidents where SIM are used involve suicidal subjects. As stated above, many of these situations include "suicide by police situations." SIM may be utilized to arrest violent subjects armed with knives or other nonfirearm-type weapons. Finally, SIM may be used to arrest subjects brandishing firearms in a nonthreatening manner. In civil disturbance situations, SIM may be used to disperse a crowd, deny access to an area, and discourage looting. SIM may also be used to target a specific individual who is providing motivation or otherwise instigating civil disorder. SIM should be considered an extended range impact weapon serving in the role of the traditional police baton to control the subject's behavior through pain compliance. Indeed, record numbers of police agencies are intending to deploy SIM devices/systems that incapacitate subjects from expended ranges.

Specialty Impact Munitions (SIM) have many classifications and descriptions which require differentiation. **Note:** a particular SIM may have more than one classification. SIM are generally classified under the following headings: high and low energy, flexible projectile, nonflexible projectile, rigid projectile, single projectile, multiple projectile, direct fire projectile, indirect fire projectile, and method of delivery.

High and low energy refers to the projectile's movement or speed and should not be confused with the degree of force that the projectile delivers to the target. Flexible projectiles are generally composed of powdered lead, lead shot, gelatin-like substances, silica housed inside a heavy cloth, canvass, or nylon bags, or flexible foam rubber. Characteristically, flexible projectiles are designed to be direct fired (see below) and conform to the contour of the surface they strike. Common projectile velocities typically travel in the 200–300 feet-per-second range.

Nonflexible or rigid projectiles are generally composed of rigid or semi-rigid materials such as wood, rubber, plastic, or dense foam material. Rigid projectiles should be relegated to the role of indirect fire (their hardness may cause serious bodily harm to include death). Common velocities for these projectiles typically travel in the 200–1000 feet-per-second range. Nonflexible projectiles may be loaded as a single projectile that are generally intended to be used as a indirect fire munition (some exceptions may be encountered; always follow the manufacturer's warnings and directions), whereas multiple projectiles are often intended to be skip fired or in some circumstances, direct fire deployed.

Direct fire projectiles, sometimes referred to as target specific projectiles, are fired directly at a subject. Direct fire munitions typically provide superior targeting capabilities. Indirect fire projectiles, sometimes known as skip fire munitions, are deployed approximately three to six feet in front of a subject(s). Typically, once these projectiles impact an area in front of a target, they will ricochet into the target at about the same angle of initial impact (**Note:** the greater the angle of deflection, the greater the decrease in velocity). Of course, the impacting surface must be conducive to producing ricochets, e.g., asphalt, concrete, stairwell landings, hallways, or other hard surfaces. Naturally soft dirt, mud, sand, grass, weeds, carpet, etc. will often disperse the projectiles energy or, at the very least, overcome any tendency to ricochet. In some limited instances, indirect fire may consist of a high angle lob delivery method. In civil disturbances situations, wooden baton rounds are sometimes fired high into the air above the crowds head in order to produce a lob effect. This procedure generates what is termed as wooden rain.

Police officers are increasingly encountering unconventional situations such as suicide assistance by police, or armed subjects directly threatening no one but refusing to put down their weapon, etc. These situations often do not

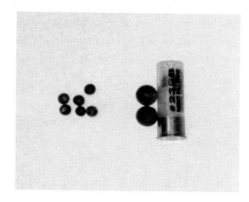

Figure 63. SIM projectiles: 12 gauge rubber buckshot and balls.

Figure 64. 37 mm SIM projectiles, left-to-right, foam rubber and wooden projectiles.

Figure 65. Cut-away view of a 37 mm foam SIM round.

call for the use of deadly force and accompanying deadly weapon platforms. Furthermore, many other use of force tools such as batons and chemical aerosol sprays are not practical options when the suspect is armed (leaving cover and closing the distance to the perpetrator often places the officer in range of the subjects weapon). Additionally, closing the distance to the subject increases both officer's and subject's jeopardy (the officer may be in range of the subject's weapon and the subject may feel forced to act as officers approach). Remember, officers may have the best of intentions but actually play a role in a fatal outcome that will certainly generate public criticism and possible litigation. This is not to say that direct intervention isn't the right thing to do.

Indeed, when properly used, less lethal options such as SIM can assist in these circumstances by avoiding tactics that are unsafe, avoiding actions performed outside accepted police practices and training, avoiding an outcome that is in conflict with the primary objective, and reducing the likelihood of death or serious injury to all involved. Finally, SIM should be considered as just another tool, an additional option to consider when seeking the successful resolution of certain critical incidents.

In the author's opinion, SIM will one day be as prominent in the field as an officer's sidearm. Indeed, it is not to farfetched to project that the public will demand the use of SIM in almost all situations. This philosophy may be generated by the judicial system as a whole, special interest groups, and families of perpetrators. The reader should not misinterpret this statement: the need for a variety of force options is necessary and has always been apparent to law enforcement officers. SIM will certainly play a huge role in future use of force continuum, and if improperly applied, may blur the lines in deadly force situations to the extent that officers will be placed in jeopardy in the interest of saving the perpetrator. A department's administration will certainly have to articulate clearly the rational, prudent, effective use of SIM before fielding any devices.

SIM necessitates the expectation that law enforcement officers will be specialists in the application of force. Given certain circumstances, deadly force may not justified, nor will it be safe for an officer to close on a perpetrator in an effort to control him or her with physical strength or close-range impact weapons. Indeed, law enforcement professionals have come to realize that they do not have to take lethal action or initiate steps that may unnecessarily escalate the use of force when a subject is armed but nonconfrontational. Thus, officers should be instructed to use less-lethal projectiles to deescalate potentially deadly situations, while reducing the likelihood of death or serious injury to all persons involved. Finally, officers must realize the value of a deescalation philosophy, to be used in all cases where confrontation does not further the mission objective.

Many police departments are already placing the use of SIM in the hands of SWAT units and training them to use SIM in these special circumstances. However, it must be remembered that many police agencies do not have SWAT teams; thus all law enforcement officers should be trained in the use of SIM. The author already believes that every police department, no matter the size, must start training SIM instructors, train officers to use SIM, purchase SIM systems for their inventories, field SIM systems for applicable use, and develop a clearly defined policy and procedure focusing on the use of SIM.

Finally, these munitions should be made available to courthouse officers in order to fit legally and socially acceptable concepts of the appropriate use of force. When properly used, SIM reduce injuries to officers and subjects, reduce the cost of liability associated with the use of force, reduce personnel complaints and associated disability pension costs, and improve the public image of the concerned agency.

Chemical Agent Munitions

Chemical agents are available in a variety of chemical mixtures and devices for use in a variety of situations. These devices consist of area devices, chemical agent ammunition, hand-delivered devices, hand launched devices, personal aerosol devices, tactical aerosol devices, and weapon-launched devices. Some devices are extremely specialized and may be dangerous to use in certain situations, while others are flexible and may be used in a variety of situations.

During courthouse violence crisis operations, it may be conducive to employ chemical agents to the interior of the structure prior to breaching and entry. Hand-delivered devices may be thrown into the openings of rooms or through windows, either singly or at coordinated multiple points in several different rooms. Another possibility is introducing the agent through an existing ventilation system (only OC should be used for this operation due to the persistent contamination qualities of CN and CS).

Chemical agents may also be used for spot control operations (after officers clear a room, they may deploy a chemical device into the room in order to discourage a subject from room hopping). Of course, a room subjected to this treatment cannot be considered secure, but merely neutralized to some extent. Frangible rounds may be fired in order to bore holes into the structure for the introduction of certain chemical agent device spray nozzles. Entry personnel may use aerosol units in their weak hand to immobilize unarmed subjects or personnel who do not appear to pose an imminent or obvious deadly force threat (in a hostage rescue operation all personnel are considered suspects and must be restrained until positive identification is made).

Figure 66. Examples of handheld OC aerosol devices.

Frangible Ammunition

There are a variety of areas where frangible ammunition are extremely valuable; for example, in tactical arenas that cannot afford collateral damage produced by misses (many studies reveal that of the rounds fired by officers in shooting confrontations, only about 17% actually hit the intended target), overpenetration, or ricochets (example tactical arenas include–nuclear facilities, airports, courtrooms, office buildings, petroleum and chemical facilities, corrections facilities, etc.). Finally, frangible ammunition normally has a maximum effective range much shorter than conventional ammunition (up to 60%).

CCI/Speer ZNT

CCI/Speer offers frangible ammunition in two calibers: 100-grain, 9mm Parabellum and 125-grain .40 S&W. These rounds are made with lead-free, clean-fire primers and feature a newly designed projectile. The projectile has a fluted copper jacket combined with a cast zinc alloy core designed to break into small pieces upon impact with steel targets, backstops, or other similar objects. While ZNT projectiles look like conventional bullets, they contain zinc alloy instead of lead, which eliminates lead dust upon impact.

Delta Frangible Ammunition (DFA)

Delta frangible ammunition (DFA) produces a line of frangible cartridges utilizing a nylon composite bullet. The nylon projectile will break apart into small pieces upon impact with hard surfaces resulting in the reduced penetration of objects which are not intended to be penetrated. DFA also has a reduced ricochet potential, reduced maximum range capability, and eliminates airborne lead contamination and lead contaminated environments. DFA is available in five handgun calibers and one (5.56) rifle caliber.

Longbow NTF

Longbow markets nontoxic frangible (NTF) ammunition in at least 15 calibers. These calibers include center fire handgun, center fire rifle, and a 12-gauge saboted slug. NTF contains no lead, thus eliminating contamination by that toxin at the firing point and at the point of impact. Indeed, bullet particles can be simply swept up and disposed of as nonhazardous material. Longbow estimates that one would have to fire 333,000 rounds of NTF to reach the same toxicity level of one round of leaded ammunition. Furthermore, as opposed to lead-free bullets in which the projectile is made of solid copper or some other metal or ceramic, Longbow's frangible bullet is made of a polymer-copper compound which completely eliminates ricochet and splash back.

Longbow's ammunition appears to be reliable (in both semiautomatic and full automatic weapons) and accurate, meaning the point of impact is very similar to that of service ammunition out to combat ranges. Indeed, Longbow designs their rounds to perform similarly to the ordering agencies' ammunition in terms of accuracy, muzzle flash, weapons function, and perceived recoil. Of course, like all other frangible rounds, Longbow's NTF is lethal if fired directly at soft flesh-type targets. Finally, Longbow's NTF round is presently being used by an impressive number of agencies throughout the United States and overseas.

Remington

Remington manufactures a lead free frangible called the "Disintegrator." The Disintegrator's lead-free bullet design provides instant and complete break-up upon impact, with no ricochet or lead accumulation. Furthermore, the totally lead-free primer eliminates the hazards of airborne lead residue in enclosed ranges. Point of impact and recoil performance reportedly duplicates that of equivalent standard duty ammunition. Finally, this round is available in 9mm, .40 S&W, and .45 ACP.

Electronic Immobilization Devices (EIDs)

Less-lethal device implementation is a key issue confronting today's law enforcement officer. Critical factors of "too much force," "the required amount of force" and/or "not enough force," are instrumental in determining the outcome of each situation. Officers are being assaulted in unprecedented numbers by individuals of a society imposing strict restraints on the police function. Thus, many less-lethal tools are being developed and utilized in order to reduce officer and suspect injuries due to the use of physical force in meeting and defeating resistance; making arrests and permitting follow-up control; reducing liability lawsuits against officers, organizations, and municipalities; and avoiding the use of lethal force when dealing with violent mentally challenged subjects or people deciding to pursue "suicide by cop" solutions. (Note: Studies and research have revealed that approximately 28 percent of all police shootings involve suicidal subjects.) Finally, these devices are generating such an interest that grant money is available and earmarked for the purchase of less-lethal tools to include EIDs.

EIDs have taken many different shapes and configurations throughout the years. Each one has a defined purpose or intended function precipitating its unique, individual form. The justification in adopting EIDs is based on understanding and education focusing on the fact that these devices are designed to be employed when and where close physical contact such as arrest or control is attempted and resistance is encountered. An EID is a personal weapon designed to be an extension of the user's hand and arm, thereby providing that individual with an intended superior amount of power. In the past, many EIDs were designed solely to repel an attacker, making the use of additional force necessary to control a suspect; this is not the case today.

Today, EIDs are designed to provide the short-term less-lethal incapacitation of a resisting or hostile individual by means of a safe, noninjurious, less-lethal force. EIDs use safe, proven, less-lethal electronic pulse wave technology to temporarily override the human body's electrical system, thereby causing confusion, disorientation, and disabling muscular response.

EIDs generate a high-voltage, extremely low amperage shock by means of a designated power source (typically a 9-volt battery). The current from the battery is triggered by a switch and flows into an oscillator which turns the current into pulses which travel through a number of capacitors which in turn shape the pulses into safe wave form. The safe waves then travel to a timer which releases current at measured intervals. The current eventually travels to a transformer which steps up the voltage for the shocking finale (approximately 45,000–50,000 volts, while the current (amperage) is reduced to 3–4 milliamps).

Amperes or current flow is the most important single factor in human electrocution. As can be seen above, the amperes generated by an EID are far below current levels that would cause the following human reactions: barely perceptible tingle (0.001 amperes), "let go" current (0.016 amperes), muscular paralysis (0.020 amperes), ventricular fibrillation (0.100 amperes), or ventricular standstill (2.000 amperes).

When applied, EID dump electrical energy into muscular tissue at a predetermined pulse rate frequency. The muscles react by performing an extraordinary amount of work, contracting and relaxing (called tetanization) violently but not in a very efficient manner (the muscles work hard but not together). This state of muscular confusion and rapid work cycle depletes the subject's blood sugar by converting it into lactic acid within a matter of seconds. As the subject's blood sugar becomes exhausted, he or she is unable to produce energy for the muscles and the body becomes unable to function. Thus, the primary design intent of this technology is to immobilize, affording safe and effective methods of control. When properly used, these devices permit an officer the opportunity to deescalate or stabilize a confrontation until such time that effective control may be achieved.

EIDs typically generate the following effects: 2 second–startles suspect; 1–2 seconds–causes a release action and minor muscle contractions; 1–4 seconds–causes a stunning action and may cause a person to fall down; and 2–5 seconds–less-lethal incapacitation state causes loss of balance, loss of control, generates confusion and disorientation). (Note: Effects will vary from individual to individual and are not 100% effective–no law enforcement tool is 100 percent effective.)

EIDs possess a number of attractive features such as: EID can be used by all officers regardless of size, strength, and speed, with equal proficiency; minimal training time is required (typically one day for a user certificate); no special skills need be acquired other than defensive blocks, holds, and takedown which are already intrinsic to most existing defensive tactics programs; it can be utilized at almost all levels of less-lethal force such as optional compliance, repelling, stunning, and incapacitation; less-lethal, short-term incapacitation reduces the chance of excessive force, enhances the officer's ability to respond to threats safely, and offers a drastic reduction of incurred liability resulting from the use-of-force as applicable to the criminal justice system.

There are a number of EIDs available to the average officer or law enforcement/security/corrections entity; for example, hand-applied devices, propelled devices, control devices, remote-control devices, and EID fencing systems.

Hand-Applied Devices

All of these devices are normally about the size of a portable telephone and are often used to force a subject to relax his or her grip on a person or object. Even the most determined subject will usually fail to maintain a grip after a period of time when the device is activated and pressed on the hand or arm. Complete take-down is also a possibility. Further, hand applied EID normally have a safety feature which disarms the electronics of the device until deployment in case a suspect successfully gains possession of the device. Frequently this safety feature consist of a wrist strap which disconnects from the device when the device is pulled free of the deploying officer's grip. The disconnection disables the device's electronic capabilities. Finally, many departments prefer hand-applied EIDs due to their concern that a person may sustain an eye injury from the barbs propelled EIDs utilize (see propelled EIDs later in the section).

EID Shields

Manufactures normally offer two types of EID shields, one shield designed for cell extractions and the other shield for riot control situations. These shields are very similar in appearance and function. They resemble full-capture shields commonly used in crowd control operations, but have an electronic immobilization feature that is effective when the shield comes in contact with a subject. These devices typically emit approximately 75,000 volts in 17 to 22 pulses per second in a 3 to 4 milliamp equivalent and do not cause burns like higher amperage electricity. Like hand-applied EIDs, these devices do sometimes leave a signature mark. Furthermore, it is not unusual for subjects to sustain secondary injuries as they bolt from the shield and fall over objects or run into objects located in the tactical arena. These devices have the additional benefit of being a psychological deterrent; experienced or knowing individuals will not want to experience or reexperience the uncomfortable effects this device generates. Of course, many people also fear electricity and may therefore be easily intimidated without actually using the device.

EID Belts

EID belts are intended to be used for prisoner transport operations or to enhance courtroom security. EID belts often resemble a heavy-duty belt which is strapped to combative or otherwise dangerous individuals prior to transport or for courtroom security measures. The belt normally comes in a one size fits all configuration and often have a "D" ring for handcuff attachment. The remote switch has dual safety activation switches designed to prevent false or accidental activations. Once activated, the switch emits a tone and there is also a built-in emergency magnetic cut-off switch. EID belts are typically activated by a remote control device that is operational out to 200 feet (line-of-sight) and 100 feet (obscured sight). Once activated, the subject will usually collapse to the ground and be incapable of running or fighting. This device, is normally powered by a 9-volt rechargeable cadmium battery which emits approximately 50,000 volts in 17 to 22 pulses per second in a 3 to 4 milliamp equivalent.

EID Batons

EID batons stun usually resemble a conventional straight handle baton. This device frequently powered by two 9-volt batteries, emits a very bright spark and approximately 150,000 volts in approximately 20 pulses per second in a 3 to 4 milliamp equivalent. This device is designed to be used in prisoner or crowd control situations.

EID Poles

EID poles are available in a number of configurations focusing on the telescoping range for model designation. These devices are normally constructed in two pieces, an insulated handle and a "hot" forward shaft designed to prevent subject grabbing. Some EID poles can be extended from 3 feet to 5 feet and other models can be extended from 5 feet to 8 feet. EID poles are

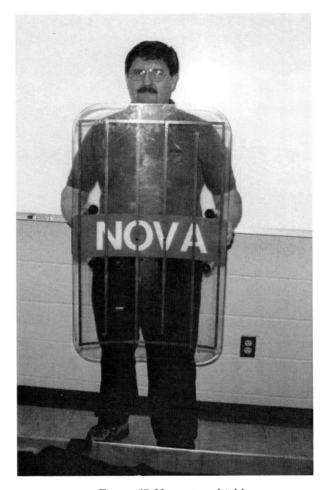

Figure 67. Nova stun shield.

typically powered by a 9-volt battery and emit approximately 75,000 volts in 17 to 22 pulses per second in a 3 to 4 milliamp equivalent.

Propelled EID Devices

Many departments do not like the fact that hand-applied EIDs require an officer to close the distance on a violent suspect and actually require a hands-on effort in order to apply the device. These departments prefer propelled EIDs, frequently called Tasers, which are designed as stand-off EID. Tasers typically have a range of 15 feet, are powered by a 9-volt battery and emit

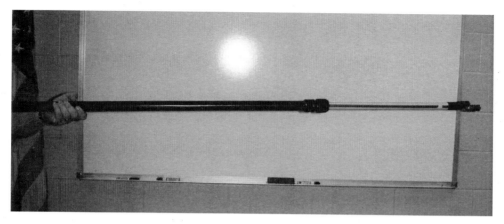

Figure 68. Nova stun pole in an extended configuration.

approximately 50,000 volts in 17 to 22 pulses per second in a 3 to 4 milliamp equivalent. Some tasers use gunpowder, priming compounds/gunpowder, or compressed nitrogen to project two (upper and lower) probes at a speed of 135 feet-per-second. Probes may be propelled at angles in order to increase the chance of the two probes hitting the target at the maximum distance. An electrical signal transits throughout the region where the probes make contact with the body or clothing. The probes are capable of penetrating two cumulative inches of clothing, including leather and most bulletproof vests. Furthermore, the probes do not have to penetrate the body to be effective; in some models, the electrical current will jump up to two inches as long as both probes are attached to a subject's clothing and/or skin.

Most models administer their electrical output automatically, for example, an initial seven seconds followed by several 1.8 second breaks for a total time of approximately 30 seconds in each cycle, ensuring the target receives the optimum output, removing user error. Alternatively, some models allow an officer to control the on/off switch. Additionally, some tasers have built-in battery checkers to provide immediate recognition of the available power supply.

Further, some tasers are single shot models, depending on easy loading and reloading characteristics if the situation dictates; other models offer a two-shot capability stating that there will be little chance to reload in most circumstances due to the close proximity of the suspect and officer. Additionally, most Tasers use an optional laser sighting system to assist with marksmanship skills.

Most tasers can be used in a backup mode as a touch-stun device after the cartridge has been fired (the cartridge may be in or out). Some Tasers disperse confetti-like microdots (neon colored and clear) when fired, for tracking purposes. These identification microdots are unique to each taser cartridge fired. Indeed, each microdot is printed with the serial number of the cartridge fired and can be used to identify the person shooting the device or for tracking down criminal misuse or stolen units. Some Taser devices also include a computer port which affords access to the unit's memory which can store the time of day and how many times the device was fired.

Furthermore, tasers are approximately the same size and weight as the hand-applied EID described above. Finally, tasers may be shaped like hand-applied EIDs, flashlights, or handguns. Many departments do not use devices that look like handguns because they believe emotionally disturbed subjects may mistake these tasers for handguns and charge officers, thus causing an escalation from less-lethal force to deadly force.

Remote-Controlled EIDs

Remotely controlled, less-lethal, anti-personnel weapons are applicable in both military and civilian environments. These EID may be used to protect assets, personnel, and facilities against intrusion from assailants, saboteurs, mob action, or insurrection. These field reloadable devices may be set up in static arrays, placed in temporary locations, or affixed to vehicles. Some of these devices fire simultaneous multiple shots into a 120-degree wide by 30 feet deep area, while other devices use an automatic sequencing plate to provide multiple shots from an accurately aimed gimbaled platform via a bore-sighted video link (operators use a joystick to control the direction and elevation of the device while viewing the target on a bore-sighted video monitor, a separate trigger switch to fire the device, and a simple display to show how many darts are left and which ones are currently active.) Once fired, each dart pair remains activated for a fixed duration of time or until manually turned off by the operator. Seven subjects, per magazine, can be kept immobilized at once by the independent circuits. The magazines are reloadable and two magazines may be stacked to increase capacity. A system abort switch will "safe" all of the darts and prevent further firing until manually reset. These remote-controlled EIDs use the same pulse wave technology as all of the other EIDs discussed.

EID Fencing Systems

These devices are less-lethal electronic fencing systems which are easily integrated into exiting fences, easily placed on top of walls, or used as a stand-alone fence. The EID fence system consists of electric wires carrying high-

Figure 69. Taser photos.

Figure 70. Gallagher power fence.

voltage electric impulses in the same manner as the other EIDs discussed above. The number of wires, distance between wires, protection zone length, and integration with existing perimeter fences are all capabilities of EID fencing. EID fence wires can also be installed vertically or at an angle in order to provide wider physical barriers that make intrusion by way of digging or climbing extremely difficult, if not impossible. The goal of an EID fence system is to provide an active intrusion detection system that reacts to an intrusion attempt, repels the intruder, and delays entry time without relying on human surveillance.

In conclusion, many agencies that have employed EID technology have confirmed a reduction of officer and suspect injuries during physical resistance encounters, a reduction of employee compensation claims, and a reduction of suspect medical injury treatment. Furthermore, EID are particularly attractive for corrections and courtroom security use where a number of less-lethal technologies are problematic. However, EID must be viewed as an alternative, not a panacea. One must comprehend when, where, and how these devices can be or could be used. It is only then that the ultimate value

---

* Note: Of course, there are a number of EIDs being developed or refined as this book is being written, for example, EID socks, cuffs, and gloves. These EIDs should be considered and tested as they become available.

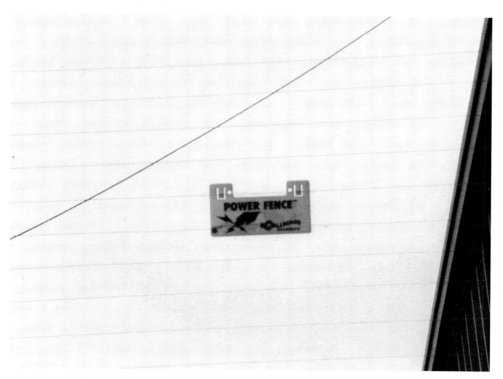

Figure 71. Sign announcing the existence of the Gallagher power fence.

Figure 72. Sign announcing the existence of the Gallagher power fence.

of such a less-lethal tool is truly realized. Used properly, at the correct moment and when other alternatives have been exhausted, the EID provides a viable and safe means to "control" a hostile confrontation on the low end of the use-of-force spectrum, thereby preventing the unnecessary use of more force and the distasteful aftermath.

Vigilance

Those who man a security post know the challenge of remaining highly alert. It is relatively easy to keep a security program focused in the immediate aftermath of a security incident, catastrophe, or after more elaborate security systems are installed and activated. However vigilance often decreases with the return of day-to-day routines. Time inevitably erodes the efficiency and effectiveness of the most competent and experienced security personnel. Even nonsecurity personnel lose vigilance and patience with security policies and procedures they once thought welcome and necessary. Operations security, security exercises and drills, and continuing security education are a must in avoiding complacency.

CONCLUSION

Now more than ever, the topic of security is on everyone's mind and protecting those inside a courthouse is a formidable task. Some experts label courthouse security operations as "low probability, high-consequence threats" due to the incalculable costs of death, facility destruction, disruption of the judicial system, negative public perception, civil/criminal lawsuits, and the resulting embarrassment of these acts. Indeed, the impact generated from a courthouse violence crisis may be isolated or widespread, predictable or unpredictable, and result in damage ranging from minimal to major. Depending on the severity of the incident, the aftermath of courthouse violence may generate a long-term impact on the courthouse and communities located in any given location. To date, there are no accurate predictions of exactly when an act of courthouse violence will occur, precisely where it will take place, or the severity of the impact.

However, effective programs may be realized by accepting the challenge of developing safe and secure courthouses. The key to safe courthouse environments places importance on the development of strong leadership, caring courthouse personnel, effective law enforcement and security operations, and participation in the design of programs and policies. Safe and secure courthouses are facilities where prevention and intervention programs are based upon careful assessment of personnel problems. While courthouse administrators and officers cannot prevent all violence from occurring, these entities can do much to reduce the likelihood of its occurrence. Through thoughtful planning and the establishment of a courthouse violence prevention and response team, many crisis situations may be averted. Additionally, when situations cannot be averted, planning will certainly prepare concerned parties for effective response measures.

Furthermore, a crisis response exercise should be held at least annually in order for all operational entities to become familiar with their specific duties and to delineate the chain of command. A real-world crisis is not the time or place for operational entities to work out these issues. It is particularly important for a courthouse's crisis response team to interface with police tactical response teams so that they can understand how important their contributions are to the law enforcement mission. All courthouse violence incidents must be treated seriously and subsequent investigations must be given priority status.

Finally, a crisis response planning document must be considered a living document and thus evaluated and periodically updated (at least annually). A properly designed, updated, practiced, and implemented planning document will ultimately increase a courthouse facility's success in saving lives. Crisis response planning should be designed as a proactive tool intended to generate a detailed analysis of possible contingency plans available to response personnel. The plan should enable intervention during a crisis to ensure safety and also focus on responding in the aftermath of tragedy. This planning document should compile elements of essential information concerning a specific target and the surrounding tactical arena into a workable format. The planning document should be made available to respective SWAT teams in order to streamline the planning effort for all SWAT entities; assist in developing the tactical operations center information display; enhance the formulation of the warning order and operations order, and assist with the development of tactical solutions. A crisis response planning process will serve a proactive role in promoting peace and harmony within the community, and in ensuring the right of courthouse staff and citizens to attend a safe courthouse environment.

Violence or the threat of violence in a courthouse complex have a profound negative impact on the court's ability to function. Therefore, appropriate levels of security should prevail in the court to protect the integrity of court procedures, to protect the rights of individuals before it, to deter those who would take violent action against the court or litigants, and to sustain the proper decorum and dignity of the court. Appropriate levels of security should also exist outside the court on all court-related functions to achieve the same end. Thus, courthouse administrators, judges, lawyers, staff members, and law enforcement officers all have a stake in proactive measures focused on quickly and efficiently responding to courthouse violence in progress and addressing the tragic aftermath that is sure to follow.

At the very least, effective courthouse security systems and operations will reap the benefits of keeping employees and the public safe, foster a professional working environment, and possibly enable a courthouse administrator to seek and receive insurance reductions and tax benefits.

Appendix A

TECHNICAL INFORMATION SOURCES

ABA Commission of Standards of Judicial Administration, Courthouse Design: A Handout for Judge and Court Administrators, January, 1975.

ABA Commission of Standards of Judicial Administration, Standards Relating to the Courts, Standards 2.46 and Standard 2.47.

Access Control & Security Systems Integration, Vol.42, No.14, Intertec Publishing Corporation, Atlanta, GA, December 31, 1999.

AJA Court Security Survey, *Court Review,* pp. 10–11, Summer, 1988.

The Appropriate and Effective Use of Security Technologies in U.S. Schools, Research Report, National Institute of Justice, Washington, DC, 1999.

Basic Training Manual and Study Guide for Healthcare Security Officers, International Association for Healthcare Security and Safety, Lombard, IL, 1995.

Blumenkrantz S., *Security Handbook,* Government Data Publications, Washington, D.C., 1989.

Bomb and Physical Security Planning, Bureau of Alcohol, Tobacco and Firearms, 1987.

Bomb Threats and Search Techniques, Department of Treasury, Bureau of Alcohol, Tobacco and Firearms, ATF 7550.2, July, 1979.

Bullets, Bombs & Schools: A Response Seminar, Ohio University, Chillicothe, OH, 1999.

Carter, Richard W., Judge, *Court Security for Judges, Bailiffs and Other Court Personnel,* 1992.

Carter, Richard W., Judge, Keeping a Secure Courthouse, *Judicature,* pp. 314–318, April–May, 1993.

Court Security: A Manual of Guidelines and Procedures, The National Sheriffs Association, NA 4471 M351, 1978.

Court Security Detection Systems, National Center for State Courts Library, 1982.

Court Security Manual, Court Security Management Course, Institute of Court Management, February, 1992.

Court Security Officers Killed at Post, *Marshals Monitor,* September, 1993.

Court Security Operations Handbook, Rhode Island Capital Police.

Courthouse Security Screening, Garrett Metal Detectors, Ram Books, 1993.

Court Security Standards, Standards for Law Enforcement Agencies, Commission on Accreditation for Law Enforcement Agencies, 3rd Ed., 1994.

Court Security: Training Guidelines, The National Sheriffs Association, May, 1991.

Court Security: Training Guidelines. The National Sheriffs Association, NA 4471 M351, 1978.

Court Security and the Transportation of Prisoners: A National Study, National Sheriffs Association, October, 1997.

Court Violence Sparks Action, *National Law Journal,* July 16, 1989.

Crutchley, Stephen, *The Security Maze,* Security Products, p. 43, October, 2002.

Danger in the Courts, *ABA Journal,* pp. 18–19, July, 1987.

DePasquale, Courting Security, *American City and County,* pp. 58–60, October, 1994.

Donalson, Paul R. & Leishman, Kathleen R., The Magnetometer, *AJA Benchmark,* Vol 14, No 4, Winter, 1991.

Early Warning Timely Response: A Guide to Safe Schools, U.S. Department of Education Special Education and Rehabilitative Services, Washington, D.C., August 1998.

Emergency Preparedness U.S.A., Federal Emergency Management Agency, June, 1998.

The Emergency Program Manager, Federal Emergency Management Agency, June, 1998.

Gallati, R.R., *Introduction to Private Security,* Prentice-Hall, 1983.

Geiger Fred A., Judge, Implementing a Court Security Program, *Court Review,* pp. 22–25, Summer, 1988.

Geiger, Fred A., Judge, Safety First: A Guide to Courthouse Security, *Judges Journal,* pp. 14–16, Summer, 1989.

Green, G., *Introduction to Security,* Butterworth Publishers, date unknown.

Guidance for Protecting Building Environments from Airborne Chemical, Biological, or Radiological Attacks, www.cdc.gov/niosh.

Hand-Held Metal Detectors for Use in Weapons Detection, Law Enforcement Standards Program, NILECJ-STD-0602.00, U.S. Department of Justice, Law Enforcement Assistance Administration, National Institute of Law Enforcement and Criminal Justice, Washington, DC, 1974.

Hazardous Materials: A Citizen's Orientation, Federal Emergency Management Agency, Emmitsburg, MD., 1993.

Hess, K.M., & Wrobeleski, *Introduction to Private Security,* West Publishing, 1983.

High Trial Threats, *Pentacle,* July, 1987.

Hougland, Steve, Conducting Searches on School Property, *Police and Security News,* Quakertown, PA., November/December, 1999.

Installation and Auditing of Security Technology, Session IV: Technical and Policy Focus Groups Group B, Cook, Peter, J., & Rodger, Robert, M., West Sussex, United Kingdom, 1996.

Johnson, Sue & Yerawadeker, Prakash, Courthouse Security, *Court Review,* pp. 4–7, Summer, 1988.

Jones, Tony L., *Booby-Trap Identification and Response Guide for Law Enforcement Personnel,* Paladin Press, Boulder, CO, 1998.

Jones, Tony L., *SWAT Leadership and Tactical Planning: The SWAT Operator's Guide to Combat Law Enforcement,* Paladin Press, Boulder, CO, 1996.

Justice Technology Monitor, Volume 2, No. 3, Capitol City Publishers, Arlington, VA., February, 2000.

Landingham, Jim Van, Microwave Network Improves Court Security and Reduces manpower, *Court Review,* pp. 18–19, Summer, 1988.

LEAA Police Equipment Survey of 1972, Volume IV, *Alarms, Security Equipment, Surveillance Equipment,* NBS Special Publication 480-4, U.S. Department of Commerce, National Bureau of Standards, Washington, D.C., 1972.

Magnetic Switches for Burglar Alarm Systems, Law Enforcement Standards Program, NILECJ-STD-0301.00, U.S. Department of Justice, Law Enforcement Assistance Administration, National Institute of Law Enforcement and Criminal Justice, Washington, D.C., 1974.

Manual for the Responding, Investigation, and Prosecution of a Hate Crime, U.S. Attorney's Office, Cincinnati, OH., 1999.

Mcghee, Terry, *Exterior Intrusion Detection-101,* Southwest Microwave, Inc., Security Systems Division, Location Unknown, 1998.

McKay, James, Judge, Courtroom Security and Criminal Sessions, *Court Review,* pp. 16–17, Summer, 1988.

McMicking, Larry, The Metal Detector and the X-Ray System, *Sheriff,* pp. 13–14, November–December, 1993.

Meeks, Bob, Courtroom Security- NSA Establishes New Committee, *Sheriff,* pp. 6, November–December, 1993.

Mercury Switches for Burglar Alarm Systems, Law Enforcement Standards Program, NILECJ-STD-0303.00, U.S. Department of Justice, Law Enforcement Assistance Administration, National Institute of Law Enforcement and Criminal Justice, Washington, D.C., 1974.

Metallic Window Foil for Intrusion Alarm Systems, NIJ Standard-0319.00, Technology Assessment Program, National Institute of Justice, U.S. Department of Justice, Washington, DC, 1980.

Model Court Security Operations Manual, The Supreme Court of Ohio/Ohio Judicial Conference Committee on Court Security, March, 1995.

NILECJ Standard for Mechanically Actuated Switches for Burglar Alarm Systems, Law Enforcement Standards Program, NILECJ-STD-0302.00, U.S. Department of Justice, Law Enforcement Assistance Administration, National Institute of Law Enforcement and Criminal Justice, Washington, D.C., 1974.

(NOVA) National Organization For Victim Assistance–1757 Park Road, N.W., Washington, D.C. 20010.

Ohio Bailiffs Association Manual, The Ohio Bailiffs Association, April, 1991.

An Orientation to Community Disaster Exercises, IS SM 120, Federal Emergency Management Agency, Emmitsburg, MD, July, 1995.

Penetrate Resistance of Concrete–A Review, NBS Special Publication 480-45, U.S. Department of Commerce, National Bureau of Standards, Washington, D.C., 1982.

Perimeter Security Sensor Handbook, Space and Naval Warfare Systems Center Electronic Security Systems Engineering Division (Code 74), July 1998.

Personal Security Handbook, U.S. Department of Justice, U.S. Marshall Service, USMS Pub No. 6, January 21, 1992.

Physical Security of Door Assemblies and Components, Law Enforcement Standards Program, NILECJ-STD-0306.00, U.S. Department of Justice, Law Enforcement

Assistance Administration, National Institute of Law Enforcement and Criminal Justice, Washington, D.C., 1976.

Physical Security of Sliding Glass Door Units, NIJ Standard-0318.00, Technology Assessment Program, National Institute of Justice, U.S. Department of Justice, Washington, D.C., 1980.

Physical Security Systems, United States Department of Energy, Washington, D.C., 1995.

Physical Security of Window Units, NIJ Standard-0316.00, Technology Assessment Program, National Institute of Justice, U.S. Department of Justice, Washington, D.C., 1980.

Planning and Procedure Manual, Ohio State Highway Patrol, 1992.

Planning for Security, *The Judges Journal,* Spring, 1983.

Preventing and Managing Riots and Disturbances, The American Correctional Association, Professional Development Department, Lanham, Maryland, 1998.

Private Security, Report of the National Task Force on Private Security, National Advisory Committee on Criminal Justice Standards and Goals, Washington, D.C., U.S. Government Printing Office, 1976.

Protecting the Courts: Training, Equipment and Personnel Issues, *Sheriff,* November–December, 1993.

Recommendations for Court Security, Illinois Sheriff's Association and Illinois Judges' Association, 1984.

The Role of Behavioral Science in Physical Security, Proceedings of the Second Annual Symposium, NBS Special Publication 480-32, U.S. Department of Commerce, National Bureau of Standards, Washington, D.C., 1977.

The Role of Behavioral Science in Physical Security, Proceedings of the Third Annual Symposium, NBS Special Publication 480-38, U.S. Department of Commerce, National Bureau of Standards, Washington, D.C., 1978.

Rosenthal, Rick, Your Public Information S.O.P.: Where good media relations translate into good public relations, *Law and Order,* Wilmette, IL., May, 1996.

Screening Out Dangerous Devices and People, *Security Management,* No 1612, June 25, 1987.

Security, *CM The Court Management And Administration Report,* Vol 1, No 11, November, 1990.

Security Lighting for Nuclear Weapons Storage Sites: A Literature Review and Bibliography, NBS Special Publication 480-27, U.S. Department of Commerce, National Bureau of Standards, Washington, D.C., 1977.

Security Planning and Procedures, National Sheriffs' Association, *Court Review,* pp. 20–24, Summer, 1988.

Security Technology Update, *Court Technology,* Vol 6, No 4, July-August, 1994.

Security in the Work Place, U.S. Department of Justice, U.S. Marshall Service, GPO: 1991-0-302-813.

Selection and Application Guide to Commercial Intrusion Alarm Systems, NBS Special Publication 480-14, U.S. Department of Commerce, National Bureau of Standards, Washington, D.C., 1979.

Selection and Application Guide to Fixed Surveillance Cameras, NILECJ-GUIDE-0301.00, U.S. Department of Justice, Law Enforcement Assistance Administration, National Institute of Law Enforcement and Criminal Justice, Washington, D.C., 1974.

Sound Sensing Units for Intrusion Alarm Systems, Law Enforcement Standards Program, NILECJ-STD-0308.00, U.S. Department of Justice, Law Enforcement Assistance Administration, National Institute of Law Enforcement and Criminal Justice, Washington, D.C., 1977.

Terms and Definitions for Intrusion Alarm Systems, Law Enforcement Standards Program, LESP-RPT-0305-00, U.S. Department of Justice, Law Enforcement Assistance Administration, National Institute of Law Enforcement and Criminal Justice, Washington, D.C., 1974.

Test Methods for Detention and Correctional Facility Locks, NISTIR 4975, U.S. Department of Commerce, Technology Administration, Washington, D.C., 1992.

Test Method for the Evaluation of Metallic Window Foil for Intrusion Alarm Systems, NBS Special Publication 480-34, U.S. Department of Commerce, National Bureau of Standards, Washington, D.C., 1978.

United States Court Design Guide, U.S. Services Administration, Public Buildings Service, 1989.

Valentine, Michael J, Judge, Judicial Security—A Shortage of Awareness, *Court Review,* pp. 14–15, Summer, 1988.

Walk-Through Metal Detectors for Use in Weapons Detection, Law Enforcement Standards Program, NILECJ-STD-0601.00, U.S. Department of Justice, Law Enforcement Assistance Administration, National Institute of Law Enforcement and Criminal Justice, Washington, D.C., 1974.

Wickizer, Jim, Recorder in the Court, *Security Management,* August, 1992.

Wise, Tony, Courtroom Tragedy, *Sheriff,* pp. 15–16, November–December, 1993.

Wong, Michael F., *Space Management and the Courts,* U.S. Department of Justice, PR 722-14, January, 1973.

Appendix B

SECURITY EQUIPMENT RESOURCES

Badge/Identification Resources
Datacard Group
11111 Bren Road West
Minnetonka, MN 55343-9015
Telephone: 952-933-0333
Fax: 952-933-7971
Website: www.datacard.com

Fargo
6533 Flying Cloud Drive
Eden Prairie, MN 55344
Phone: 800-459-5636
Fax: 952-941-9470
Website: www.fargo.com
Email: sales@fargo.com

TEMTEC, Inc.
100 Route 59
Suffern, NY 10901-4910
Telephone: 914-368-4040
Fax: 914-368-4099

J.A.M. Plastics, Inc.
1804 N. Lemon Street
Anaheim, CA 92801
Telephone: 800-844-8424
Fax: 714-773-4330
Website: www.jamplastics.com
Email: jamplastics@earthlink.net

Key Control Resources
Morse Watchman
2 Morse Road
Oxford, CT 06478
Telephone: 203-264-4949
Fax: 203-264-8367
Website: www.morsewatchman.com

Explosive/Narcotics Detection Technology Resources
IDS Intelligent Detection Systems Inc.
152 Cleopatra Drive
Nepean, Ontario, Canada K2G 5X2
Phone: 613-224-1061
Fax: 613-224-2603

ITI Ion Track Instruments
205 Lowell Street
Wilmington, MA 01887
Phone: 978-658-3767
Fax: 978-957-5954

Integrated Security System Technology
MADAHCOM
50 West 23rd St.
New York, NY 10010
Telephone: 212-620-4413
Fax: 212-620-4439
Email: sales@madah.com
Website: www.madah.com

Interactive Visual Imaging
Interactive Tactical Group
Boston, MA
Telephone: 888-752-4205
Email: info@tacticalvr.com
Website: www.tacticalvr.com

Intrusion Detection System Sources
Access Denied, Inc.
1280 South Williams Drive
P.O. Box 814
Columbia City, Indiana 46725-0814
Telephone: 219-244-3692
Fax: 219-244-6131
Website: www.ultradog.com
Email: rjbagan@ultradog.com

Axcess, Inc.
3208 Commander Drive
Carrollton, TX 75006
Telephone: 972-407-6080
Fax: 972-407-9085

Cortex Vision Systems, Inc.
P.O. Box 14282
Research Triangle Park, NC 27709
Phone: 919-361-9606
Fax: 919-572-2471

Deggy
600 Brickell Avenue, Suite 604
Miami, FL 33131
Telephone: 305-377-2233
Fax: 305-377-8711
Website: www.deggy.com
Email: dsales@deggy.com

Designed Security Inc.
Route 6, Box 835
Bastrop, TX 78602
Telephone: 512-321-4426
Fax: 512-321-9181

Detex Corporation
302 Detex Drive
New Braunfels, TX 78130
Telephone: 830-629-2900
Fax: 830 620-6711
Website: www.detex.com

ECSI International, Inc.
790 Bloomfield Avenue, Bldg. C. Suite 1
Clifton, NJ 07012
Phone: 973-574-8555
Fax: 973-574-8562

Extreme CCTV Surveillance Systems
#2-6221 202 St.
Langley, BC Canada V2Y 1N1
Telephone: +1.604.533.6644
Fax: +1.604.533.6610
Website: www.ExtremeCCTV.com

FSI FLIR Systems, Inc.
9 Arrow Lane Amherst, NH 03031
Phone: 603-424-4752
Fax: 603-424-8941

Kaba Ilco Inc.
7301 Decarie Blvd
Montreal, Quebec H4P 2G7
Telephone: 514-735-5410
Fax: 514-735-8862
Website: www.ilcounican.com
Email: Mburnie@mtl.ilcounican.com

Racon Security Solutions
12628 Interurban Avenue South
Seattle, WA 98168-3383
Phone: 206-241-1110
Fax: 206-246-9306

Radionics
340 El Camino Real-South, Building #36
Salinas, CA 93901
Telephone: 800-538-5807
Fax: 831-796-1892
Website: www.radionics.com

Southwest Microwave
9055 South McKemy Street
Tempe, Arizona 85284-2946
Telephone: 480-783-0201
Fax: 480-783-0401
Website: www.southwestmicrowave.com

Total Recall Corporation
50A South Main Street
Spring Valley, NY 10977
Telephone: 800-659-7793
Fax: 845-425-3097
Website: www.totalrecallcorp.com
Email: Jordan@totalrecallcorp.com

Locking Device Resources
OSI Security Devices
1580 Jayken Way
Chula Vista, CA 91911
Phone: 619-628-1000
Fax: 619-628-1001
Website: www.omnilock.com
Email: sales@omnilock.com

Metal Detection Sources
CEIA USA
9177 Dutton Drive
Twinsburg, OH 44087
Telephone: 330-405-3190
Fax: 330-405-3196
Website: www.ceia-uas.com

Control Screening
35 West Pittsburgh St.
Greensburg, PA 15601-2323
Telephone: 724-837-5411
Fax: 724-837-5425
Website: www.controlscreening.com
Email: dcunningham@controlscreening.com

Fisher M-Scope
200 W. Willmott Road
Los Banos, CA 93635
Telephone: 209-826-3292
Fax: 209-826-0416
Website: www.fisherlab.com
Email: info@fisherlab.com

Garrett
1881 W. State St.
Garland, TX 75042
Telephone (972) 494-6151
Fax (972) 494-1881

METAL-TEC
3500 Fairlane Farms Road, Suite #3
West Palm Beach, FL. 33414
Phone: 561-790-0111
Fax: 561-790-0080

METOREX, Inc.
Princeton Crossroads Corporate Center
P.O. Box 3540
Princeton, NJ 08543-3540
Phone: 609-406-9000
Fax: 609-530-9055

PerkinElmer
10E Commerce Way
Woburn, MA 01801
Telephone: 781-939-3989
Fax: 781-939-3993
Website: www.perkinelmer.com

Robotic Resources
Cybermotion
719 Gainsboro Road, NW
Roanoke, VA 24016
Phone: 800-762-6848
www.cybermotion.com

Security Film For Windows
A-1 American
3144 N. Main Street
Dayton, OH. 45405
Phone: 937-274-2800
Fax: 937-274-3800
www.A-1 American.com

X-Ray Screening Resources
EG&G
4630 Montgomery Avenue, Suite 500
Bethesda, MD 20814
Phone: 301-951-0457
Fax: 301-951-0217

HEIMANN Systems GmbH
186 Wood Avenue South
Iselin, NJ 08830
Phone: 732-603-5914
Fax: 732-603-5995

PerkinElmer
10E Commerce Way
Woburn, MA 01801
Telephone: 781-939-3989
Fax: 781-939-3993
Website: www.perkinelmer.com

Rapiscan Security Products
Washington National Airport
Hanger 3, Room 115
Washington, DC 20001
Telephone: 703-416-9571
Fax: 703-416-9573
Email: Bailey@rapiscan.com

SAIC Science Applications
International Corporation
16701 West Bernardo Drive
San Diego, CA 92127
Phone: 800-962-1632
Fax: 619-646-9718

VIVID Technologies, Inc.
10E Commerce Way
Woburn, MA 01801
Phone: 781-939-7800
Fax: 781-939-3993

INDEX